WOMEN'S ROLES IN TWENTIETH-CENTURY AMERICA

Recent Titles in
Women's Roles in American History

Women's Roles in Seventeenth-Century America
Merril D. Smith

WOMEN'S ROLES IN TWENTIETH-CENTURY AMERICA

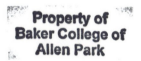
Martha May

Women's Roles in American History

GREENWOOD PRESS
Westport, Connecticut • London

Library of Congress Cataloging in Publication Data

May, Martha.
  Women's roles in twentieth-century America / Martha May.
    p.   cm. — (Women's roles in American history)
  Includes bibliographical references and index.
    ISBN 978-0-313-34015-4 (hard copy : alk. paper) —
ISBN 978-0-313-08772-1 (ebook)
    1. Women—United States—History—20th century.
2. Sex role—United States—History—20th century. I. Title.
  HQ1426M393   2009
  305.40973'0904—dc22   2009006068

British Library Cataloguing in Publication Data is available.

Library of Congress Catalog Card Number: 2009006068
ISBN: 978-0-313-34015-4
ISSN: 1553-507X

First published in 2009

Greenwood Press, 88 Post Road West, Westport, CT 06881
An imprint of Greenwood Publishing Group, Inc.
www.greenwood.com

Printed in the United States of America

∞™

The paper used in this book complies with the
Permanent Paper Standard issued by the National
Information Standards Organization (Z39.48-1984).

10 9 8 7 6 5 4 3 2 1

For Paul,
and for Isaac,
as he charts his own course

Contents

Series Foreword

Women's history is still being reclaimed. The geographical and chrono-logical scope of the Women's Roles through History series contributes to our understanding of the many facets of women's lives. Indeed, with this series, a content-rich survey of women's lives through history and around the world is available for the first time for high school students to the general public.

The impetus for the series came from the success of Greenwood's 1999 reference *Women's Roles in Ancient Civilizations*, edited by Bella Vivante. Librarians noted the need for new treatments of women's history, and women's roles are an important part of the history curriculum in every era. Thus, this series intensely covers women's roles in Europe and the United States, with volumes by the century or by era, and one volume each is devoted to the major populated areas of the globe—Africa, the Middle East, Asia, and Latin America and the Caribbean.

Each volume provides essay chapters on major topics such as:

- family life
- marriage and childbearing
- religion
- public life
- lives of ordinary women
- women and the economy
- political status
- legal status
- arts

Country and regional differences are discussed as necessary.
  Other elements include

- introduction, providing historical context
- chronology
- glossary
- bibliography
- period illustrations

The volumes, written by historians, offer sound scholarship in an accessible manner. A wealth of disparate material is conveniently synthesized in one source. As well, the insight provided into daily life, which readers find intriguing, further helps to bring knowledge of women's struggles, duties, contributions, pleasures, and more to a wide audience.

Preface

Women played critical roles in twentieth-century American life. As workers, parents, artists, and in many other forms, women offered their energies, insights, and strengths in periods of crisis and prosperity. This book examines those diverse roles through a topical and chronological narrative, considering the major contributions and the obstacles women confronted as individuals and citizens.

The first chapter explores the changing nature of women's work, as new opportunities and options drew a growing number of women into the paid labor force. Women's domestic labor played an equally important part of that story, allowing women to extend family income and nurture their children. The constraints of race and class remain an essential part of that history, as the differences among women both complicated and enriched women's lives. Chapter 2 considers the importance of family roles for women in a century when many families reconsidered gender roles, individual needs, and family responsibilities.

Women's changing political roles serve as the focus of Chapter 3. When the century began, women nationwide could not vote; by 2008, women ran for the nation's top offices, held significant Cabinet positions, and articulated the special interests of their gender. Chapter 4 focuses on the place of women in popular culture and the arts, as creators and subjects of music, film, literature, and dance. As women's roles changed during the century, the laws that provided access and protection also provoked debate and dissention, the subject of Chapter 5. In Chapter 6, women's extraordinary gains in education in the twentieth century become apparent. Women's position in the nation's mainstream religions also changed significantly, the topic of Chapter 7. A historical introduction, timeline, photos, and selected bibliography round out the coverage.

Acknowledgments

The many achievements of women in the twentieth century persist as an extraordinary legacy of endurance, optimism, and strength. From every decade, the talent, intelligence, and courage of individual women offer inspiration to all of us who continue to work to increase opportunities for our daughters and our sons. Trying to include every element of women's accomplishments has proved to be a daunting task, and one I know remains incomplete. Other historians will keep filling in the gaps of our knowledge, adding to our appreciation of women who have made our history.

Wendi Schnaufer, the editor of this series, deserves special thanks for her patience and persistence. Thanks also go to Burton Peretti for making work life easier, and to my colleagues Joshua Rosenthal, Leslie Lindenauer, Wynn Gadkar-Wilcox, Katherine Allocco, and Michael Nolan for their good humor and insightful conversations. Paul McManus helped in a multitude of ways, and I'm also grateful for the support of Dr. David Sperling and Barbara Selleck. Randall and Marissa Smith tempered doldrums with pizza. Isaac May labored as a diligent and inspired research assistant. This book also owes a lot to my family, that extended network of folks—Boo, Celie, Bill and Sis, Rusty, Terry and Allison, Stevie—and everyone else who claims our kin, who provided many gracious lessons about life, endurance, and love.

Introduction

When Cornelia Pearl May of Culpeper, Virginia, was born in the second year of the new century, few American citizens imagined the extraordinary course of the years ahead. As a child, Pearl saw the nation enter a World War. When she was a young woman, she bobbed her hair, raised her skirts, and danced to the radio. Pearl married and became a new mother in the early thirties; then, she witnessed her husband and her brothers scramble for work, and a decade later, go off to another war. At middle age, Pearl Hill went to work in a variety of jobs, as a salesclerk, a writer, and family entrepreneur. By the time Pearl died in the 1980s, she had seen space flight, bad television sitcoms, the computer, and satellite communications. The world that her descendents inherit offers new opportunities and challenges for women.

One of Pearl's great-nieces, Lillian May, understands the dramatic changes in female roles. Her childhood included international air travel, her own computer, frequent trips to museums and the theater, and sports. Because she excelled in math and science in school, Lily found teachers and mentors eager to encourage her in careers in medicine or engineering. Exposure to "women's studies" in high school and college meant a thoughtful evaluation of gender. No one doubted that Lily would attend college, or questioned her decision to undertake graduate work. As the nation entered into another new century, Lillian May eagerly participated in activities that would have been unusual for a woman of Pearl's era.

The remarkable transformation of American women's possibilities in the twentieth century remains one of the most exciting and provocative stories in American history. Within one hundred years, women moved from lacking the right to vote throughout the nation to opening new realms of women's political leadership. In the first decade of the twenty-first century, two women have been Supreme Court Justices, two have been Secretaries of State, and the country has had a female Speaker of the House of Representatives.

However, women continue to face what has been called the "double bind." Every advance can easily be answered with less salutary statistics. Few women head Fortune 500 companies. In professions that have historically been predominantly male, such as engineering or the building trades, women continue to be underrepresented. Women's wages remain remarkably resistant to decades of attempts to equalize earnings. College-educated female graduates may do better than their mothers in the comparison with male peers, but they too will receive smaller paychecks. After a century, women still confront persistent barriers to economic equality with their male counterparts in professions, services, and trades.

The "double bind" also permeates education, despite impressive achievements by women. Women have held the presidencies of the nation's most prestigious colleges and universities and now make up the majority of college undergraduates. Nevertheless, women remain in the minority among school administrators and in the top ranks of college faculty. The "chilly climate" in the classroom, where boys and girls experience differences in praise, speaking time, and encouragement, persists despite a decade of educators' efforts. The competence of women in science and mathematics continues to generate debate, even as women head scientific panels and win Nobel Prizes for research.

Sexuality and family life also define women's lives in ways that do not limit men. In the 2008 Presidential campaign season, those differences came into sharp focus. At one campaign event, hecklers chanted "iron my shirt" at Democratic candidate Hillary Clinton, for example. When Republican Vice Presidential nominee Sarah Palin appeared at rallies in high heels, commentators noted the height of her shoes and the shape of her legs. Both women heard persistent questions about their families, and ironically, both gained support by using their families to legitimate their candidacies. For Clinton, that tactic meant referring to her years as First Lady as preparation for the presidency and reliance on her husband, President Bill Clinton, as a campaign surrogate. Governor Palin of Alaska put her children on display as she defined herself as a "hockey mom." In 2008, it was difficult to imagine comparable strategies for male candidates.

As the campaigns suggested, physical attractiveness and display remained controversial issues among those who study and write about gender. When Hillary Clinton wore a relatively low-cut blouse for a political event, reporters discussed whether it was appropriate. At the same time, television dramas and situation comedies in 2008 routinely feature actresses playing professional women with décolletage. Which standards applied to which women, and whether professional women could wear sexy clothing, seemed confusing at best. The question reflected a persistent debate among women about how to deal with sexuality. In the 1970s, anthropologist Gayle Rubin suggested that women's sexuality could contain playful, joyous expressions of creativity and identity. That point has been echoed by many writers in the years which followed, as they noted the pleasure some women derive from fashion, cosmetics, or flirtation. Other feminists worry that the social construction of sexuality through such vehicles as advertising, film and television, and pornography tends to demean women by portraying them as sexual objects. As women attempt to define their goals and achievements, it remains unclear how much they can make personal, authentic choices and how much larger social definitions and constraints define their options.

Any discussion of the challenges faced by women as a group can obscure factors that differentiate women's experiences. Since the legalization of slavery in colonial America, women from Africa, those of African descent, and other women of color have confronted laws, practices, and attitudes that impose a secondary status and significant barriers to real equality. Women from Latin and South American, and those from Asian nations, and their descendents, have also faced restrictive laws, overt discrimination based on their identity, and persistent cultural biases. Class, too, has mattered in the access to education, job training, child support, and health care. For Americans, regional identities create fewer distinctions among citizens than in 1900, but Texans would vehemently declare their differences from New Englanders and Californians would notice how they are dissimilar from Midwesterners. Throughout the twentieth century, region has shaped education, working life, and the nature of family networks in the lives of women.

The differences among women present a special challenge for historians of the twentieth century, as the nation witnessed the development of many strong cultures within, or in contrast to, a dominant "American" culture. The larger dimensions in national life, from the anxieties of the Great Depression to the "domestic containment" of the 1950s, did not diminish communities or cultures in America with distinctive traditions and mores. What is perhaps most telling is how such cultures informed American society with increasing vigor. Today students have days off for the Jewish holidays, bosses reschedule meetings for colleagues fasting for Ramadan, and revelers hoist green beers for St. Patrick's Day and drink tequila and cerveza for Cinco de Mayo. Women proudly claim their particular heritages, which can define expectations about family or work.

Another persistent divide among women stems from changing perceptions on the nature of domestic responsibility. Throughout the twentieth century, most Americans defined women's primary role as wife and mother. Protective legislation reinforced that perception by limiting women's work hours; wage levels also reflected the belief that men supported families while women worked to sustain themselves. Even as women increasingly entered the labor force, families continued to organize chores based on notions of what was acceptable for men or women. By the end of the century, more men took care of children or changed diapers, tasks commonly rejected by their grandfathers as new parents. Yet sociologists determined that women still confronted a "double day" of paid work and housework far more frequently, and for more hours, than did their husbands. When asked to rate their personal happiness, married women continue to rank as the least satisfied of single or married men and women.

If the young American woman in the twenty-first century finds more opportunities than her great-grandmother of 1900, in short, she still shares a number of her ancestor's concerns about gender roles. Trying to sort out how life has changed, and how women make choices about their lives, has been an important task for historians of women and the family for the past forty years. In that time, very sketchy histories of women's contributions have led to nuanced investigations of all aspects of women's experiences. Scholars have also explored the ways in which gender shapes men's choices, and how gendered interactions have profound social and political consequences. Women's history, in short, is not just about women, but about how a society changes, and the meanings people attach to all aspects of their lives.

Chronology

1900	Margaret I. Abbott is the first American woman to win an Olympic gold medal by winning a nine-hole golf tournament.
1901	Annie Taylor is the first person to go over Niagara Falls in a barrel and survive.
1902	Elizabeth Cady Stanton, a pioneer of women's rights and women's suffrage, dies at the age of 87.
1903	Maggie Walker of Richmond, Virginia, becomes President of the St. Luke's Penny Savings Bank.
	The National Women's Trade Union League is formed.
1904	Amanda Clement of Iowa umpires a male baseball game and is paid for her work.
	Journalist Ida Tarbell writes *The History of Standard Oil*.
	Mary McLeod Bethune founds the Daytona Normal and Industrial Institute for Negro Girls.
1906	Lula Olive Gill wins a horse race in California as a paid jockey.
	Susan B. Anthony dies before women's suffrage is achieved.
1907	First organized women's bowling league begins in St. Louis, Missouri.

1908	Portia School of Law opens in Boston as a women's law school
	In *Muller v. Oregon*, the Supreme Court upholds laws that provide special protections for female workers.
	Manufactures of shampoo urge users to wash their hair at least every two weeks.
1909	First female automobile race takes nine drivers from New York to Philadelphia.
	International Ladies Garment Workers Union organizes a strike of 20,000 women workers to protest wages and conditions in the New York City garment trade.
1910	Madame C. J. Walker opens a beauty school and salon in Indianapolis; she will become the first female millionaire in America.
1911	In New York City, a fire at the Triangle Shirtwaist factory kills 146 workers.
1912	Maria Montessori's *The Montessori Method* is published in the United States.
	Women workers strike in Lawrence, Massachusetts in the textile trades for "bread and roses."
	Girl Scouts are founded by Juliette Gordon Low.
1913	Women's suffrage parade in Washington, DC, includes 5,000 marchers.
1914	Birth control activist Margaret Sanger is indicted for using the United States mail to distribute birth control information.
	Women's basketball rules change to allow women to play half court, replacing the earlier standard of playing on one-third of the court.
1915	Aimee Semple McPherson begins her evangelical work.
	International Conference of Women at The Hague is created to advocate peace among warring nations.
1916	Jeanette Rankin of Montana is the first women elected to the U.S. House of Representatives.
	National Women's Party is created.
	Evelyn Burnett becomes the first champion platform diver.
	Ruth Law sets a solo flight record, traveling nonstop from Chicago to Hornell, New York.
	Film actress Theda Bara stars in "A Fool There Was!"

1918	Margaret Sanger opens a birth control clinic in Brooklyn, New York.
	Author Willa Cather publishes novel *My Antonia*.
1919	Actress Mary Pickford, "America's Sweetheart," establishes United Artists with Charles Chaplin, D. W. Griffith, and Douglas Fairbanks.
	Writer Dorothy Parker helps establish the Algonquin Roundtable of writers in New York City.
	Crystal Eastman organizes the First Feminist Conference.
1920	Nineteenth Amendment is ratified, assuring women's rights to vote in federal elections. African American women are barred from voting in states that have adopted methods to disenfranchise black voters.
	Philadelphia women's hockey team competes internationally.
	Theresa Weld Blanchard is the first American woman to win an Olympic medal for figure skating, placing third.
1921	Helen Meany wins the first of many springboard diving championships.
	Bessie Coleman is the first licensed African American pilot.
	First Miss American contest is held in Atlantic City, New Jersey.
	Bryn Mawr Summer School for Women Workers begins.
	Lila Acheson Wallace creates *Readers' Digest* with her husband.
1922	Florence Allen of Ohio is the first woman to become a judge on a state supreme court.
	Rebecca Latimer Felton of Georgia becomes the first woman to serve in the U.S. Senate, occupying the office for slightly more than a day in November.
1923	National Women's Party founder Alice Paul introduces an Equal Rights Amendment, which asserts that "men and women shall have equal rights throughout the United States and every other place subject to its jurisdiction." The proposal generates heated debate among women activists.
	Bessie Smith records blues for Columbia Records.
	Edna St. Vincent Millay wins the Pulitzer Prize for Poetry.
1924	Native American women gain the right to vote in federal elections.

Helen Mills wins gold in both singles and doubles tennis in the Olympics.

Artist Georgia O'Keefe marries artist Alfred Stieglitz.

1925   Nellie Tayloe Ross becomes governor of Wyoming, and Miriam A. Ferguson becomes governor of Texas. Both follow their husbands into office.

The Society of Women Geographers is founded.

Zora Neale Hurston publishes the literary magazine *Fire!* with Langston Hughes.

Short skirts are popular.

Martha Graham founds her own dance company.

Florence Sabin is accepted as the first female member of the National Academy of Science.

1927   Helen Wills begins eight years as the world's female tennis champion.

The Carter family of Virginia records their first traditional song.

Builder Kate Gleason creates concrete community housing in Sausalito, California.

Gerber introduces canned baby foods with its first selection, strained peas.

Director Dorothy Arzner makes her first movie, *Fashions for Women.*

1928   Women in Puerto Rico receive voting rights.

Genevieve Rose Cline of Ohio is appointed as a federal judge to the U.S. Customs Court.

Sonja Henie wins the first of her three Olympic gold medals for figure skating.

Anthropologist Margaret Mead publishes *Coming of Age in Samoa.*

1929   Mildred Wirt writes the first Nancy Drew mystery.

The applicator tampon is introduced.

1930   Anne Morrow Lindbergh with her husband Charles sets a transcontinental flying record for speed.

Baseball Commissioner Judge Landis bans women from playing professional baseball.

Bette Davis makes her first movie, *Bad Sister.*

1931   Social worker Jane Addams wins the Nobel Peace Prize.

1932	Hattie Wyatt Caraway of Arkansas is appointed to the U.S. Senate and wins election in 1933.
	Babe Didrikson of Texas wins the national women's track and field team championship.
	Women's Lacrosse Association is founded.
	Amelia Earhart flies solo across the Atlantic.
	Babe Didrikson wins three gold medals at the Olympic games. Two African American women, Louise Stokes and Tidye Pickett, are barred from competition.
1933	Frances Perkins is appointed to Franklin Roosevelt's Cabinet as Secretary of Labor, the first woman in a presidential cabinet post.
	Eleanor Roosevelt became First Lady.
	Lena Horne starts her singing career at the Cotton Club in Harlem.
1934	Florence Allen is named to the Sixth Circuit Court of Appeals, the first female judge on a U.S. appellate court.
	Ella Fitzgerald enters a singing contest at the Apollo Theater in New York and wins.
1935	Mary McLeod Bethune creates the National Council of Negro Women.
	The Aid to Dependent Children Act is passed.
	Nylon fabric is introduced by DuPont.
1936	Olympics allow women gymnasts to compete.
	Margaret Mitchell publishes *Gone with the Wind.*
1937	Female trainer Mary Hirsch sees her horse win the Kentucky Derby.
	Writer Edith Wharton dies.
1938	The Fair Labor Standards Act establishes minimum wages for women and men, without regard to gender.
	Billie Holliday first performs the song "Strange Fruit."
1939	Marion Anderson performs at the Lincoln Memorial after being barred from the DAR Convention Hall because of her race.
	Hattie McDaniel wins an Academy Award for Best Supporting Actress in *Gone with the Wind.*
1940	The Republican Party endorses the Equal Rights Amendment.

1941	Congressional representative Jeanette Rankin casts the only vote against war with Japan.
1942	Internment of Japanese Americans begins.
	The Women's Auxiliary Army Corps (WAACs) is formed.
1943	The All-American Girls Professional Baseball League is created and teams begin to tour.
	Norman Rockwell illustrates "Rosie the Riveter" for the *Saturday Evening Post* cover.
1944	Helen Taussig pioneers surgery for infants born with heart defects.
1945	Eleanor Roosevelt is appointed to the U.S. delegation to create the United Nations.
	Pearl S. Buck wins the Nobel Prize for Literature.
1946	United Nations establishes a Commission on the Status of Women.
	Alice Coachman is the first African American woman allowed to compete on the U.S. All-American Track and Field team.
	Benjamin Spock publishes *Baby and Child Care.*
1947	Althea Gibson wins the first of ten straight American Tennis Association championships.
	Gerti Cori wins the Nobel Prize for work with husband Carl on human energy theories.
	Fashion designer Dior introduces the "New Look."
1948	Women's roller derby is broadcast on television.
1949	Margaret Chase Smith of Maine is elected to the U.S. Senate, the first woman to win a seat without a prior appointment to Congress.
	Burnita Shelton Matthews is appointed to the federal trial bench.
1950	U.S. Census Bureau recognizes that women may use their original last name after marriage.
1951	Barbara Johns and other students in Prince Edward County, Virginia, protest inferior conditions in their segregated school.
	I Love Lucy appears on television.

1952   Author Lillian Hellman testifies before the House Un-American Activities Committee and refuses to "name names."

Physician Virginia Apgar creates the Apgar score to assess infant's health at birth.

1953   Clare Booth Luce is named as U.S. Ambassador to Italy, the first woman to receive a major diplomatic post.

Tenley Albright wins the world female figure skating championship.

Alfred Kinsey publishes *Sexual Behavior in the Human Female*, which becomes a best seller.

Ethel Rosenberg is executed for treason after husband Julius at Sing Sing prison.

1954   Schools are ordered to desegregation with "all deliberate speed" by the Supreme Court in its *Brown* v. *Board* decision.

1955   Rosa Parks refused to comply with a Montgomery, Alabama, law requiring African Americans to give up their bus seats for white passengers. Her refusal sparks the Montgomery Bus Boycott.

Louise Boyd flies over the North Pole, the first woman to do so.

The Ladies' Professional Golf Association holds its first championship.

1956   Althea Gibson becomes the first African American to win a Grand Slam championship, in France.

1957   Althea Gibson wins Wimbledon in England and the U.S. National Championship. She ranks as the top female tennis player in the world.

African American students attend Central High School in Little Rock, Arkansas.

1960   Carol Hess performs the first double jump in women's figure skating.

Wilma Rudolph wins three Olympic gold medals for track and field.

G. D. Searle markets an oral contraceptive.

Ruby Bridges enters New Orleans elementary school and is segregated in a class of one.

1961   Jane Jacobs publishes *The Death and Life of Great American Cities*, challenging city planners.

President John F. Kennedy creates the President's Commission on the Status of Women.

Women Strike for Peace is formed.

Charlayne Hunter enters the University of Georgia.

First Lady Jacquelyn Kennedy becomes a role model for fashion and "pillbox" hats.

1962   Female attorney Constance Baker Motley represents black student James Meredith in his attempt to gain admission to University of Mississippi.

Dolores Huerta works in the creation of the Farm Workers Movement.

Rachel Carson publishes *Silent Spring*, which warns of pending environmental hazards.

1963   Congress passes the Equal Pay Act, requiring equal pay for women and men performing equal work. This is the first federal law directly prohibiting sex discrimination.

Julia Child begins broadcasts as "The French Chef" on Boston Public Television.

Betty Friedan's book, *The Feminine Mystique*, documents the growing discontent of college-educated women.

Maria Goeppert Mayer wins the Nobel Prize for physics with Hans Jensen.

Four African American girls are killed in a bombing at a Birmingham, Alabama, church.

Vivian Malone enters the University of Alabama.

1964   The Civil Rights Act prohibits discrimination on the basis of race and sex. It includes Title VII, establishing the Equal Employment Opportunity Commission.

Fannie Lou Hamer challenges the credentials committee at the Democratic Convention.

Designer Rudi Gernreich introduces a topless swimsuit for women.

Patsy Mink of Hawaii is elected to the U.S. Senate, the first Asian American women in Congress.

1965   The Supreme Court asserts a constitutional protection for privacy rights for married couples in *Griswold v. Connecticut.*

Donna De Varona becomes the first woman sportscaster for ABC.

Photographer Dickie Chapelle dies while working in Vietnam.

White "go-go" boots are popular with young women, who also prefer mini-skirts.

1966   The National Organization of Women is founded and challenges laws that discriminate against women.

Billie Jean King wins the women's singles event at Wimbledon, her first major championship.

Women play in an intercollegiate basketball tournament.

1967   The Supreme Court's decision in *Loving* v. *Virginia* prohibits state laws barring marriage between people of different races.

Katherine Switzer is prohibited from running in the Boston Marathon.

Paper dresses are marketed.

Muriel Siebert is the first woman to have a seat on the New York Stock Exchange.

1968   Diahann Carroll stars in *Julia*, the first situation comedy featuring an African American protagonist.

1969   The Supreme Court rules in *Weeks* v. *Southern Bell*, ending regulations on the conditions and hours of women's work.

California institutes the nation's first "no fault" divorce law.

1970   Cathy Rigby becomes the first American to win a medal in international gymnastics competition.

Anna Mae McCabe Hays is promoted to General, the first woman to reach that rank in the U.S. Army.

1971   In *Reed* v. *Reed*, the Supreme Court overturns a law that automatically makes men the administrators of wills.

The National Women's Political Caucus is formed.

1972   In *Eisenstadt* v. *Baird*, the Supreme Court clarifies access to contraception for all adults.

Women are allowed to run in the Boston Marathon.

Title IX of the Education Amendments Act requires equal access for students attending schools, colleges, and universities receiving federal funding.

Shirley Chisholm, an African American member of the House of Representatives, campaigns for the presidency.

1973	The Supreme Court rules in *Roe* v. *Wade* that women may, in consultation with their physicians, terminate a pregnancy.
	The U.S. Tennis Association makes prize money equal for men and women.
	Tennis star Billie Jean King beats male player Bobby Riggs in the "Battle of the Sexes."
1974	The first shelter for female victims of domestic violence opens in St. Paul, Minnesota.
	Ella Grasso of Connecticut becomes the first woman elected as governor in her own right.
	Congress outlaws sexual discrimination in housing and credit.
	Little League allows girls to play ball.
1976	Dorothy Hamill wins an Olympic gold medal for women's figure skating.
	Kitty O'Neil sets a land speed record for women by driving 300 mph.
	Shirley Muldowney wins a National Hot Rod Association event.
1978	The Pregnancy Discrimination Act bars employers from firing a woman based on pregnancy.
	Melissa Ludtke, a reporter for Sports Illustrated, sues to gain access to male athletes in their locker rooms for interviews, a standard practice for male reporters.
	The Women's Professional Basketball League plays its first game, with the Chicago Hustle and Milwaukee Does.
	Janet Guthrie finishes the Indianapolis 500 in eighth place.
1979	Nancy Lopez wins Rookie of the Year on the LPGA.
	Billie Jean King wins her 20th Wimbledon title in tennis.
1980	The International Women's Sports Hall of Fame is created.
1981	The Supreme Court reasserts a military draft for men only in *Rostker* v. *Goldberg.*
	Sandra Day O'Connor is named to the U.S. Supreme Court by President Ronald Reagan.
	Betty Ellis becomes the first woman to officiate at a professional soccer match.

Maya Lin wins the design competition for the Vietnam War Veterans Memorial.

The first in vitro fertilization occurs in the United States.

AIDS is identified and begins to spread in the United States.

1982   Brenda Berkman becomes the first female New York City firefighter.

The Equal Rights Amendment, passed by Congress in 1972, fails to win ratification in the states.

1983   Martina Navratilova becomes a Grand Slam winner in tennis.

Sally Ride is the first American woman in space.

1984   Congressional Representative Geraldine Ferraro is nominated as the Democratic candidate for the vice presidency, running with Walter M. Mondale.

Georgeann Wells-Blackwell becomes the first woman to dunk a basketball in an NCAA intercollegiate game.

Joan Benoit wins the first women's Olympic marathon.

Mary Lou Retton wins the all-around gold medal at the Olympics in gymnastics.

Kathryn Sullivan becomes the first woman to take a space walk.

1985   Wilma Mankiller becomes the first female chief of the Cherokee nation.

1986   The Supreme Court holds that sexual harassment creates a hostile work environment and violates Title VII of the 1964 Civil Rights Act.

Jackie Joyner-Kersee wins the Olympic Heptathlon.

1988   Stacy Allison is the first American woman to climb Mount Everest.

1989   The Supreme Court upholds the ability of states to deny public funding for abortions in *Webster* v. *Reproductive Health Services*.

Chris Everett becomes the first tennis player to record 1,000 wins.

Barbara Harris becomes America's first female bishop.

1990   Martina Navratilova wins her ninth Wimbledon title.

Congress passes the Americans with Disabilities Act.

1992	Supreme Court nominee Clarence Thomas is challenged in his confirmation hearings for sexual harassment.
	Mae Jemison, the first female African American astronaut, goes to space.
1993	Janet Reno of Florida is named as the first female U.S. Attorney General.
	Ruth Bader Ginsburg is confirmed to the U.S. Supreme Court.
	The Family and Medical Leave Act allows employees to take unpaid leave to care for children or other family members.
1994	The Violence Against Women Act creates penalties against stalking and other crimes of sexual violence.
	Picaboo Street wins the World Cup for downhill skiing, the first American woman to do so.
1995	Myrlie Evers-Williams is elected head of the NAACP.
	Over 40 percent of American women have some college education.
1996	Sergeant Heather Johnsen becomes the first woman soldier to guard the tomb of the Unknown Soldier at Arlington National Cemetery.
1997	The National Basketball Association hires female referees.
	The National Women's Basketball Association begins.
	Madelyn Albright becomes the first female Secretary of State.
	Jody Williams wins the Nobel Peace Prize for her work to ban land mines.
	Major General Claudia Kennedy becomes the first three-star female general in U.S. history.
	Pat Henry sails around the world solo.
1998	The Supreme Court declares that harassment of gays and lesbians violates Title VII of the 1964 Civil Rights Act.
	Cynthia Trudell is appointed head of the Saturn division of General Motors.
	Lilith Fair, an all-female concert series, earns over $28 million.
2000	In *United States* v. *Morrison*, the Supreme Court rules that victims cannot use the Violence Against Women Act to sue attackers in federal court.

Hillary Clinton becomes Senator from New York, the first former First Lady elected to Congress.

Body piercing and tattoos become increasingly acceptable for women.

2001   Condoleezza Rice is named National Security Advisor.

Anne Mulcahy is appointed head of Xerox Corporation.

2005   Condoleezza Rice becomes Secretary of State.

2006   Nancy Pelosi of California is elected Speaker of the U.S. House of Representatives.

Indra Nooyi becomes CEO of PepsiCo, a Fortune 500 company.

2007   Senator Hillary Clinton of New York is a major candidate for President.

2008   Governor Sarah Palin of Alaska is the Vice Presidential nominee for the Republican Party.

1

———∽∽∽———

Women and Work

Of the many changes in women's lives in the twentieth century, few were as dramatic or significant as the expansion of women's opportunities for work. At the beginning of the century, the typical female laborer still toiled in the home as a domestic servant. One hundred years later, women worked as physicians, astronauts, clerical workers, police officers, soldiers, ministers, and engineers, among many other jobs and occupations.

The transformation of women's labor resulted in part from the larger shifts in the American economy away from the production of heavy manufacturing toward consumer goods and services. The factors that increased women's labor outside the home were the result of complex and sometimes contradictory dynamics. Some women responded to new opportunities for work; others challenged legal or social barriers to win the right. An even greater number took advantage of shifting technologies or attitudes, and sometimes both, to find a good job.

Throughout the century, however, key characteristics of women's paid labor remained remarkably consistent. Women's wages continued to be less than those of men, and not until the twenty-first century would a significant, albeit small, proportion of women earn more than men in comparable jobs. Most "women's work" also occurred in occupations primarily populated by women. Scholars have referred to the latter as a "dual labor market" or, more colorfully, as a "pink collar labor force." Regardless of the definition attached, the segregation of work paralleled social assumptions about family life and gender roles in which men would work for pay, and women, after marriage, would tend their homes. Race further divided women's work, as African American women, those from South and Latin America, and other women of color faced prohibitions and barriers based on antagonistic laws and customs. Each of these elements that shaped twentieth-century women's labor would be challenged by individuals, activists, and labor and reform organizations. Not until the last decades of the century would those struggles begin to bear fruit in the form of improved laws and opportunities for the majority of women workers.

THE PROFESSIONAL WOMAN, 1900–1930

Many specialized fields of work, from medicine to law and academia, began to professionalize in the late nineteenth century. Historians have noted that the movement for creating professional credentials allowed those working in these arenas to structure knowledge, ethics, and standards of practice. In disciplines such as medicine, an accredited education and licensure might be a new guarantee for patient safety. As professionals seemed to promise the public improvements in service, however, they also gained control over admission to their respective areas of expertise, the numbers of professionals, and in turn, rates of compensation. For some aspiring Americans, access to a profession through merit and education promised a life of prosperity, while others who hoped to enter confronted quotas and prohibitions.

For women, the movement toward professionalization created new opportunities in subjects that might be associated with women or the home, such as teaching, library work, or social services. Barriers remained in fields identified as supposedly male provinces. The presumption that men would work and women remain in the home remained one rationale for discrimination.[1] When women entered professions such as medicine, increasingly structured as a hierarchy that placed male doctors in charge of female nurses, they struggled to retain the unique niches created by the first female physicians. Women doctors had practiced since Elizabeth Blackwell became the nation's first female medical school graduate in 1857. Blackwell opened the Women's Medical College of the New York Infirmary for Women and Children with her sister Emily, and soon other medical schools enrolled women. The University of Michigan admitted female applicants in 1870, the first state school to do so. When Johns Hopkins University opened its medical school in 1893, donor Mary Elizabeth Garrett provided nearly $500,000 to ensure the admission of female applicants. Other doors opened as well. Physician Mary Harris Thompson read a scholarly paper at the annual meeting of the American Medical Association and published it in the association's *Journal*. By 1900, the Women's College of Philadelphia, the University of Michigan, and the Female

Medical College of Pennsylvania produced nearly one thousand female doctors, including over one hundred African American practitioners.

Despite such dedication, women found entrance into medicine daunting. In 1910, women constituted only 10 percent of the profession. In the following decades, most medical schools used quotas to limit the number of female entrants to 5 percent of each class. Once a woman received a medical degree, the next obstacle she encountered was finding an internship; many hospitals refused to consider applications from women. Although World War II resulted in an increase of women medical school students, to 12 percent, by 1945 those numbers had returned to the dismal prewar single digits. Medical schools gradually opened to women, with Harvard finally accepting female candidates in 1945; the last medical school to allow entrance to women, Jefferson Medical College of Philadelphia, did so in 1960.

Women hoping to pursue a legal career confronted even greater barriers. Although some states still allowed women to read law rather than attend a law school, few permitted women to practice. Myra Bradwell challenged restrictions in Michigan in the 1870s, but her initial effort ended when the U.S. Supreme Court ruled in 1873 that women needed to "fulfill the noble and benign offices of wife and mother."[2] Law practice, according to the Court, made such obligations impossible. Illinois disagreed, however, and began admitting women to the bar. Bradwell entered practice in 1885, but for many women attorneys, the restrictions continued to be daunting. In 1910, fewer than 1,500 women lawyers had entered the profession; five years later, only 3 percent of attorneys nationally were female.

Similar difficulties arose in other fields socially defined as masculine prerogatives. In science and engineering, women labored in laboratories and studied in classrooms but found fewer mentors, employers, and sponsors, despite the worldwide fame of Nobel Prize winner Marie Curie. Mathematicians such as Charlotte Barnum, Winifred Merrill, and Mary Frances Winston Newson, each of whom received PhDs in mathematics prior to 1900, taught only sporadically in their field. Only with the entrance of more women, and the immigration of female scientists and mathematicians from Europe, did opportunities slowly evolve. As women entered academia in growing numbers in the 1920s, many universities shifted standards for promotion and hiring. The "standards" of research and scholarship for hiring, tenure, and promotion favored individuals able to devote uninterrupted time to research. These implicitly disadvantaged women with families, forcing women to find congenial husbands or satisfy themselves with the lower ranks of academia.[3]

Aspiring female dentists and veterinarians faced the same type of exclusions. Although women had practiced as dentists since the late nineteenth century, many limited their patients to women and children. As late as 1945, four major dental schools, including Harvard, refused to accept women applicants. Women hoping to practice veterinary medicine had few options for training; as late as the 1960s, women comprised fewer than 5 percent of the profession. Those who earned the DVM included Mignon Nicholson, the first woman recorded as graduating from a private veterinary school, who finished a program in 1903. Elinor McGrath, from Chicago's Veterinary College, and Florence Kimball, a Cornell University graduate, completed their degrees in 1910 and opened private practices on small animals. In the 1930s, women trained at Kansas State University, Michigan State, and Washington State in order to work on livestock, in public health, or in meat inspection. The slowly increasing numbers of women veterinarians led to the creation of the Association of Women Veterinarians in 1947, with the very overt goals of sharing "knowledge, support and friendship."[4]

One arena previously connected to masculine acumen offered new opportunities to women with entrepreneur drive and skill, that of business. Martha Matilda Harper, for example, moved to Rochester, New York, and began to sell hair tonic door to door. She earned enough to open her own beauty shop and decided to emphasize luxury care for the affluent. As her clientele grew, Harper leased her name and idea to others, and so developed the idea of franchising. Maggie Lena Walker, the first female bank president in the United States, developed a penny savings bank from a mutual aid society. That institution in Richmond, Virginia, evolved into the only bank for African Americans, the Consolidated Bank and Trust. By World War II, the Consolidated was one of only six African American banks in the nation. Madame C. J. Walker, the nation's first self-made female millionaire, earned her wealth from beauty products and an astute business sense. Born Sarah Breedlove, Walker developed the "wonderful hair grower" and subsequently a hair straightening product for African American women. Breedlove grew up in poverty in Louisiana. After her first husband died, she moved to St. Louis, working as a laundress. In attempting to relieve a scalp ailment, she experimented with hair treatments. She moved to Denver and sold hair products for another female entrepreneur, but returned to St. Louis to marry C. J. Walker, a journalist. She also opened her own business, the "Madame C. J. Walker Manufacturing Company." By 1917, Madame Walker owned the most successful and largest African American business in America.

Other women entrepreneurs also found their success in beauty products. Elizabeth Arden began life as Florence Nightingale Graham in Canada, but after moving to New York in 1908, she embarked on a career in beauty treatments. With a partner, Elizabeth Hubbard, the young woman opened a salon and renamed herself "Arden," attempting to invoke the "ardent" search for youth and love. Her salon, and her name, appealed to middle-aged women who longed to regain their beauty. Arden's formula for a unique approach to the customer was also used by other female entrepreneurs, including Helena Rubenstein and Hazel Bishop.

Women's needs or desires also served as springboards into business for other women. Lena Himmelstein, a Lithuanian immigrant, initially earned an income by designing and sewing clothes for pregnant women. Her styles were flattering, and Himmelstein added a line for larger women in 1910. Her stores, marketing under the name Lane Bryant, continue in operation. Carrie Marcus Neiman, the daughter of German immigrants to Texas, worked selling blouses in a Dallas department store. After she married Abraham Lincoln Neiman, she and her brother Herbert became partners with Neiman in a new store featuring women's fashions. Neiman Marcus's status depended on Carrie Neiman, and after her divorce from Al Neiman, she and brother Herbert ran the company.

One American entrepreneur in the early twentieth century remains remarkable for her skills, the animosity she generated, and her legend. Hetty Green became known as the "Witch of Wall Street" as much in derogation as in praise for her investment skills. She inherited substantially from what her father had made in the whaling business in New Bedford, Massachusetts, but gained a public reputation after suing unsuccessfully to acquire control of her aunt's estate. Even without that income, Green astutely parlayed her income into a fortune through careful investments and a notorious frugality. When she died in 1916, she was America's wealthiest woman, worth approximately $100 million.

Gender clearly circumscribed opportunities in the first half of the century. Even in professions open to women, advancement or treatment at work differed for men and women. In journalism, the reporting of women such as Ida Tarbell and Ida B. Wells won national attention, but most female reporters found themselves relegated to feature pages and society columns. Tarbell's investigation of Standard Oil contributed to antitrust action against millionaire John D. Rockefeller; Wells campaigned ferociously against lynching in print and in person. These women took the tradition of "scribbling women" writers and combined it with women's increasing access to public spaces and reform. They still seemed to be interlopers on male tradition, however, and a journalist's exposure to indelicate matters and danger led some editors to make less challenging, and career-making, assignments.

WORKING FOR WAGES

In 1900, America remained primarily an agricultural nation. With a population of seventy-six million people, nearly ten million men, women, and children still labored on farms and in fields, even though the industrial expansion of the nineteenth century made the United States a global economic force. The transition from a rural, agricultural society to an urban, industrial nation in the early twentieth century affected nearly all aspects of American life. One part of this change was the arrival of nearly twenty-six million immigrants, mostly from Southern and Eastern Europe, drawn by work, religious freedom, and the urgings of friends, neighbors, and family already in America. By 1920, the majority of Americans lived in or near a city, and nearly 40 percent worked in manufacturing. For women, the changes in work offered opportunities, as increasing capacity in industry and the growing service sector required more and more workers. As women and men entered the twentieth-century industrial labor force, however, some old barriers remained, and new ones appeared. The differentiation between male and female waged workers grew more distinct, with women largely restricted to the lowest-paying jobs in the clerical, sales, and service fields.

In 1900, the "typical" working woman was a young woman who left the labor force once she wed. Over half of the female laborers in the first years of the century were either foreign born, the children of foreign-born parents, or African American. Few found representation from unions to protect them from long hours or low wages; instead, the evolution of laws providing some safeguards from dangerous conditions or stipulating maximum hours of work came from a coalition of reformers and female activists. Progressive era women reformers joined with working women in organizations such as the Women's Trade Union League and the National Consumers' League to establish minimum hours.

In New York, a 1909 strike by women garment workers mobilized nearly 20,000 workers in the textile trades eager for better conditions. The International Ladies Garment Workers' Union (ILGWU) worked with the Women's Trade Union League (WTUL), and each considered the strike a success, although it ended without a conclusion settlement. Instead, shop owners reached individual agreements with their workers, a patchwork of promises that did not extend to all garment workers. On March 25, 1911, a fire in the Triangle Shirtwaist Factory, located on the fifth floor of a building near Washington Square in lower New York, resulted in the deaths of 146 women workers. A public outcry led New York legislators to establish a Factory Investigating Committee and establish safety standards for workers. Although New York responded to the tragedy, it had little impact on other female factory workers laboring in other parts of the country.

Some employers such as H. J. Heinz and Edward Filene provided paternalistic environments in shops and factories. For most women in industry, however, jobs required tending machines doing repetitive tasks, usually in poorly lit, badly ventilated, and dirty facilities with limited breaks. Wages tended to be a third lower than those of men, and sometimes less. Bureau of Labor reports, for instance, found that in 1911 the median wage for men in the New York clothing factories was $10.50, and for women, only $5.50.[5] In agriculture and domestic service, more frequent sites of women's work, wages were even lower and conditions less favorable. Women who picked, hoed, plowed, and ditched in the postwar South might earn 50 cents a day to a man's 65.[6] Domestic service remained the worst option, with little time for personal needs, low wages, and constant interference and supervision by the employing family. The notorious Lizzie Borden of Fall River, Massachusetts, provided an instructive example of the disregard for servants at her 1893 trial for the murders of her father and stepmother. Lizzie did not remember the name of the woman employed in the Borden household; she called every successive maid "Bridgette," never bothering to learn any real names.

In the first part of the century, women's waged labor continued to be structured around key elements such as the life cycle, race, and economic need. Single women worked outside the home for pay, but with some notable exceptions, the typical married woman did not. In 1890, only 5 percent of all married women labored outside the home. Despite slowly increasing numbers of married women re-entering the labor market, prior to 1940 most women remained housewives or supplemented family earnings by other means. Race played an important role in women's decisions about work, however. African American women continued to work for pay, most commonly in domestic services and agricultural labor; between 1890 and 1930, 90 percent of all black women workers could be found in those areas of the economy.[7] On the eve of the Depression, married African American women were still three times more likely to be employed than married white women.

Women's labor patterns also varied in immigrant communities. In some neighborhoods and regions, married women were far more likely to work for pay outside the home before the 1930s. In Passaic, New Jersey, for example, a predominantly Jewish community reflected the tendency of married Jewish women to work more frequently than other New Jersey women, and so labor force participation rates for the married women in Passaic rose to over 20 percent of all married women. The opposite story comes from Italian families in the Greater New York region, who tended to keep wives and daughters out of the labor market. When women did work, Italian immigrant families found employment that maintained family networks and relationships.[8]

The mechanisms that created and perpetuated variations in opportunities for women included laws that restricted women or required men to support families, traditional ideas about family structures, religious teachings that celebrated particular family ideals, and economic needs. For women seeking wage work, the notion that the home remained the ideal

Women workers on Erie, Pennsylvania, drill presses in 1918. AP photo.

sphere of feminine influence still shaped many of the options open to them. Although many women at the turn of the century worked prior to marriage, attended college, worked as volunteers in charities and reform agencies, and lived outside of domestic seclusion, defenders of women's homebound role insisted that women's entrance into the labor force would result in weak, debilitated children.[9] This adamant assertion from an American Federation of Labor speaker echoed the sentiments shared by many regardless of class or gender. The domestic ideal reinforced the belief that women were, at best, temporary workers. Consequently, for some women, notions of propriety led them to leave work despite a desire to continue earning. For others, working after marriage meant challenging friends and family who might think it unsuitable.

The laws and hiring practices applied to women after the turn of the century utilized the domestic ideal to reinforce the perceived differences between men and women. In law, the belief that all women would eventually become wives and mothers served to sustain *protective legislation*, laws that mandated specific hours, conditions, and wages for women workers. Such laws began in the late nineteenth century, as Massachusetts set women's work hours to 10 per day in 1874. When these provisions, won on a state-by-state basis by female reformers and workers, were challenged in the Supreme Court in 1908, the Justices affirmed the need for different laws for men and women workers, concluding that women needed "especial care that her rights may be preserved." The case *Muller v. Oregon* not only asserted the constitutionality of difference, but also provided a legal explanation for safeguarding women's household roles. Ironically, the laws designed to help women workers also limited their labor, something that would be a matter of debate between women reformers and workers until the 1970s. Nevertheless, states passed protective statutes; by 1914, twenty-seven states had maximum hours laws, and after 1920, fifteen states had passed minimum wage laws for women.

The domestic ideal served to legitimize other restrictions as well. Increasingly, employers defended lower wages for female workers on the basis that most were single, and that unlike men, they did not support families. Married women worked for "pin money," a little extra to buy luxuries, some claimed, and that notion became more commonplace as consumer goods multiplied in the 1920s. Most intriguing of all, however, was the connection between domesticity and the evolution of clerical labor.

By the 1890s, new improvements in typewriters and the growth of business created a demand for lower-waged clerical labor. Simultaneously, education began to change, as school districts consolidated to create large high schools with expansive curriculums. Clerical training emerged as a popular offering, allowing young women to find work with better hours, and in cleaner environments, than in factories. Young men, on the other hand, found themselves on a managerial path that led to on-the-job training or, by the 1920s, a Masters in Business Administration.[10] Young women who became secretaries typed, filed, and took transcription, but advanced only within the secretarial ranks. They also provided domestic touches to the male office, answering the telephone, serving food and beverages when asked, and, according to *Ladies Home Journal*, radiating "the office with sunshine and sympathetic interest."[11] Many firms developed policies that restricted clerical positions to women while excluding them from more lucrative posts in accounting or marketing. The wage gap between young men and women, initially only 14 percent, grew dramatically as each worked within their separate tiers of new firms in the 1920s. Even with comparable education and years of experience, men earned 40 percent more than women, a result of occupational segregation.[12]

The first real change in women's labor in the twentieth century came as married women gradually entered the labor market, despite barriers. A variety of factors served to push and pull them into waged work. From the late nineteenth century, many working-class wives supplemented family income through informal means, such as taking in boarders, doing piecework, or cleaning laundry. Opportunities for such work slowly diminished with the spread of manufacturing, the lessening of immigration after 1914, and growing commercialization. The expansion of a consumer economy served as an additional lure; in Muncie, Indiana, "Middletown" families cited their need for such items as radios, toasters, refrigerators, cosmetics and beauty products, and, of course, a car, as increasing their budgets. The working wives of Muncie explained their jobs as necessary for their families, to compensate for a husband's unemployment, to buy clothes and goods for children, or to improve the family's standard of living.[13] Many husbands still expressed a sense of being diminished and less manly when their wives worked, and neighbors criticized. Nevertheless, the 1920s became a turning point for the work of married women.[14]

The Great Depression, beginning in 1929 and stretching through the 1930s, brought hardship to all but a few Americans. As the economic crisis worsened from the fall of 1929 into 1930, families on farms and in manufacturing cities such as Detroit or Gary, Indiana, experienced the consequences acutely. Unemployment in manufacturing rose above 70 percent in many manufacturing towns, and men fought to find work. On farms, milk, livestock, grain, and produce no longer earned enough at market to make it worthwhile to transport; families who had held farms for generations confronted foreclosure. By the end of 1932, journalists struggled to describe the desperation experienced by many Americans, using terms such as *decrepit, hopeless,* or *exhausted.* Ironically, in the nation's worst economic crisis, women workers as a distinct group in the labor force fared better through these years than men.

The segregated nature of the labor market meant that by the 1930s, few women remained in heavy manufacturing, the sector of the American economy hit hardest during the Depression. The clerical and service areas in which most women were employed suffered less from the constrictions of the labor market than others, and recovered more rapidly. As a result, male unemployment at the peak of the Depression, in 1932, stood at four times that of women, and women's wages actually rose by 63 percent in comparison to those of men.[15]

Women did face pressure to leave the labor force when it was perceived that they "took" jobs from men. In some professions, women found it harder to get work. Men entered the teaching profession again, for example, and the number of female teachers nationwide declined by 13 percent as a result. The Economy Act of 1932 contained Section 213, which mandated that only one family member could work in the federal civil service; overwhelmingly, families decided to give up the work of women (The act was repealed in 1937.) States followed suit, and many local governments also initiated policies to limit jobs. One county in Washington State banned married women from government jobs and ended up freeing almost fifty positions for the 83,000 recorded unemployed. Public school teachers faced tightened restrictions on marriage as well. In 1931, the National Education Association found that 77 percent of districts surveyed would not employ married teachers, and 63 percent dismissed women who wed.

The sentiment against hiring married women extended into the private labor market. Employers found many reasons to exclude married women from their workforces; 65 percent of banks, 84 percent of insurance companies, and 63 percent of public utilities reported doing so as late as 1939. As the worst effects of the Depression lessened somewhat after 1935, however, the anxiety over married women's competition abated slightly. Section 213 of the Economy Act was repealed, for example, and it became increasingly obvious to most observers that women rarely competed with men for the same jobs because of continuing divisions of labor. In addition, men showed no eagerness to fill the clerical positions or service roles generally occupied by female workers. As a result, the labor force participation of married women continued to rise slowly throughout the decade. The growth remained "slow and evolutionary."[16] Yet it was also clear that the forces pulling women into paid employment, from the urban necessity for wages and the development of new jobs in the service and clerical sector to the consumer-oriented market, continued to lure more women to work outside their homes. By 1940, a significant number of married women workers (estimated at more than 40 percent) already lived comfortably because of a husband's earnings; many cited a better standard of living for the family as their primary reason for work.[17]

Although the Depression did not signal a major setback for women as a group within the workforce, for individual women, the unemployed, and women of color, the 1930s frequently brought a desperate search for a job, a place to stay when unemployed, or some way to keep going. Examining the plight of such women in the early years of the Depression, writer Meridel LeSueur commented on the lack of mission services for women, and asked, "What happens to them? Where do they go?"[18] Tramping or traveling from town to town in search of work could be dangerous, as reporter Adela St. John discovered when she tried it for her newspaper for two weeks. The stigma of poverty and the absence of aid forced New York's homeless women to "give up," journalist Emily Hahn wrote in 1931. African American women found it difficult to find work, as jobs once open to them went to white workers.

Charities, social welfare agencies, and churches struggled to provide help for the women, men, and children devastated by the nation's economic catastrophe. Relief finally arrived as the New Deal began in the first days of President Franklin Roosevelt's first term in March 1933. Roosevelt's "First One Hundred Days" included legislation to restore stability in banking, stop foreclosures on family farms, and give aid to the cities coping with record numbers of the hungry and homeless. For women, the New Deal meant work programs, assistance, and some new rights. Much of the New Deal legislation still permitted divisions by race and gender, or explicitly created exclusive programs segregating blacks and whites, or reinforced stereotypes of a "domestic ideal" for women. Some New Deal programs, such as the Civilian Conservation Corps, employed only men. The National Industrial Recovery Act (1933) provided minimum wage rates by industry, but set different standards for men and women and did not cover agricultural or domestic work. Other New Deal agencies such as the Public Works Administration gave higher wages to male workers. Even at its peak, the Works Progress Administration (WPA) only offered between 12 and 16 percent of jobs available to female workers. Pressure from women within the Roosevelt administration sometimes resulted in improvements or alternatives for women. By 1935, many jobs programs had been transferred to the WPA, where Ellen Woodward assumed charge of a new Women's and Professional Projects Division. Hilda Worthington Smith used her friendship with Eleanor Roosevelt to establish a small program for women like that of the Civilian Conservation Corps (CCC) run through the National Youth Administration. When she finally secured a small stipend for the women workers, they earned half of what their male counterparts in the CCC did.[19]

Odd coalitions of conservatives, female reformers from groups such as the National Consumers' League, and male trade unionists from the American Federation of Labor campaigned for protections for home and family in labor legislation. In arguing about the National Industrial Recovery Act of 1933, the Social Security Act of 1935, or the Fair Labor Standards Act of 1938, this strange alliance insisted that single women occupied a distinct niche in the labor market, supporting only themselves. Men, on the other hand, provided for families and deserved recognition for their obligations. By encoding these gender roles into New Deal legislation, legislators perpetuated what has been called a "gendered right to earn."[20] "The practical effect," it has been argued, "was to restrict women's access to economic citizenship."[21] Put more simply, women's opportunities for equal pay and equal work opportunities included an additional obstacle after the 1930s, that of federal reinforcement of gender differences.

New activists emerged to tackle the barriers to fair employment for women in the 1930s, however. The protection for union membership afforded by Section 7(a) of the National Industrial Recovery Act in 1933, and subsequently by the Wagner Act in 1935, resulted in more women joining older unions, such as the ILGWU, or new ones under the emerging Congress of Industrial Organizations (CIO). By 1940, nearly 800,000 women belonged to unions.[22] The CIO organizers worked among groups traditionally ignored by the AFL, from Mexican immigrants in California's canning industry to African American women in Virginia's tobacco warehouses. In Chicago, Baltimore, Cleveland, and other cities, African American women created Housewives Leagues. Through the leagues, they launched a "Don't Buy Where You Can't Work" campaign to force business to hire African

American workers. Housewives, daughters, sweethearts, and other female family members played another significant role in the labor movement in female auxiliaries. During the Flint, Michigan, United Auto Workers' (UAW) strike against General Motors in 1937, the "sit-down" strikers required the food, coffee, and solidarity of female kin. Not allowed to join the striking workers, some two hundred women occupied a sewing room of Fischer Body Plant No. 1 and closed the entire plant when over 300 Fischer workers sat with them. Women's auxiliaries provided a means for unions to prolong strike benefits, promote union ideals, and deepen a community's commitment to strike goals.[23]

As with many examples from women's history, the women's auxiliaries for unions in the 1930s illustrate the contradictory issues facing women. Female activists in the auxiliaries played critical roles in Flint and other cities in winning recognition for the UAW and other CIO unions, and in bettering the earning power of working families. As they engaged in auxiliary work, however, women tacitly promoted their own secondary status as nonworkers. At times, women openly criticized their passive roles; one Flint participant declared, "Just being a woman isn't enough anymore. I want to be a human being with the right to think for myself."[24] Unable or unwilling to resolve the apparent conflict between women's responsibilities to their families and their individual interests, unions did little to explore alternatives.

Unions in the 1930s also acted to limit the labor or participation of African American women with disturbing frequency. Although some CIO organizers attempted to cross racial lines, other organizers quickly abandoned black workers to win a contract. In 1939, the Tobacco Workers International successfully unionized Liggett and Myers in North Carolina, but agreed to the loss of jobs for African American employees. In 1933, the ILGWU signed a Boston contract that excluded black workers, but by the end of the decade, they had begun to recruit African American members and officers. Union protection for African American women workers, or for other women of color, remained haphazard at best.

Among the most prominent and vocal organizers in the 1930s was the Communist Party, which openly challenged the limits of the New Deal. The Party offered soup kitchens, campaigned against lynching in the South, and asserted the equality of black and white workers. Its members also tried to organize workers into unions without regard to craft, race, or gender. The Sharecroppers' Union, for example, resulted from efforts in the South; in the North, Communist Party members created Unemployed Councils, combining neighborhood connections between women and communities of unemployed men, to lead challenges against evictions.

The New Deal also meant advancement of a particular sort. Roosevelt's administration included the nation's first female Cabinet member,

Secretary of Labor Frances Perkins, and more women in higher levels of administration than ever before. Political consultants such as Mary McLeod Bethune, a member of President Roosevelt's informal "Black Cabinet," used both position and publicity for advocacy. Bethune became the Director of the Negro Division of the National Youth Administration. The First Lady, Eleanor Roosevelt, emerged as an even more dynamic and politic defender of the rights of women and African Americans and an extraordinary role model for generations to follow. Even the energetic Mrs. Roosevelt spoke in favor of programs and laws that supported women's domestic roles, as she encouraged new possibilities for professional women.

WORLD WAR II

Historians have long identified World War II as a major turning point for women's work in the twentieth century, as the demands of the wartime economy lowered barriers and drew married women to jobs in record numbers. This interpretation focuses on only part of a larger story, however. The expanding role of the federal government from the 1930s onward was a critical dynamic in shaping new opportunities for women. Continued involvement by the government in the postwar economy contributed to the nation's prosperity and a robust job market, and the federal government became a major employer of women and people of color.

Historians have also pointed out that the trends in women's employment were in place before World War II. The war crisis provided temporary opportunities and more dramatically signaled the shifts in work patterns that were already underway. Before the war, married women's labor force participation rates rose slowly but steadily. During the war, when 75 percent of new workers were married women, and in the decades to follow, older married women and those with school-aged children sought work in record numbers. Simply, the true "revolution" in women's work in the twentieth century lay not in women entering the labor market, but in white married women's paid employment. And, married women's labor in the postwar period simply "exploded."[25] Historians rightfully point out that World War II increased opportunities for women who had already been in the labor force. Some re-entered work because of high wages and less stigma; others went back to a job because their children no longer needed supervision after school. At the very least, the entrance of Rosie the Riveter into wartime work indicated that many women wanted or needed work at good wages.

During the war, few working women or their employers could have fully anticipated the changes that lay ahead. When the nation entered the war in late 1941, mobilization began to divert resources into war production, as the government acted to recruit men into military service and encourage other workers to replace servicemen in defense industries. Both consumer-based production and heavy manufacturing were retooled to make goods needed for the war, from canned food, shoes, and uniforms to bombs, aircraft, and destroyers. Between 1941 and 1944, an additional eight million women would join the workforce; in 1945, women constituted 36.1 percent of the civilian workforce.[26] Most found work in traditional female employment, such as clerical or domestic labor, but the need for workers in previously male-dominated sectors of the economy drew women into ship building, munitions work, steel milling, and the assembly of Jeeps and other heavy production. Before the war, women had made up less than 20 percent of the manufacturing workforce; by 1945, women constituted a third of it.

Women still faced contradictory messages about work, despite the importance of their role in wartime industries. As war mobilization increased in 1942, the War Manpower Commission and the Office of War Information encouraged women to contribute to the war effort by taking a job. Messages were carefully tailored to overcome prejudices, but at the same time advertisements reminded workers that such work was for the duration of the war only. At the same time, as production needs increased, older claims that women lacked the physical or intellectual capacity for industrial labor disappeared. Women instead read government posters that compared their sewing skills to using rivet guns. The Office of War Information declared that the war had "disproved" the idea that "women have no mechanical ability."[27] If they could do the work of men, however, women still needed to remember why they were doing it. The Office of War Information persistently asserted that women's industrial work was a patriotic contribution to victory, not a permanent change. *Yank* magazine, produced by the War Department for soldiers, reminded readers in 1944 that "the girls who are holding a job left by a serviceman know that under the GI Bill of Rights the man can get it back if he wants it."[28] Working women also learned that they should retain their allure and recall that their femininity, not their skill, attracted men. Barbara Gould Night Cream, for example, advertised that its product would keep women beautiful when they took a mechanical job in wartime, reminding its customers of the soldiers who dream of "coming back to YOU as beautiful as ever."[29] It has been noted that a woman worker learned that "she was not primarily a worker but just a woman who happened to work; her participation in the labor force was not motivated by self-actualization or self-reliance, but by patriotism and the desire to win the approval of men."

Advertising and propaganda also connected women's work for the war effort with household production and consumption. Ironically, as women

Women work on the wing of a bomber in a West Coast factory during World War II. Courtesy of the Library of Congress.

were hearing that they could do the work of men, they also heard that the labor they did at home had value beyond the emotional nurture it provided for husbands and children. "Liberty gardens" meant supplementing the food supply, getting vitamins into the younger future citizens, and defeating the Axis with every radish and cabbage. Companies also told women that purchases connected housekeeping to the war. Canon Towels allowed savings that would be put to "war savings bonds," while Chef Boy-ar-dee's canned foods meant that mom could build "the builders of victory, backing up the men over there" with "foods that build strength and endurance and courage."[30] Wartime housewives preserved the nation at home with frugality and careful labor as they were transformed into a new type of war worker.

Women even learned that the content of work, once described by employers and by many workers as innately male, could shift. Jobs that had a significant content of heavy work could be restructured. In 1943, the National Industrial Conference Board found in a study of 155 plants that many had revised production jobs to require less strength. In the process, the work frequently demanded less skill, a growing concern to unions and male workers who had received higher wages under the prior classifications. Whether in retaliation for what they perceived as a threat to jobs and manhood, or because of culture, some male workers responded to women on the assembly lines and shop floors with hostility, sexual innuendo, or physical intimidation.[31]

War work began to dismantle other prejudices that had prohibited certain women from jobs in specific companies or skills. In Lowell, Massachusetts, for example, the Merrimack Mills never hired Catholic women for clerical positions in the front office until a 1941 strike ended the practice.[32] Native American women found jobs in the aircraft industries of the West; African American women still found many jobs closed to them; however, when they were hired, often the positions entailed dangerous, difficult, or dirty tasks. From a study of African American women's employment in World War II it was concluded that "whatever the hierarchy of preference ... black women could always be found at the bottom."[33] The UAW discovered in a 1943 survey that of 280 manufacturers, only 74 offered jobs to African American women. The Wagner Electric Company of St. Louis rejected the 1945 Executive Order for fair hiring; American Telephone and Telegraph (ATT) provided only a few jobs outside of food and service work to black women applicants. Typically, employers accepted African American women as new workers when other available laborers, usually white women and African American men, were scarce. Even with African American women on shop floors or production lines, some employers retained racially segregated restrooms. White female employees also contributed to the exclusion of black women by refusing to work with them. Strikes in 1943 and 1944 in Detroit, Baltimore, and Dan River occurred when white workers tied improvement of working conditions to limit or segregate African American women's jobs.[34]

Even with such discrimination, African American women did improve their overall position in the labor force, as many found better paying jobs, the chance to leave Southern agricultural work, and opportunities to avoid domestic service. The total number of African American women in manufacturing tripled, from 6.5 percent to 18 percent. Like their white counterparts, African American women would confront the loss of jobs at the end of the war. Because many had been hired after other workers, however, they had little protection from seniority rules; racial discrimination would also mean that after the war, many job possibilities remained or became closed. Employment in less desirable service or domestic positions, or in unskilled labor, once again became the recourse of many African American women.

A smaller but equally visible number of women served the nation in uniform during World War II. Women's "auxiliary" war service developed in Europe during World War I; in the United States, advocates proposed a comparable branch of women providing support services for the Armed Forces. Supporters hoped that an official women's branch would solve the problem of volunteer dieticians, nurses, ambulance drivers, and other personnel during World War I, who lacked housing, safety, and recognition.

When presented with a bill to establish the Women's Army Auxiliary Corps (WAAC) in May 1941, however, Southern Congressmen objected loudly. After Pearl Harbor, the WAAC bill passed in 1942. The Women's Naval Reserves (Women Accepted for Volunteer Emergency Service, or WAVES) followed, along with the Marine Corp Women's Reserves and the Coast Guard Women's Reserves (SPARS, or, after the Coast Guard motto, Semper Paratus, Always Ready). Women pilots worked with the Army Air Corps, as the Women's Field Ferrying Service, and trained as flyers in the Women's Flying Training Detachment. In 1943, these divisions were combined into the WASP (Women's Airforce Service Pilots); women pilots worked under military command but received civil service pay. The WASP were not recognized as part of the official Army Air Corps effort until 1979, when veterans received military benefits.[35]

The WAAC structure revealed the subsidiary nature of the organization, and the assumption that WAAC's would be clerical workers, typists, and secretarial workers. Oveta Culp Hobby, appointed as the first Director by Secretary of War Henry Stimpson, supervised a force in which the top rank was Major. No woman from the WAAC was to be allowed to command men. Technically, women were barred from combat positions, and initially the service was not under Army command. In 1943, Congress authorized the Women's Army Corps, or WACS, as part of the regular Army. In practice, the demands of the war soon allowed women to expand the duties they performed. By war's end, women had flown B-17's in support missions, served on hospital ships in the Pacific, provided support services in malarial conditions on Pacific Islands, and worked on the Manhattan Project. Sixteen WACs earned the Purple Heart; over 500 won the Bronze Star for meritorious conduct. Over 150,000 women between 1942 and 1945 pioneered the development of America's first official female military unit.[36] The WAC included African American women. Officers trained with whites, but units were segregated and typically served black Army units. The WAVES prohibited black women's service until December 1944; the SPARS were opened to black women in October 1944. In each case, the opportunity to serve came after activists pressed the Departments of the Army and Navy for women's inclusion.

The war's end signaled "reconversion" to a peacetime economy and the shift from the emphasis on defense production to consumer goods. "Rosie" the wartime worker was now supposed to go home, welcome her soldier husband to domestic bliss, and occupy herself with motherhood, housekeeping, and other "womanly" duties. Advertisements and magazine stories emphasized women's new responsibilities. In "Diapers for Flight Six," a female pilot happily becomes a flight attendant; in "Mission for Henry," a female engineer delights to hear her husband's plans for her to design "a baby carriage with retractable wheels." Most poignant, perhaps, was an ad featuring a small girl tugging at her mother's work overalls, plaintively asking, "Mommy, when will you stay home again?"[37]

Many women workers reported their desire to remain in the workforce, however. Surveys by the Women's Bureau found that nearly three in four female laborers expressed interest in remaining on the job. Many found that impossible, however, as employers fired them, downsized, or changed job classifications to exclude women. Some companies, such as the Ford Motor Company, openly discriminated against women by ignoring their years of work, placing them in jobs they were not trained to do, or requiring new, strict medical exams.[38] Unions frequently did fail to protect female members. By 1947, over three million women had been "let go" or left the workforce, as the number of women in the workforce returned to the same level as 1940. As important, the gains made in women's wages during the war declined as women were forced out of heavy manufacturing and lost the protection of equal wages for doing work previously done by men. In two years, the real wages of 90 percent of the female labor force was less than it had been during the war.[39] For African American women, and for other women of color, the elimination of war jobs signified even more significant changes. Clerical work remained largely unavailable to them, and domestic service, always the work of last resort, became the only option for many.[40]

In the postwar period, advertisements, television shows, and women's magazines celebrated the domestic ideal of a breadwinning husband, a wife content in housekeeping, and cheerful, obedient children. Women of all classes and races learned that their highest achievement was, according to two psychologists, a healthy dependency on men and personal sacrifice for their families. That family was supposed to represent a haven of security in the anxious atomic age of "duck and cover." And as Americans ideally followed this domestic prescription, in practice, many married women returned to the labor force.[41]

The postwar resumption of women's paid work represents a curiosity of sorts when contrasted with the apparently enthusiastic domesticity of the 1950s. Even domesticity could contain covert messages about independence, however. I Love Lucy, one of the most popular television shows of the decade, featured a housewife constantly conniving to escape domesticity and join her husband at work. The role, played by Hollywood's very successful businesswoman, Lucille Ball, heralded and diminished women's housebound role simultaneously.[42] In a similar fashion, married women's entrance into the labor force in the 1950s occurred primarily among women with older, independent children; in families with higher incomes; in sectors that did not compete with male workers; and through the expansion of part-time labor. It was clear that despite the domestic imagery that World War II had helped in the erosion of the practical barriers against married women's waged work. One economist noted, "the bars vanished sometime after the early 1940s and by the 1950s were rarely encountered."[43]

Women's labor force participation rose dramatically between 1950 and 1960, from 29 percent to 40 percent of all women. At mid-decade, nearly one in four of mothers with children under twelve had a job, an even more telling statistic. By 1965, one-third of mothers with children under six were working outside of the home. The majority of female employees continued to fill the "pink collar" sector of the labor force, however, in work done primarily by women. One in three women workers occupied a position in clerical or service fields.

Married women's work rates did not slow during the remainder of the century. From the 1970s until 2000, employment by married women grew steadily; by 1991, 64 percent of all married American women worked, a marked contrast with the 5 percent who had in 1900. During the same period, men's labor force participation declined slightly, so that by century's end, the genders appeared to be moving toward greater equity in frequency of work, if not wage levels. Some economists have speculated that such leveling may be the result of the growth of the service industries and the decline of manufacturing in the United States by the late twentieth century.[44]

WOMEN'S CAREERS AND PROFESSIONS, 1929–1966

A worried young mother wrote to the feminist writer Betty Friedan. "I've tried everything women are supposed to do," she complained, as she described her life as a housewife. Something was wrong, she insisted, as she described what Friedan called "the problem that has no name." The young woman wondered, "who am I?" voicing the concern shared by other women through the 1950s and early 1960s as they struggled to define a more satisfying, less constraining role. In 1963, Friedan's popular book, *The Feminine Mystique*, described the dilemma of a generation of college-educated women who aspired to something more than diapering babies and mastering new recipes for their working husbands.[45]

Increasingly more and more women found a solution in work, and for many women, in a career. Between the 1930s and the 1960s, women who entered professions continued to face restrictions based on gender, as well as more subtle discrimination in job assignments and career tracks. Despite obstacles, women continued to enroll in law and medical schools, become architects and scientists, and run successful businesses. Between 1960 and 1980, women's employment as a whole advanced, as women claimed almost twenty million new jobs. Much of the change would occur as women began to find employment in areas once dominated by male employees.[46] By 1980, the majority of women were in the labor force. Their presence and persistence eroded old barriers, as new laws helped ensure access. By 1986, women were nearly 18 percent of physicians, 18 percent of attorneys and judges, 23 percent of scientists, 36 percent of university and college professors, and nearly 39 percent of executives or administrators.[47] African American women and women of color had shared in the advance; by 1980, almost half of all African American women held white-collar jobs.[48]

The expanding opportunities for careers came after decades of continued restrictions and persistent obstacles. The 1930s slowed the progress women had made in many professions. During the Depression, many young women could not afford college; fewer than 12 percent of women under twenty-one received any higher education during the decade. Without the credentials increasingly required in some fields, jobs were more difficult, if not impossible, to secure. Ironically, in areas that were identified as women's professions, such as social work, library work, and nursing, the numbers of female professionals increased between 1930 and 1940. In contrast, teaching, medicine, and higher education became more restrictive, as employers privileged male job seekers.[49] In journalism, women found encouragement from a special supporter, Eleanor Roosevelt. The First Lady began to hold news conferences exclusively for female reporters and openly supported the work of Lorena Hickok, Ishabel Ross, and Ruth Finney. Reporters and photographers such as Anne O'Hare McCormick, the first woman to win a Pulitzer Prize for foreign coverage; Dorothea Lange and Margaret Bourke White, who captured the images of the Depression; and Freda Kirchwey, who became publisher of The Nation, received respect and fame for their efforts. Notable women in research, such as Ruth Benedict and Margaret Mead in anthropology, and Mira Komarovsky and Helen Merrill Lynd in sociology, contributed to social science.

Despite the prominence of a few, however, for many professional women the Depression meant continued difficulties. Those who remained persistent found better luck by the end of the decade, and the full employment economy of World War II offered many opportunities. Even with such a roller-coaster experience, women in predominantly female professions fared better than those in traditionally male jobs. Women in nursing, librarianship, and once again in teaching enjoyed a relatively steady job market. In law, women continued to face exclusion, and remained marginalized as fewer than 5 percent of the legal profession. In medicine, the demands of the war forced reluctant medical schools to admit women. By 1945, nearly 15 percent of first-year medical students were female, and even Harvard had accepted its first women.

After the war, the return of male students reduced women's opportunities in nontraditional fields. Once again, women's participation in law slipped to under 5 percent of the total number of attorneys; in medicine, the newly available positions closed again. Crowded out by men eager to take advantage of the GI Bill, women in the late 1940s and early 1950s found fewer spots on college campuses and professional programs. For the first time in the century, women's percentage of doctoral degrees declined, and women were told to shape their vocational plans for marriage. A 1957 study by the National Manpower Commission discovered that 95 percent of doctors, lawyers, scientists, and architects were male; only in journalism had women made substantial gains.[50]

Women seeking professional careers, much like their wage-earning sisters, did not remain out of the labor force, however. Even with the difficulty of gaining access to certain fields, women continued to challenge existing boundaries. It has been suggested that even as American society appeared to erect new domestic barriers, a more subtle acknowledgement of women's contributions in business and professions appeared.[51] Female executives such as Helena Rubenstein and Elizabeth Arden, along with Bonwit Teller's Dorothy Shaver and Margaret Rudkin of Pepperidge Farm, became more visible. Women in government, from Maine's Senator Margaret Chase Smith to Oveta Culp Hobby, Eisenhower's head of Health, Education, and Welfare, continued the legacy of activism from the New Deal. Eleanor Roosevelt remained the most visible woman in America, a constant champion for women's governmental work.

In 1953, Roosevelt broke with women reformers who had long supported protective legislation, and endorsed the Equal Rights Amendment first introduced decades earlier by Alice Paul and the National Women's Party. The proposal had split women's groups in the 1920s, with most reformers insisting that legal equality would undermine the gender-based protections essential for working women. Roosevelt's change of heart signaled an important transition. Many women activists still contended that protective legislation remained important, and trade unions continued to advocate laws that provided exceptions for women based on hours or conditions of work. Through the Truman and Eisenhower administrations, the Women's Bureau supported protective laws, while professional associations such as the National Federation of Business and Professional Women's Clubs and the National Women's Party championed gender-neutral laws. The political differences echoed longstanding debates about women's rights and obligations to their families. Roosevelt's new stance suggested that it might be possible to find a new common ground.

The 1961 Presidential Commission on the Status of Women developed from this debate. The newly appointed head of the Women's Bureau, Esther Peterson, convinced Kennedy to convene the commission as a response to support from women and labor; she also hoped to dampen demands for the ERA. Eleanor Roosevelt, as the Chairperson, died in 1962, soon after the Commission began. When the Commission completed its work, it suggested strengthening protective laws and monitoring to ensure elimination of gender bias in the civil service. Peterson also used the Commission to promote legislation to eliminate wage differences. In 1963, President John F. Kennedy signed the Equal Pay Act, which prohibited wage differentials for work requiring "equal skill, effort and responsibility and which are performed under similar working conditions."[52]

The Equal Pay Act did little to change the segregated nature of the American workforce, or to eliminate discrimination in the private sector. Yet, it has been suggested that it did serve as one of many factors leading to new demands by women for meaningful equality in the workplace. The movement for women's rights developed from the sheer numbers of women in the workforce by 1960, from the prominence of calls for justice from the Civil Rights Movement, from the baby boom entering college and the workforce, from the needs of a consumer culture which flourished best on dual-earner family incomes, and the ideals of change in the 1960s. From the 1960s until the end of the century, women slowly gained access to professions that had been largely closed to them, won protection against harassment and discrimination, and improved the wage differential between men and women. Perhaps most important, by century's end, few young women believed that any job or profession should exclude women solely on the basis of gender.

NEW RIGHTS FOR WORKING WOMEN, 1960–1980

In the 1960s, American women experienced a series of startling changes. For African American women in the South, the Voting Rights Act of 1965 restored the right to cast the ballots that had been denied under Jim Crow laws. A generation of young white women who entered colleges and universities in unprecedented numbers read the new books by authors Betty Friedan and Helen Gurley Brown, *The Feminine Mystique* and *Sex and the Single Girl*. Both upset notions of calm domesticity and reticent feminine charm. In the 1960s, married and single women entered the labor force in increasing numbers, but in this decade, laws and a political movement asserted new rights. Women began to alter their expectations about work, career, and family.[53]

As women's labor force participation grew during the 1960s, and more married women entered the workforce, mothers with young children also left home for work. The movement of mothers into part- or full-time work marked a reappraisal about the permanency of marriage, as divorce rates skyrocketed after the 1950s. Some women also cited the necessity of two incomes for buying a home, securing retirement, or, in a society bursting with consumer goods and credit, the good life.[54] Gradually the

U.S. Army nurses played a critical role during the Vietnam War. Capt. Gladys E. Sepulveda and Second Lt. Lois Ferrari waited in Cam Ranh Bay in South Vietnam in 1965 to transfer to the field hospital in Nha Trang. AP photo.

number of women in jobs outside the home began to near the numbers of men at work; by 1990, almost 60 percent of married women worked, while 78 percent of married men did. More remarkable still, women's wage gap narrowed, so that by 1990 women as a group earned 75 percent of what white men received. In closer comparisons that compare educational and work experience, the gap becomes even smaller. In the first decade of the twenty-first century, young women in major cities such as New York would surpass their male counterparts in earnings.[55]

Laws providing for equal treatment for female and male workers allowed women more effective remedies than the protective legislation once favored by unions and female reformers. In 1964, the Civil Rights Act faced hostile Southern Senators, and one, Howard K. Smith of Virginia, added "sex" to its provisions to ensure its defeat. When the bill passed, the provision of Title VII prohibited discrimination in employment on the basis of race, color, religion, national origin, *and* sex. Although Title VII did not immediately dismantle older protective legislation, it did create an Equal Employment Opportunity Commission (EEOC) empowered to administer and enforce the law. Moving initially with caution, the EEOC failed to challenge job ads that specified the sex of applicants ("help wanted male, and help wanted female"). In protest, activists created a new organization to promote legal reform, the National Organization of Women, in 1966. Other political organizations and activists pressured Congress and state legislatures for sexual equality and protection in law. In 1965, President

Lyndon B. Johnson issued Executive Order No. 11246, and in 1967, Executive Order 11375, to substantiate the idea of affirmative action and provide special protection against sexual discrimination. In 1972, Congress passed Title IX of the Education Amendments, outlawing discrimination in educational programs receiving federal aid. And in the same year, the Equal Rights Amendment finally passed. Signed by President Richard M. Nixon and sent to the states for ratification, the amendment stirred controversy about public bathrooms, marriage for gays and lesbians, and public morality. Despite an extension of the ratification deadline by Congress, the amendment failed in 1982. Legal questions about work and discrimination remained the province of Congress and, when willing, the courts.

In the 1960s, the Supreme Court handed down several major decisions that provided new rights for working women. In *Weeks* v. *Southern Bell,* the Court found in 1969 that employers could not limit women's employment on arbitrary attitudes about women's capabilities. The Court found seniority rights based on gender a violation of law in the same year in *Bowe* v. *Colgate Palmolive.* By 1971, the Court applied the Fourteenth Amendment to a gender discrimination case in *Reed* v. *Reed,* as Ruth Bader Ginsburg, subsequently the Court's second female Justice, argued before the Court. *Philips* v. *Martin Marietta Corporation* (1971) established that employers could not refuse to hire a female applicant solely on the basis that she had young children; *Cleveland Board of Education* v. *LaFleur* (1974) made it illegal to force pregnant women to take maternity leave.

The controversial issue of pregnancy and work led to the passage of the 1978 Pregnancy Discrimination Act. Ironically, one of the first cases the EEOC would enforce under the act involved a workingman who used the law to assert his right for medical coverage for his pregnant wife. The law ended the longstanding practice of replacing pregnant workers, however, and ensured women that work and family lives might be less at odds. In 1993, the Family and Medical Leave Act provided up to twelve weeks of unpaid time off for the birth or adoption of a child for parents, or for a family medical emergency, offering further protection for workers. Sexual harassment in the workplace also secured the courts' attentions, and a series of decisions made it clear that women could find redress in law. In *Meritor Savings Bank* v. *Vinson* (1986), the Supreme Court found that an abusive work situation amounted to sexual discrimination. By 1993, the Court elaborated in *Harris* v. *Forklift Systems* and ruled that victims of harassment did not need to suffer physical or serious psychological harm in order to make a claim for damages. Employers were held responsible for failing to supervise competently and intervene in harassment in *Burlington Industries* v. *Ellerth* in 1998. States, too, initiated codes mandating training for supervisors about sexual harassment and fair employment practices.

The legal protections remained imperfect. Parental leave laws that do not provide for lost wages have been criticized by wage-earning women and unions that represent them, for example. Sexual harassment continued to be an issue many women confronted as part of their working lives. The lack of affordable, safe childcare remained another problem frequently cited by working mothers. A national daycare system passed by Congress in the early 1970s was vetoed by President Nixon; since then, little progress has been made to introduce a similar initiative on the federal level. Instead, solutions to the dilemma of combining the responsibilities of motherhood and work have focused on "the mommy track," an idea that suggests that women scale their ambitions to accommodate family life; part-time employment; and home-based work. Professional women with high salaries resort to full-time home care for their young children; wage-earning women with minimum wages make do with family or, for some, substandard services.

Despite the problems, women remain in the workforce. Several key factors that have changed the nature of women's work since the early 1970s have been identified. Many young women plan a career or anticipate a lifetime of work, no longer anticipating the prospect of years at home as a wife and mother. The result has been better skills, which allow women to compete with male job applicants for a wider range of jobs and higher wages. In colleges, women no longer cluster in disciplines defined as those most appropriate for women, but increasingly venture into all fields of study. Even science and engineering, areas that have historically recruited few women, actively sought women as students and employees in the final decades of the century. The federal census of 2000 revealed a small number of categories in which women remained under 10 percent of all employees: firefighting, electrical engineering, and contracting, along with the very few women in tool and die manufacturing, continued to be almost solely male occupations.

As new opportunities appear in women's working lives, older questions remain unanswered. Does paid work, as it has been organized in the United States during the twentieth century, ignore the importance of family life, or would connections between home and work intrude into workers' privacy? Should workers be able to labor at home? Would such work increase "flex time," or endanger children and risk work protections? Americans struggling to reconcile issues of work, family, and economy may well find that some part of the answers lie in the history of women's work.

NOTES

1. Alice Kessler-Harris, *Out to Work: A History of Wage-Earning Women in the United States* (New York: Oxford University Press, 2003).
2. *Bradwell v. State of Illinois*, 83 U.S. 130 (1872).
3. Bonnie G. Smith, *The Gender of History: Men, Women, and Historical Practice* (Cambridge, MA: Harvard University Press, 1998).

4. Association for Women Veterinarians Foundation, http://www.vet.ksu.edu/AWV/about.htm.

5. Leslie Tentler, *Wage-Earning Women* (New York: Oxford University Press, 1979), 19.

6. Jacquelyn Jones, *Labor of Love, Labor of Sorrow: Black Women, Work, and the Family from Slavery to the Present* (New York: Vintage, 1985), 94.

7. Ibid.

8. Elizabeth Pleck, "A Mother's Wages: Income Earning among Married Italian and Black Women, 1896–1911," in *A Heritage of Her Own: Toward a New Social History of American* Women, ed. Nancy F. Cott and Elizabeth Pleck (New York: Touchstone, 1979), 367–392.

9. Philip S. Foner, *From the Founding of the American Federation of Labor to the Emergence of American Imperialism* (New York: International Publishers, 1998).

10. For example, the University of Pennsylvania's Wharton School of Business opened in 1881.

11. Nancy Woloch, *Women and the American Experience* (New York: McGraw Hill, 2006), 388.

12. Claudia Goldin, *Understanding the Gender Gap: An Economic History of American Women* (New York: Oxford University Press, 1990), 111–114.

13. Robert and Helen Merrell Lynd, *Middletown: A Study in Modern American Culture* (New York: Harvest Books, 1959), 29.

14. Goldin, *Understanding the Gender Gap*, 12.

15. Woloch, *Women and the American Experience*, 447.

16. Susan Ware, *Beyond Suffrage: Women in the New Deal* (Cambridge, MA: Harvard University Press, 1981), 28; Goldin, *Understanding the Gender Gap*, 120.

17. Winifred D. Wandersee Bolin, "The Economics of Middle-Income Family Life: Working Women during the Great Depression," *Journal of American History* Vol. 65, No. 1 (1978): 29.

18. T. H. Watkins, *The Hungry Years: A Narrative History of the Great Depression* (New York: Macmillan, 2000), 65.

19. Lois Scharf, *To Work and to Wed: Female Employment, Feminism, and the Great Depression* (Westport, CT: Greenwood Press, 1980), 361; Sharon Hartman Strom, "Challenging 'Woman's Place': Feminism, the Left, and Industrial Unionism in the 1930s," *Feminist Studies* Vol. 9, No. 2 (1983): 359–386.

20. Alice Kessler-Harris, *In Pursuit of Equity: Women, Men, and the Quest for Economic Citizenship in 20th-Century America* (New York: Oxford University Press, 2001), 21.

21. Ibid.

22. Woloch, *Women and the American Experience*, 449; Strom, "Challenging 'Woman's Place,'" 365.

23. In 1955, the CIO merged with the AFL. The CIO accepted the AFL's arguments for higher male wages at this point.

24. Quoted in Strom, "Challenging 'Woman's Place,'" 364.

25. Goldin, *Understanding the Gender Gap*, 120.

26. Marc Miller, "Working Women and World War II," *New England Quarterly* Vol. 53, No. 1 (1980): 42; Susan M. Hartmann, *The Home Front and Beyond: American Women in the 1940s* (Boston: Twayne, 1982), 21.

27. Elaine Tyler May, "Pushing the Limits, 1940–1961," in *No Small Courage: A History of Women in the United States*, ed. Nancy F. Cott (New York: Oxford University Press, 2000), 476.

28. The advertisement is available at the National Women's History Museum site exhibition, "Changing Images of Women's Roles," http://www.nwhm.org/Partners/exhibitentrance.html; Barbara Friedman, "'The Soldier Speaks': *Yank* Coverage of Women and Wartime Work," *American Journalism* Vol. 22, No. 2 (2005): 71.

29. Bilge Yesil, "Who Said This Is a Man's War? Propaganda, Advertising Discourse, and the Representation of War Worker Women during the Second World War," *Media History* Vol. 10, No. 2 (2004): 103–117.

30. Ibid., 109.

31. May, "Pushing the Limits," 477.

32. Miller, "Working Women," 54; May, "Pushing the Limits," 480.

33. Karen Anderson, *Wartime Women: Sex Roles, Family Relations, and the Status of Women during World War II* (Westport, CT: Greenwood Press, 1981), 84.

34. Ibid.

35. Natalie J. Stewart-Smith, "Women Air Force Pilots of World War II," New Mexico Military Institute, http://home.earthlink.net/~reyesd99/stewartsmith/contents.html.

36. Judith Bellafaire, "The Women's Army Corps," Center for Military History Publication 72–15, http://www.army.mil/CMH/brochures/wac/wac.htm.

37. Mary Ryan, *Womanhood in America* (New York: Franklin Watts, 1973).

38. Nancy F. Gabin, *Feminism in the Labor Movement: Women and the United Auto Workers, 1935–1975* (Ithaca, NY: Cornell University Press, 1990).

39. May, "Pushing the Limits," 493.

40. Jones, *Labor of Love, Labor of Sorrow,* 258–259; May, "Pushing the Limits," 503.

41. Elaine Tyler May, *Homeward Bound: American Families in the Cold War Era* (New York: Basic Books, 1999).

42. Joanne Meyerowitz, *Not June Cleaver: Women and Gender in Postwar America, 1945–1960* (Philadelphia: Temple University Press, 1994); Mary M. Dalton and Laura R. Linder, *The Sitcom Reader: America Viewed and Skewed* (Albany: SUNY Press, 2005), 5.

43. Goldin, *Understanding the Gender Gap,* 375; Meyerowitz, *Not June Cleaver.*

44. David A. Cotter et al., "Women's Work and Working Women: The Demand for Female Labor," *Gender and Society* Vol. 15, No. 2 (2001): 429–452.

45. Betty Friedan, *The Feminine Mystique* (New York: Norton, 1963).

46. Cotter et al., "Women's Work and Working Women."

47. Margaret L. Cassidy and Bruce O. Warren, "Family Employment Status and Gender Role Attitudes: A Comparison of Women and Men College Graduates," *Gender and Society* Vol. 10, No. 3 (1996): 312–329.

48. Delores P. Aldridge, "African-American Women in the Economic Marketplace: A Continuing Struggle," *Journal of Black Studies* Vol. 20, No. 2 (1989): 129–154.

49. Ware, *Beyond Suffrage,* 73.

50. Eugenia Kaledin, *Mothers and More: American Women in the 1950s* (Boston: Twayne, 1984), 70.

51. Meyerowitz, *Not June Cleaver.*

52. Cynthia E Harrison, "A 'New Frontier' for Women: The Public Policy of the Kennedy Administration." *Journal of American History* Vol. 67, No. 3 (1980): 642.

53. Julie A. Matthaei, *An Economic History of Women in America: Women's Work, the Sexual Division of Labor, and the Development of Capitalism* (New York: Shocken Books, 1982); Goldin, *Understanding the Gender Gap*; Kessler-Harris, *Out to Work.*

54. Lizabeth Cohen, *A Consumer's Republic: The Politics of Mass Consumption in Postwar America* (New York: Alfred A. Knopf, 2003).

55. Goldin, *Understanding the Gender Gap.*

2

———— ∞∞ ————

Women and Family

Controversy surrounds family life in the early twenty-first century. Politicians, pundits, and people gathered around dinner tables debate who should be allowed to marry, adopt children, or care for foster children. Others argue about who is properly "American," and whether the children born in the United States to immigrants without proper documentation should still be counted as citizens. School districts continue to discuss whether to include books such as *Heather Has Two Mommies* in their libraries. James Dobson's popular organization, Focus on the Family, promotes firm family discipline and spanking children, while the American Academy of Pediatrics denounces physical punishments. At any holiday, gatherings of kin find a variety of step, blended, single-parent, same-sex, traditional, multicultural, and other forms of family, who may define "family values" differently from the family celebrating the same holiday next door.

American families have retained a remarkable diversity over the course of the past century. Immigrant traditions, economic differences, and regional variations shaped domestic options and forms in distinctive ways, allowing, and in some cases forcing, families to adapt, rely on networks of kin or neighbors, or to forge new accommodations of work or assistance. As wives, mothers, and daughters, women played perhaps the most significant role in the changing dynamics of family life, as options for women shifted during the course of the last century. Confronted with the conflict between family obligations and personal fulfillment, women continually faced difficult decisions, attempts to balance demands of home and work, and efforts to combine motherhood and career. Whatever they chose also meant new arrangements for those at home, from day care and dual career incomes to tighter family budgets.

The national debates over family life have also shaped some of the choices and options available for women. Since the first decade of the twentieth century, reformers fought for governmental protection, regulation, and aid for some families and particular members of the family, such as children, the elderly, and "dependent" mothers. A substantial number of employers prior to 1941 prohibited or discouraged married women's employment, slowing or shifting opportunities. In each case, some women enjoyed an advantage; daughters won the jobs their mothers could not take, for example. State pensions for widowed mothers gave "virtuous" mothers small subsidies so that they could remain at home with their children, but white women keeping company with men, and African American women, typically failed the social workers' tests. Throughout the twentieth century, questions of family economics and personal autonomy continued to place some women at odds with the definitions of family that dominated governmental reforms and regulations. Employers, too, could play a significant role within local or regional economies. In Lowell, Massachusetts, married women's work outside of the home remained part of the community dynamic for a better part of the century; in a rural community such as Culpeper, Virginia, few married white women labored outside of the home until after World War II, while African American wives frequently worked as domestic servants or farm workers.[1]

The idea of a "proper" women's role in the family would be the subject of an expanding media as well. Advertising, pulp magazines, radio, and television did not operate with conniving male executives meeting in dark rooms plotting to ensnare women in domesticity, of course. Nevertheless, each utilized idealized images to sell products, shows, and stories (and more products). As advertisers established market strategies in the 1920s, they discovered that in order to "tell it to Sweeney," the man on the street, they could feature glamour and focus on the "true" consumer, a woman.[2] She wanted the illusion of happily ever after and needed to be reminded to "bring him home" to Wonder Bread, if necessary. Advertisers often separated the domestic ideal into elements of seduction and sexuality, fear, and fulfillment. Some consumables presented women with the promise that the product would make them desirable or marriageable. Ivory soap told women that "Most men ask 'Is she pretty' not 'Is she clever'" in 1924, while Pepsodent toothpaste in 1943 confidently asserted that it could guarantee "How to catch a husband." Ivory made sure that women worried about whether "his eyes [will] confirm what his lips are saying" in 1925, and Dryad antiperspirant in 1949 depicted a woman waiting by a telephone "alone—because she doesn't know." None were as distressing as the 1969 housewife, however, who could at least be reassured by Del Monte that her green beans "don't go soft on you."[3] Throughout much of the century, advertisers confirmed that women would find happiness in home and marriage, as long as they used the right products. Discontent with housework or marriage could be solved easily with another purchase.

Motion pictures also reinforced domesticity and family roles for women. Films such as pioneer director Dorothy Arzner's 1933 *Christopher Strong*, with Katherine Hepburn as a pilot, or 1940's *His Girl Friday*, with Rosalind Russell as a reporter, offered capable female characters and found audiences. The "maternal melodrama" and films that featured more bucolic domesticity dominated the film market directed at women, however, and even movies that featured strong female performers usually ended with a marital message. In *Woman of the Year* (1942), for instance, the extraordinary achievements of Katherine Hepburn's character, Tess Harding, finally matter less than her ability to please her husband and make his breakfast. In the latter years of the century, as films featured far more adventurous roles for women, domesticity remained intact in films such as the animated *Shrek, The Incredibles,* and *Happy Feet,* and thrillers from *Mr. and Mrs. Smith* to *Fargo.*[4]

As advertising and film continued to use domesticity and the family as a central motif, the content of work within the home changed during the twentieth century. New technologies and devices, "improved" products, and shifting ideas about health, safety, and child care meant differences in the labor of women in the home. In 1900, affluent women in urban areas typically had access to electricity, ice boxes for refrigeration, washing machines, canned food, vacuum cleaners, and indoor plumbing. The 1925 study of Muncie, Indiana, by Robert and Helen Merrell Lynd, *Middletown,* revealed that almost a fourth of that town's residents lacked indoor toilets, however. It would take a century for over 95 percent of Americans to finally relieve themselves of outdoor toilets.[5] As the century progressed, more devices and conveniences became available to less advantaged women and to those in rural areas. After World War II, the development of extensive highway networks allowed more families easier access to an ever-expanding variety of goods and services.

The spread of convenience technology and consumer goods did not mean less housework. As historian Ruth Schwartz Cowan demonstrated in her pioneering work *More Work for Mother,* changing household technologies meant increasing standards of cleanliness, fewer workers engaged in housework, and more time spent in using the new devices. In the nineteenth century, for example, rugs were taken outside and beaten several times a year. With the development of vacuum cleaners, one woman could clean her carpets every day, if she chose, or if advertisers suggested that she should. An array of products began to appear that made it obvious that any piece of lint or dirt on the carpet offended guests and must be removed immediately with cleaners, sprays, and rotating devices. By the end of the twentieth century, the housewife guarded against germs as well and vigilantly removed offending bacteria from all surfaces. Her diligence led physicians to worry that she had become too successful, contributing to the creation of germ-resistant bacteria, and in turn, a host of bacteria-bearing products began to appear.[6]

Finally, married women's entrance into the labor market and the growing numbers of working mothers after World War II increased pressure on the other adults in the family—usually, a husband—to contribute to domestic labors. Numerous studies suggest that even as the number of children in the family increases, husbands' contributions to housework and childcare remained under half of what women typically performed. By 2006, married women spent an average of almost thirteen hours a week in child-centered activities, while married men reported fewer than seven. This represented a significant increase from men's average of three hours per week in child care in 1965, however. What has been most notable in such studies remains the number of total hours of work done by women, averaging over seventy per week in household chores, child care, and paid labor for working mothers by 2006. Exhaustion, stress, and a lack of personal time became a new version of what feminist Betty Friedan once termed the "problem that has no name." Solutions remained varied, depending on employers, families, and location, into the new century.

Historians examining the changes in family life over time have frequently noted the complexity of "the family" as a social relationship. In fact, how families are organized, who belongs and who is determined to be an outsider, what kind of work is performed, and who does that work are issues that continue to intrigue scholars. In American families of the twentieth century, the household increasingly became viewed as a private haven of emotional connections, rather than a place of work and the renewal of resources, despite the labor performed at home. The content of work differed, however, not only by decade but also by class and location. At the turn of the century, rural Southern women in sharecropping families may have lived in cabins with dirt floors, no running water, and no electricity, whereas New York City matrons among the economic elites supervised servants. African American women continued to confront segregation in housing, schools for their children, and in the stores where they shopped. For Native American, Asian, or Latina women, racial policies in government and employer prejudice often combined to constrain family choices from where to live to what members in the family might work. If twentieth-century women learned from experts and advertisers that an ideal mother and wife behaved, bought, or thought certain things, women's actual family lives frequently remained at odds with the dominant prescriptions.

MARRIAGE AND MOTHERHOOD IN THE EARLY TWENTIETH CENTURY

Frances Willard, the founder of the Women's Christian Temperance Union, declared simply in 1888 that "the mission of the ideal woman . . . is to make the whole world homelike."[7] By the late nineteenth century, a growing array of women's organizations, clubs, and reform agencies provided the means for women to transform domesticity into public action. From the General Federation of Women's Clubs to the National Association of Colored Women's Clubs, women challenged the nineteenth-century ideal that virtuous women occupied the private worlds of household and family, while more rugged and public realms of government and business belonged to men. Many women involved in reform organizations embraced the idea of "municipal housekeeping," which declared that women's domestic skills and spiritual inclinations especially suited them to clean up politics and cities.

The concept of "municipal housekeeping" served to legitimate women's entrance into new arenas of public life through clubs, reform associations, and government. The importance of this ideology in linking ideas of home life with women's public roles has sometimes obscured two other issues, however. First, while some women in the middle and advantaged classes had been segregated into limited social spaces, those defined for "proper" women with virtuous attitudes, other women in working classes, or the poor already had access to city areas defined as "public" or "male." Working-class wives might take a drink with husbands at saloons, for example, despite the fact that saloons tended to be predominantly male settings. Race and class also shaped public space. Before World War I, for instance, only working-class viewers enjoyed the motions pictures; after the war, even the most moral middle-class woman might agree to "take in a picture."[8] As the century progressed, the spaces open to women appeared to increase, a result of women's growing employment and shopping outside of the home and expanding transportation networks. Whether women of all classes could walk alone as they chose where they chose, however, remains an unanswered question.

The idea of a "private" household, the second issue that reformers appeared to challenge, developed in the nineteenth century from domestic writers such as Catherine Beecher, ministers such as her brother Henry Ward Beecher, and women's magazines such as *Godey's Lady's Book*. The emerging middle class in the nineteenth century used domestic ideals to distinguish itself from other segments in society, from declining numbers of craft workers to the evolving industrial working class.[9] The glorification of the home by writers did not change the ways in which households remained connected to markets, government, and all other aspects of life, however. States regulated marriage, divorce, and child custody as well as marital obligations for support and domicile; the market fulfilled the needs for subsistence and earnings and played a role in which family members worked and when. Religions, schools, neighbors, and other outside influences also touched the "private" family, which was never very private at all. Yet nineteenth-century writers, ministers, and other advocates of the domestic hearth did succeed in establishing a common assumption that somehow the family *was* private. That notion rested primarily in a shift in emphasis from the economics of family to its emotional components; in *The American Woman's Home*, Catherine Beecher and Harriet Beecher Stowe labeled the key domestic sentiments as "intelligence, virtue, and happiness." The continuing presumption that the family should be a locus of nurture and emotional sustenance shaped debates over women's work, the development of household technologies, governmental policies, and attitudes about marriage and childrearing. As late as 1992, a political candidate's wife had to prove that she could indeed bake cookies, a final symbolic connection between housework, family, and women's roles as wives and mothers.[10]

Even as arguments about the private family solidified, a variety of "experts" and reformers during the late nineteenth and early twentieth century sought to intervene in family matters. Progressive era activists worked to regulate child labor and to establish protective labor laws for working women; others such as Lillian Wald and Alice Hamilton championed public health, better housing, and improved sanitation. Budget analysts examined poverty and standards of living to determine family needs; educational reformers challenged one-room schools. Each measure, from new ideas about juvenile delinquency to the passage of a federal Pure Food and Drug Act, touched family life substantially and affected the lives of women as wives and mothers.[11]

As Progressive-era reformers championed "home life," the movement to bring science to housework intensified through the late nineteenth century. The development of home economics as a field of study began during the late nineteenth century. Its origins lay in the establishment of colleges under the Morrill Land Grant Act of 1862, which required coeducational offerings and training in "mechanical arts." Western colleges attempted to provide some courses in "domestic science," but other universities such as Cornell and Wisconsin staffed classes in "hygiene" only. A second stimulus came from the efforts of Beecher and others such as Fannie Farmer to elevate housework and cooking into scientific or professional study. More rigorous academic programs followed when Ellen Swallow Richards, the first female professor at the Massachusetts Institute of Technology, became the central proponent of university and college courses on home management. Richards had developed a specialty in food and sanitation, and in the 1890s pioneered food services such as the New England Kitchen and school lunch services for the poor in Boston. In 1899, she and other educators met in Lake Placid, New York, to share research and work; by 1908, the group had formed the American Home Economics Association. The Association worked to establish professional standards for academic review and to promote scholarship among its members.[12]

Home economists produced texts on proper diets, costs of living, how to feed babies, adequate home decoration, and a vast array of topics connected to household work, child care, and the emotional well-being of family members. College and university programs in home economics concentrated on educating a new generation of experts in home efficiency and household management, but many also emphasized preparing public school teachers. In 1913, the Bureau of Home Economics was created within the U.S. Department of Agriculture, a reflection of a growing focus on rural and farm families. In 1914, the Smith-Lever Act provided for cooperative extension services, including home economics courses, which offered demonstrations for farm women in canning, pest control, and sanitation. The Montgomery Ward Company provided additional funding for home demonstrators between 1916 and 1923.[13] The Smith-Hughes Act in 1917 added additional opportunities for education, establishing vocational programs and funding for public schools. Unfortunately, the law segregated both vocational training and individual programs from mainstream school curriculums; gradually "voc ed" became perceived as less demanding intellectually and academically. Students, too, typically faced separation into gender appropriate courses, with trade courses reserved for males, and home economics populated by young women.[14]

Despite such obstacles, advocates of scientific housekeeping and professors of home economics won increasing acceptance for new standards of home work. Women's willingness to adapt to the techniques and methods advocates favored stemmed in part from the growing importance of expertise in the twentieth century. Businesses and advertisers joined physicians and home economists in promoting the importance of sanitation, refrigeration, and the eradication of bacteria. New appliances and new technologies became part of the "scientification of housework."[15] Ironically, with each innovation the amount of time spent in housework increased rather than decreased as the demands for cleanliness and order intensified.

Nor did iceboxes, vacuums, electricity, and running water arrive for every American housewife in the early twentieth century. African American women in the American south continued to face backbreaking labors whether on a farm or in a city. One observer in 1896 described the day of a domestic laborer, filled with heavy lifting of coal, pots, water, and wood, the turning of mattresses and scrubbing of laundry. Immigrant women in Northern cities faced similar circumstances, managing an equal number of draining tasks from carrying water from cisterns to scrubbing floors and steps.[16] In cities where water lines allowed indoor plumbing for the suburbs, poor neighborhoods sometimes continued to deal with privies and pumps, as well as unpaved streets littered with garbage of all kinds. Class and race, which for Americans at the turn of the century included those categories that would later be termed "ethnicity," determined much of the housewife's lot.

For many middle-class women, the image of illustrator Charles Dana Gibson's "Gibson Girl" captured the ideal for life. Active, educated, involved in appropriate civic affairs (and perhaps even a settlement volunteer), this young woman planned to marry. Unlike the generation of women dedicated to reform who determined to remain single, the typical woman viewed marriage as personally and socially desirable. Courtship in the middle and advantaged classes continued to be carefully controlled by etiquette and convention, and after marriage, the young husband and wife occupied what still amounted to relatively separate social spheres. Challenges to this decorum came from women who questioned sexuality and the conventions of marriage, such as Charlotte Perkins Gilman, Ellen Key, and Crystal Eastman. The idea of "feminism," raised for the first time in these decades, served not simply to advocate votes but to claim a new role in the home. In 1912, New York feminists created a club they called "Heterodoxy," seeing it as a refuge for women who were "not orthodox" in outlook. Through the activism of women, the expansion of women's roles and education, the beginnings of consumerism, and America's growing prosperity, the middle-class woman in 1920 would describe herself as more active and more engaged in the world than her forerunner in 1900.[17]

In her household, an icebox and ringer washer were only two of the new appliances that promised to make housework more efficient. As more homes received electricity, the possibilities of adding conveniences multiplied. Yet by 1920, only slightly more than a third of American households had electrical systems for anything more than lighting, and not until the 1940s would most families be able to use the wide range of devices flooding the markets, from electric washing machines to refrigerators and electric fans.[18] The arrival of new technologies paralleled a second change in the lives of middle-class and advantaged wives, the increasing difficulty in retaining domestic servants. As job opportunities in industry expanded for the young immigrant women who had typically filled positions in domestic service, fewer and fewer willingly accepted the exhausting work as household servants. The women seeking household help bemoaned the "servant problem" and accepted the possibility of technological solutions.

Other shifts in household life also transformed the work of middle-class women. Through the late nineteenth century, servants, vendors, or shopkeepers brought groceries, foodstuffs, and other necessities to the home. Dressmakers, milliners, and physicians called when needed. In the twentieth century, consumers would learn to go out to shops and services, managing "errands" around a series of stores and providers. The department store promised to make this easier by centralizing many kinds of purchases in one place, a concept that has persisted throughout the century in a variety of forms, from shopping malls to "big box" stores.

Life in working-class households varied depending on income, a family's religion, and traditions, region, and race. Skilled workingmen, such as engineers or train conductors, sometimes earned enough to provide their families the same comforts found in the middle-class home. Unskilled workers faced more dire prospects; agricultural workers, sharecroppers, and transient workers confronted the most dismal situations in providing for families. As a result, for daughters and mothers in the working class, subsistence remained an important concern in the first decades of the century. Economists continued to find large numbers of working-class families laboring beneath standards of "health and decency."[19] Depending on a family's country of origin, mothers worked to supplement family earnings by taking in boarders, doing laundry, or doing piece work. Daughters might be sent into the workforce to supplement family earnings. Immigrant families usually preferred to keep mothers at home and utilized the lower earnings of children. The significant exception to this pattern would be African American families, who typically sent their children to schools for as long as possible; African American married women's labor force participation rates remained statistically distinctive until after World War II.

Religion and tradition shaped family life for many working-class American families in the first decades of the twentieth century. Jewish immigrant families, for example, tried to maintain religious laws such as keeping kosher kitchens, observing holidays, and allowing men to study the Torah. Italian families preferred to send young men into the workforce and to closely proctor young women; many kept strong ties to the Catholic Church, with resulting family traditions quite different from those of Jewish neighbors. Saint's Days provided special occasions for Catholic wives to organize festivals and parades. Slavs, Slovaks, Slovenes, Dalmatians, Croatians, Lithuanians, Latvians, and other immigrants also arrived with distinctive customs that shaped diet, household habits, and family traditions. Even entertainments for young women might depend

on family tradition, with Jewish families preferring to have daughters cha-
peroned, and Italian daughters relegated to more home-centered events.[20]

Progressive reformers throughout the period worked assiduously to
undermine many of these differences, insisting that immigrant customs
and standards of cleanliness should reflect "American" values. When
reformers such as Jane Addams and Mary Simkovitch spoke openly about
the effects of low wages on family life, other social workers in Charity Organization Societies, in some social settlements, or in associations such as
the National Consumers' League and the National Child Labor Committee condemned the inadequate home life of many immigrants. Settlement
worker Mary McDowell recalled that she had once sailed in to immigrant
homes to order women to improve their surroundings; she credited her
work with settlements as changing her attitude about the difficulties
working-class wives faced in their daily chores. Regardless of a growing
awareness that low wages, insufficient incomes, and substandard housing
made it impossible for the most diligent wife to turn a dingy tenement
apartment into a model home, however, reformers continued to assess
working-class domestic life through middle-class ideals. One Sicilian wife
explained that in Italy, she washed clothes infrequently, but in the United
States, "one must wash two or three times a week."[21] Reformers insisted
that a good wife baked bread, rather than purchasing it at a nearby bak-
ery; children's clothes were always to be clean and pressed, even if there
were hardly the means to do so.

For the children of immigrants, domesticity and family life also became
a point of rebellion. The "second generation" often rejected traditions,
clothing, or customs for more "American" values, fashions, and mores.
Many also objected to the practice of daughters handing most of their
pay packet to parents, or deferring to brothers for education. The lives of
young working women in early twentieth-century New York have been
found to be "dramas of control, resistance, acquiescence, and subterfuge"
over wages, family supervision, and American styles.[22] Young women
increasingly preferred the more commercialized entertainments of the
city, from Coney Island to movies, theater, and dance halls.

These ventures by working-class women opened new possibilities for
other women in the 1920s. The dance halls, dark movies theaters, and
entertainments such as the Tunnel of Love at Coney Island were perfect
for courting couples, who might find the occasion to touch, hold hands, or
even more. By the early 1920s, dance clubs, movie palaces, and amusement parks "toned downed" the overtly sexual aspects of their offerings;
now "tamed for the middle class," public entertainment "promised self-
fulfillment for women through consumerism and an ideology of companionate romance and marriage." The tea dance of polite couples replaced
the "tough dancing" performed by working-class youths, in which a

woman had placed her arms around the man's neck while he held her close, and they moved together in time (or not) to the music.[23] By the 1920s, a heterosexual culture supplanted the ideal of separate spheres for men and women.

An emphasis on sexuality in the companionate marriage of the 1920s also replaced older notions that women possessed only maternal instincts or were "passionless." Historians continue to debate the shifts in attitudes about sexuality at the turn of the century and whether women anticipated sexual pleasure as a part of their marital relationships. What is clear is that some did; letters between couples reveal expressions of passion, playfulness, and enjoyment in intimacy. The expectation that women should be eager sexual companions in marriage may have been privately expressed before the 1920s, but during that decade, sex became public. Movies featured the exotic vamp Theda Bara, the dashing Douglas Fairbanks, and the overtly seductive Rudolph Valentino, while titles such as *The Danger Girl* (or, *Love on Skates)*, *Bedroom Scandal*, and *Back to Batching* lured viewers to new tales of romance. Pulp magazines offered readers stories such as "A Primitive Lover" and "Playboy of a Back Street," while advertisers tantalized customers with promises of satisfactions beyond product efficiency. The pioneering study of sexuality, *Intimate Matters* (1998), suggested that the 1920s represented a distinct break with America's sexual past: Americans experienced a new view of "erotic expression that can be defined as sexual liberalism."[24]

The "new" companionate marriage of the 1920s no longer cast husband and wife as partners in charge of separate realms, but as buddies sharing bed and life. The ideal union of the 1920s combined romance and sex, as the relationship between the husband and wife became the primary concern of family life, replacing the nineteenth-century stress on the bonds between mother and child. Following the popularization of Sigmund Freud's ideas about sexuality, sociologists, physicians, and other family "experts" declared that a good marriage depended upon a fulfilling sexual union. The wife's role as agreeable companion and sexual partner signaled both new emphasis on the woman as individual and women's rising expectations of marriage. Her role retained some ambiguity, however. The wife's duty was still as support for her man, and her responsibility centered on his nurture. Keeping a marriage viable depended upon the wife, on her attractiveness, her skill with entertaining, or keeping the children orderly and affectionate. In short, the wife of the 1920s companionate marriage had to work at her marriage to ensure her husband still liked and desired her.

Marriage changed in other ways during the 1920s. Childbearing and childrearing "modernized," at least according to the experts connected with each. The birth control movement, spearheaded by Margaret Sanger over a decade earlier, allowed women access to information and the means to limit family size. The diaphragm became increasingly popular as a means of contraception for women. Until 1937, the American Medical Association provided little education or support for contraceptive information; most women received birth control from clinics run by women and contraception advocates. A key incentive came from the federal courts, which in 1936 prohibited federal bans on contraceptive information in *United States* v. *One Package of Japanese Pessaries*. By 1942, when Planned Parenthood officially formed, nearly eight hundred such clinics existed throughout the country. In the same period, women's ability to end a pregnancy became more limited as numerous state laws restricted abortion to cases involving danger to a woman's life, something her physician alone was to decide.[25]

Childbirth for middle-class women moved from the home into the hospital. Several factors influenced women's decisions to forego home birth, from the potential benefits of a sterile environment to the promises of painless delivery with "twilight sleep." The anesthesia, a combination of morphine and scopolamine, slightly reduced the pain of childbirth, but rendered women largely incapable of remembering the event. While they did not recall a painful delivery, however, mothers and their physicians became increasingly concerned about the effects of the medication on infants, whose respiratory systems had less ability to cope with the powerful drugs. The use of "twilight sleep" continued for several decades, but its popularity waned substantially.[26] Nevertheless, women in labor still hurried to the hospital to give birth; gradually even the poorest Americans abandoned the practice of using midwives until the home birth movement of the 1960s and 1970s.

Childrearing was also becoming the realm of experts, seeming to grow in complexity as the numbers of children in families decreased. In 1900, middle-class families had fewer than three children, and working-class families an average of three to five, although "large" families of up to ten children were not unusual. As the century progressed, every segment in American society would reduce the number of dependents; even during the "baby boom" years after World War II, the number of children in individual families did not skyrocket.[27] A variety of authors and "authorities" had long offered parents advice on childrearing. By the 1920s, many of these held advanced or medical degrees, so that their apparently scientific reasoning supposedly surpassed the natural instincts of any mother. Sociologists Robert and Helen Merrill Lynd noted that in the 1920s, mothers in Muncie, Indiana, remained eager to "lay hold of every available resource" on how to raise children properly, including guidance from the Visiting Nurses Association, pamphlets from the Massachusetts Society for Mental Hygiene, and school home economics programs. One mother told the Lynds that in the past "one did not realize there was so much to be known about the care of children." She declared that she was "afraid of making mistakes" without the right advice.[28]

Special concern centered on adolescent and youth. During the 1920s, the period of life between age fifteen and twenty-five was endowed with new meaning, a time when, for the middle class, the youth deserved time for special pastimes, including, perhaps, an unchaperoned date using the family car. Young women could choose between a variety of role models, from the flapper, represented on movie screens by Joan Crawford, to the sexy vamp portrayed by Theda Bara, or the sweet young thing, Mary Pickford. The image of youth differed from two decades before; author F. Scott Fitzgerald characterized it as dancing till dawn, kissing and petting, and never telling. Romanticized and commercialized, youth became a period of indulgence and leisure, but only for those who could afford it.

Beyond the fun and almost self-indulgent dissatisfaction of youth lay new dilemmas for Americans. Prosperity was not as widespread as many hoped, and wages during the decade had not kept up with an expanding supply of credit and consumer goods. The restrictions on immigration imposed in 1924 did little to improve conditions for American workers. Migrating African American families moving from the South to the industrial North found fewer jobs and more discrimination than they had

Marion Wolcott Post worked as a photographer for the Farm Security Administration during the New Deal and visited migrant worker camps to record conditions. This mother and child were photographed in 1940 at the Okeechobee migrant camp in Belle Glade, Florida. Courtesy of the Library of Congress.

hoped; Latino families confronted deepening restrictions in parts of the West and Southwest. Perhaps most chilling of all, as Joan Crawford danced onscreen in *Our Dancing Daughters*, Muncie, Indiana, women openly wore their Ku Klux Klan robes to christenings and community parades. Even *Middletown*, it seemed, harbored both the bucolic and abhorrent sides of the 1920s.[29]

THE GREAT DEPRESSION, WAR, AND DOMESTICITY

The Great Depression spread slowly over the nation between 1929 and 1933, as economic failure engulfed agriculture, banking, and manufacturing. Some families maintained a reasonable standard of living throughout the decade, and a few remained indisputably wealthy. For many Americans, the Depression meant hard times, ranging from doing without to hunger and homelessness. Working-class and poor families faced the most difficult challenges; dislocation, separation of family members, and other stresses were common. These burdens meant that wives often had to sustain emotionally drained husbands, and mothers were forced to divide food among hungry children. Women learned to "make do," yet the real dilemmas of finding resources placed wives and mothers in challenging positions.

Housewives extended the family income as far as possible, budgeting carefully with measures such as buying day-old bread and mending old clothes. Many food companies featured special recipes to extend the food dollar. Kraft's Ritz cracker "mock apple pie," for instance, allowed bakers to replace expensive apples with crackers to simulate the look, if not the taste, of a real apple pie. For some families, the economic crisis made an already tenuous existence in poverty worse. Sharecroppers in the rural South, the poor in Northern cities, and the displaced farm families of the dustbowl plains confronted real hunger. When journalists and government observers toured the South and witnessed the brutal conditions of sharecroppers' families, most wrote in astonishment that such degradation still existed in the United States. The wives and families captured in photographs by Walker Evans, published subsequently as *Let Us Now Praise Famous Men* with writer James Agee, shocked readers. The portraits of migrant women and their families in or on their way to California's agricultural fields taken by Dorothea Lange, and of farm families in the South by Margaret Bourke-White, held the same power. The mothers recorded in these photographs became symbolic of the worst of the Depression.[30]

In 1935, the Social Security Act, which established Aid to Dependent Children, promised assistance for the neediest, but moralism and racism limited the benefits available for children and their mothers. The federal government initially provided only a third of the funds for the poor, and allowed states to refuse aid to certain mothers. Among those excluded from assistance were mothers who had given birth outside of marriage, many who were African American, and any who might seem to be keeping "improper" company. Other New Deal programs held similar restrictions for families. Federal and state laws passed at the beginning of the Depression had limited government employment to one family member. The majority of New Deal programs favored male workers, providing higher wages and better jobs; segregation by race remained the norm. Scholars reviewing the New Deal legacy for women have concluded that the programs provided needed help, but assumptions about male and female roles in family life played a critical role in placing women at a disadvantage as workers, wives, and mothers. Legislators encoded the belief that men should be primary breadwinners and did little to provide for situations when they were not; laws also contained qualifying language that upheld notions of morality or behavior. Despite such restrictions, state support enabled some women to struggle toward independence from abusive husbands or survive when families were unable to help.[31]

For some married women, a solution to the economic crisis meant going back into the labor force. Ironically, women's work, segregated into areas that predominantly employed women, suffered less from unemployment than did the occupations that traditionally hired men. Although married women's employment did not grow substantially in the 1930s, those married women who did work for pay experienced a new set of worries. For those with unemployed husbands, tensions might surface at home over a wife's role as family breadwinner, as husbands reported feeling "unmanned" and shamed by not fulfilling their masculine roles. Women using existing child care expressed guilt over working, one historian has noted, and often attempted to find rationales for needing day care.[32] By 1939, as the decade came to an end and the worst of the Depression seemed to be over, nearly eight million Americans still earned less than the new minimum wage, and an estimated 40 percent of families continued to live in poverty.[33] It would take another crisis to lift many out of poverty and put the nation on a new road to prosperity.

As the United States entered World War II on December 8, 1941, Americans could not foresee the vast consequences of their new global commitment for themselves and their families. Between 1941 and August 1945, over 400,000 American men and women died of war-related causes, and over 650,000 were injured or wounded. Americans would inter Japanese American citizens in camps and surveil German-American families for the duration. African Americans serving their country were segregated from white troops, and Europeans were "warned" of their differences. Neither the nation, nor the world, would be the same in 1945 as it had been in 1939 or 1941. The same might be said for American women and their families.

When the war began, women faced a distinctive set of challenges in family life. Japanese American and German American families dealt with relocation or investigation, and frequently wives and mothers had to maintain family cohesion. Other women confronted the absence of male family members during the war, and the injury or loss of a husband or children. Jewish American families, and others with direct European ties, worried about relatives who could not emigrate to safety.

The internment of Japanese Americans originated with Executive Order 9066, which required all Japanese and Japanese Americans living in the western states to evacuate to temporary "relocation" stations. Between March and November 1942, approximately 110,000 men, women, and children moved through the fifteen temporary stations, many of which were unsanitary and not suited for large numbers of people. By October 1942, the population of interned Japanese Americans, of whom three-fourths were United States citizens, were housed in guarded camps behind barbed wire. For the families confronting such conditions, the communal life forced upon them created difficulties in retaining traditions, autonomy, or connection. Legal challenges to internment proved unsuccessful until 1945, when Mitsuye Endo successfully claimed that her forced relocation, despite her citizenship, her brother's military service, and her secretarial work in civil service, violated her liberties. The Supreme Court finally agreed; the majority decision held that relocation was an "unconstitutional resort to racism." Relocation centers closed, but many families had lost their farms and businesses. Reparations would finally be awarded in 1988.[34]

All Americans faced rationing and conservation of resources, from silk to rubber and gasoline. Advertisements and government propaganda assured housewives that their work at home contributed to the war effort; conservation of resources allowed soldiers to receive the food and supplies they needed. "Victory gardens" of vegetables also became popular in 1943, and an estimated twenty million Americans planted seeds in small urban plots, in flower boxes, and rooftop gardens. The work of preserving the bounty of such labors fell to women, who purchased canning supplies in record numbers.[35]

Even in the face of war pressures, the marriage and birth rates began to climb; a marriage boom between 1941 and 1943 reflected the common decision many couples made to wed before a man "shipped out." By 1943, rising birth and divorce rates indicated the consequences of such decisions. When the war ended, marriage, babies, and divorce would all become popular. The consequences for the nation included a baby "boom," the largest cohort of births in national history, from 1943 until

Even in relocation camps such as Manzanar, women worked to maintain stability for their families. Yaeko Nakamura chose games in 1943 with her children. Courtesy of the Library of Congress; photograph by Ansel Adams.

1964. The age of first marriage also fell, with women marrying by an average age of twenty at the end of the decade. Most Americans increasingly believed that marriage was a natural part of life, and nine out of ten wed at some point in their lives. Yet divorce rates also rose with every decade; by the 1960s, divorce lost much of the stigma previously associated with "correspondents" and the "Reno" or "quickie" divorce of the past.

As the war ended in 1945, both the nation and the families that soldiers returned to went through a period of readjustment. Jobs and housing reflected the surge of young men into the economy. Women who had gone to work "for the duration" frequently found themselves without jobs, replaced by veterans. Scarce housing became another problem for families, forcing many to "make do" by living with parents, in makeshift Quonset huts, or in other temporary shelters. Gradually the nation reabsorbed workers and builders created new housing, but with significant differences. Married women did not remain out of the workforce and slowly began one of the most significant transformations in American life, the prevalence of dual-earner families. At the same time, Americans moved out of cities and into suburbs, redefining the ideals of what many would characterize as "the good life." Postwar Americans increasingly focused on consuming the vast array of goods and services available in an extraordinarily prosperous economy. The "purchaser as citizen" could bolster the national economy by spending a paycheck *and* by charging on her credit card.[36]

WOMEN'S FAMILY ROLES IN A CONSUMER AGE

In the 1950s, women's roles seemed almost contradictory. On one hand, advertisers, magazine editors, and radio and television shows featured strong encouragements for domesticity and women's household role. At the same time, however, more married women continued to enter the workforce. What should, or would, women be? Dedicated home-makers like Donna Reed, content that "father knows best," or ambitious women, "not June Cleaver?"[37]

The domestic ideal of the 1950s served as a social prescription, a powerful ideology that may not have described the life of any one woman, but that became part of the framework within which women understood the female experience. During the 1950s, white middle-class women faced a domestic imperative as strong as it had ever been historically. Following the war, advertisers and employers urged women to settle down with their sweethearts, have babies, and enjoy the many consumer items that a prosperous nation now produced. Stories ran in magazines such as the *Saturday Evening Post* that stressed the importance of family life. The sol-dier had sacrificed his years, perhaps his life, to ensure the protection and stability of the family. His sacrifice took precedence over women's needs for self-expression in a career, or financial advancement. If women had to remain working, stories suggested, she should take a job more appropriate for women. Thus, in a story called "Diapers for Flight Six," a pilot becomes a stewardess; in another, a woman leaves the Women's Army Corps to be a happy secretary. In "A Mission for Henry," a female engi-neer and pilot delights in a soldier telling her that he keeps "visualizing you in a rose-covered backyard, wearing simple coveralls and designing a baby carriage with retractable wheels." War work had been temporary, women heard. A coffee ad proclaimed "when you've done your bit for Uncle Sam, it's Maxwell House Coffee time...." Another showed a little girl saying to a woman in overalls, "Mother, when will you stay home again?"[38]

Women were repeatedly told by magazines, movies, and even by col-lege presidents that their best role, their true calling, was in the home as wife and mother. In their 1947 bestseller, *Modern Woman: The Lost Sex*, psychologists Marianna Farnham and Ferdinand Lundberg declared that women's emotional health depended upon men. Even film makers chimed in with movies such as *Sorry, Wrong Number*, *Double Indemnity*, and *The*

Postman Always Rings Twice, featuring women who betrayed men by abandoning their docile role as earnest wives or mothers. Feminist Betty Friedan would later recall that, "it almost didn't matter who the man was who became the instrument of your feminine fulfillment."[39]

It has been suggested that white Americans saw domesticity as the embodiment of security in the midst of their troubled world. The home became an emotional fortress, and even in its architecture now seemed walled off, private and self-contained, a haven where satisfaction and safety melted the worries of the postnuclear age. The man would be king of the castle, and his beautiful wife—male college students agreed in a poll that she was supposed to look like Grace Kelly, and college-educated, trim, and welcoming—cared for the family's comfortable suburban spread as she occupied herself with baking, meetings with a volunteer group, keeping the house lovely, and chauffeuring the kids in the station wagon. Dad went off to work at a corporate job and came home from the city to a good martini or a Manhattan, a leisurely cigarette, and a steak, all guilt free. The kids waited, not demanding but ready to share their achievements and discoveries. The family went to church or synagogue on the weekend, the parents played bridge or golf, and enjoyed the good life. That family image was, and remains, a powerful ideological framework. Yet the family fallout shelter would be perhaps the most powerful metaphor for the contradictions of family life in the 1950s, capturing both the prospects of domestic tranquility and the specter of danger beyond.

Within the household, technology and consumption continued to transform family patterns. For example, frozen vegetables became widely available in the 1950s, changing the bland winter diet to one of peas and cherries in March. Frozen dinners also appeared, promising convenience if not great taste. Manufacturers offered American housewives the latest time-saving gadgets, and the result was more time spent in housework. Perhaps even more significant, Americans increasingly described housework as an emotional contribution, a measure of love rather than a task that had some economic place in the family's subsistence. It wasn't so much that housework made wages go farther, Americans believed, as housework reflected the nurture that a good woman provided her family. Yet the housewives of the 1950s spoke in contradictory ways about their home labor and the material abundance that seemed to surround them. Housewife June Traven recalled a washing machine that became a "big thrill"; Eileen Hanley remembered that she "loved my little house, loved decorating it, choosing the drapes. We were the first on the block to have kitchen appliances that weren't white, and that matched: we had an avocado-colored General Electric refrigerator and range. Very nifty." Despite these satisfactions, Traven revealed that she "was determined to make homemaking represent a good job," but noted, "a lot of it was simple boredom." Hanley put it another way: "once the house was finished I found myself very lonely." Repeatedly the memories, diaries, and letters of white housewives in the 1950s returned to this revelation of dissatisfaction. While many women described the importance of friendships with other women, or closeness with their husbands, they also mentioned a lingering sense of emptiness, boredom, and loneliness. Jill Morris of Long Island remembered that marriage and children had been her "driving goal," yet after five years of marriage and two kids, she said, "here I was in my nice house, with nothing to do."[40]

Children particularly were supposed to deepen domestic attachments, but as a number of historians and sociologists now suggest, childrearing became a more difficult task for the twentieth-century woman. As families grew smaller, emphasis on the development of each individual child began to increase. By the 1950s, a new generation of child specialists such as Benjamin Spock, Mamie Clark, and Arnold Gesell published rules for maternal interaction, urging women to be more involved with the mental development of their children. Too intensive mothering would be dangerous, however. In 1947, author Philip Wyllie declared that mothers threatened society in *A Generation of Vipers*. The image of the emasculating mother permeated films, from 1955's *Rebel Without a Cause* and Alfred Hitchcock's *Psycho* (1960) to 1962's classic *The Manchurian Candidate*.[41]

Despite the demands of housework and child care, many women in the 1950s described themselves as content. If marriage was any measure of women's response to domesticity, American women voted with wedding bells, marrying at a younger average age, nineteen, than any generation before. Yet as author Brett Harvey noted humorously, even the clothes of the 1950s reflected the contradictions of women's roles, in this case between sensuality and reserve. Harvey wrote that "fifties clothes were like amour. . . . our cinched waists and aggressively pointed breasts advertised our availability at the same time they warned of our impregnability."[42] Such fashions illustrated how the contradictions of the 1950s for women extended into the realm of sexuality, a mixed message of freedom and restraint, of titillation and prohibition. The ideal marriage, for example, required the wife to be an enthusiastic sexual partner, and simultaneous orgasm became a prominent concern of sexual counselors. The Kinsey Report on women's sexuality appeared in 1953, and it bolstered the notion that American women sought sexual satisfaction. But if sexual incompatibility marred the union, family counselors and marriage "experts" still told the unhappy couple to stay together. Studies of couples during this period found that most did precisely that, despite rising divorce rates. Individual happiness in marriage, the fulfillment of the self, remained less important than the family.

An American family watches a tabletop radio television in 1948. AP photo.

The "traditional family" and the ideal woman of the 1950s proved to be largely myths, ideologies that suggested more about what people hoped for than what their lives had actually become. This was particularly true for the millions of Americans who did not find themselves reflected in advertisements or college curricula. Poverty remained a persistent national problem despite a decade of prosperity. In 1960, one-fourth of the nation's families ranked under or near a national poverty level. African American families in the South, or in the North for that matter, faced legal or social limitations that white neighbors did not. And even beyond that were hidden revolutions. Lesbians and gays began to organize and advocate new rights through the Daughters of Bilitis and the Mattachine Society. Labor organizing among Latino workers in New Mexico and California created new challenges to residential segregation and workplace discrimination.[43] Mexican American families won the right to desegregated schools in California in 1946 in *Mendez* v. *Westminster*, successfully convincing the Court that students should not be divided on the basis of national origin. The Supreme Court decision in *Brown* v. *Board* in 1954, and the Montgomery Bus Boycott in 1955 and 1956, made clear that opportunities would not belong exclusively to one segment of American society.

The 1960s and 1970s proved to be decades of extraordinary change for all American women. The passage of the 1964 Civil Rights Act not only insured prohibitions against racial discrimination; almost by a quirk, one resistant Southern senator had inserted provisions against sexual discrimination in hopes of making the bill less viable. Instead, the act became a significant protection against gender bias and a foundation for further legal change. By 1978, the Pregnancy Disability Act made it illegal for employers to dismiss women workers during pregnancy. Legal challenges also allowed women to receive credit without a spouse and to gain better access to Social Security funds after divorce or widowhood. In *Loving* v. *Virginia*, the Supreme Court ended state bans against marriage between partners deemed to be of different races. By 1972, an Equal Rights Amendment passed Congress, and with the signature of President Richard M. Nixon, went to the states for ratification to the Constitution. Most controversial of all, the Supreme Court ruled in 1973 that women had a right of privacy to decide, with their physicians, to terminate a pregnancy. *Roe* v. *Wade* would subsequently provoke another movement of Americans dedicated to the elimination of abortion.

These changes that occurred in women's legal rights reflected a more fundamental transformation in ideas and attitudes about women within society. Even within the domestic ideology of the 1950s, the discontent of some women emerged in subversive forms. The popular situation comedy, *I Love Lucy*, scholars have noted, featured the housewife Lucy in her repeated attempts to escape the household and join husband Ricky at work. Both male and female viewers could get a good laugh; husbands might find it reassuring that Lucy failed every week, and wives were encouraged by the fact that Lucy kept trying. Audiences also knew that Lucille Ball was actually no ditz, but an astute working woman who owned Desilu Studios with husband Desi Arnaz, another subtle reminder domesticity was not all that it appeared to be.[44]

Other indicators of discontent appeared as well. On November 1, 1961, nearly fifty thousand housewives and other women mounted a one-day protest over atmospheric nuclear testing. Women Strike for Peace, organized by Bela Abzug, Amy Swerdlow, and others, successfully continued protests until 1963. When called to appear before the House Committee on Un-American Activities in 1962, hundreds of women attended the hearings. As mothers testified about the importance of milk not tainted by strontium 90, others offered bottles to their infants. The Committee was overwhelmed by such clearly politicized motherhood.[45] By the time Betty Friedan wrote about "the problem that has no name," the dissatisfactions of middle-class housewives in the early 1960s, women readers eagerly purchased Friedan's 1963 analysis of *The Feminine Mystique*.

The maturing baby boomers, the tumult of the political unrest of the 1960s, and movements for individual rights combined in the 1960s to foster new attitudes toward sexuality and marriage. From the Kinsey reports on human sexuality in 1948 and 1953 and the arrival of Hugh Hefner's *Playboy* magazine in 1953 to Helen Gurley Brown's 1962 *Sex and the Single Girl*, Americans engaged in a more public discussion on premarital sexuality and sexual pleasure. The availability of new contraception in 1960, the oral birth control pill, also played a role in the steady erosion of older sexual mores. Throughout the 1960s, Americans debated free love (as if it were a new idea), cohabitation, and the nature of marriage. By the late 1960s, many had moved past the "summer of love" to what in the 1970s would be celebrated by Nena and George O'Neill as "open marriage."[46]

The development of a women's movement in the 1960s gave theoretical and political shape to new ideas about women's roles. American couples increasingly wanted to separate procreation from sexuality as pleasure. As women's work outside the home increased, and as women gained greater control over their fertility, many women also asserted their equality in marriage. The idea of a companionate marriage, with the husband as first companion, would be increasingly rejected by women, who sought more equitable roles inside and outside of the home. For poor families, new programs, such as Head Start, Medicaid, Medicare, and the revamping of welfare, along with the nation's War on Poverty (1964) began to have an impact. The Welfare Rights Movement, led primarily by women, also raised issues of practices that had targeted mothers as immoral or unworthy. For lesbians, too, the women's movement allowed for greater opportunities to claim rights in public and in private. Couples who had lived as "friends" became more willing to reveal their commitments to family members, if not coworkers.

During the decade, radical newspapers and publications flourished, allowing women to explore issues of sexuality, gender roles, housework, and childrearing from a feminist perspective. From the more mainstream magazine *MS* to newspapers such as *Off Our Backs*, writers considered the history and the consequences of gender discrimination. Women tried out new ideas or old notions, and the ripples throughout American culture were felt in a variety of ways. Some women, for example, refused to take a husband's name upon marriage, a personal choice that has continued in an ever-expanding array of her-his name options. Cohabitation, a radical prospect in the 1960s, became commonplace for unmarried couples by the end of the twentieth century. "Reproductive rights," the idea that women should have a significant role in determining the means and timing of birth control, abortion, and gynecological care, shaped ideas of patient access and patient rights.

As the women's movement flourished, advertisers and television executives noticed and responded. By the middle 1970s, advertisements and television shows featured products and plots that suggested women did more than cook and clean. *That Girl*, which ran between 1966 and 1971 and starred Marlo Thomas, offered viewers the first single heroine on television. *The Mary Tyler Moore Show*, from 1970 to 1977, went further, with a working single woman as the main character who, although funny, struggled to be taken seriously. In 1968, the Philip Morris tobacco company introduced a cigarette marketed for women called Virginia Slims, and advertisements declared boldly "you've come a long way, baby!" A decade later, Enjoli perfume had women singing, "I can bring home the bacon, fry it up in a pan, and never ever let you forget you're a man, 'cause I'm a woman."[47]

While the women's movement seemed welcome for some, other Americans believed it caused great harm to families and to the nation as a world power. George Gilder, a conservative writer, complained in his 1981 book *Wealth and Poverty* that feminism endangered the masculine ethos that allowed the military to protect American interests internationally. Through the 1970s, conservatives who had pursued the ideals of small government as part of the Republican Party or other organizations aligned with social conservatives opposed to the Equal Rights Amendment or distressed over *Roe* v. *Wade*. Such opponents included Phyllis Schlafly, who founded the Eagle Forum in 1972 as a vehicle for organizing protests against "radical feminists." The National Right to Life Committee formed in 1973, leading a growing campaign to overturn *Roe* v. *Wade* and limit the availability of abortions. By the late 1970s, minister Jerry Falwell announced his "Moral Majority" and defended the importance of "family values." Many of the supporters of the "traditional family" denounced changes in gender roles and advocated the return to a nuclear unit in which husbands resumed the dominant role in family decisions.

Issues of gender and family remained controversial for the remainder of the twentieth century. Adherents of "traditional family values" and social conservatives sought to overturn abortion case law, custody law that appeared to favor single mothers or gay parents, and create legislation on preferred marriage forms. The debate on gender roles and family life played a significant role in elections on both the state and federal levels from the 1980s until 2000.

A frequently overlooked aspect of changes in American life, or one heavily coded in discussions about welfare reform and urban poverty, was the growing crisis of African American families. From the 1960s onward, rates of unmarried pregnancies skyrocketed among young African American women, as the number of available partners for marriage declined because of incarceration, unemployment, or death. The numbers of

Americans continue to debate the issue of abortion. A 2006 rally in Jackson, Mississippi, led to a confrontation between activists. AP photo/Rogelio V. Solis.

never-married African American women also rose significantly; by 1990, one out of three remained unwed. In 1940, three in four African American children lived in two-parent families; by the end of the century, only one in three did. Although single mothers offer the same love and nurture to their children that other parents provide, they face additional challenges economically, socially, and emotionally. In particular, many African American women face the "double day" of work and child care without assistance from a spouse.[48]

The demands of work and family concerned more Americans by the 1980s, as the numbers of working mothers continued to rise. Proposals for a national day care system failed in 1971, when President Nixon vetoed legislation by claiming that it would fail to keep families together. States continued to regulate day care on an individual basis, with varying standards and differing types of inspection. Employers with a need for highly skilled workers tended to move more rapidly to create child-care facilities that promoted child development, but for poorer workers, finding care remained haphazard. Writers debated what could or should be done, with suggestions varying from the creation of a "mommy-track" for professionals to flexible time. As the discussions continued, families contended with the problems of expensive care, transporting children, and managing schedules.

New reproductive technologies also changed family dynamics at the close of the twentieth century. In vitro fertilization made it possible for couples to become parents; surrogacy has provided new avenues for childbearing and childrearing for others. Artificial insemination has also become more commonplace, and single "mothers by choice" celebrate a new type of domesticity. Gay and lesbian parents also found wider acceptance, legally and socially, in many states.

Perhaps the most dramatic trend of all by the late twentieth century lay in the decline of marriage itself. Decreasing marriage rates did not mean that American disapproved of or rejected the idea of family life, but increasingly younger Americans delayed marriage, older Americans did not remarry, and more Americans remained single than at any point in our history. After 1975, white and African American women were increasingly unlikely to marry before age twenty-five. By 2005, less than half of the nation's 111 million households contained married couples. Ironically, one in five Americans over age fourteen could claim to have been divorced at least once.

NOTES

1. Joanne L. Goodwin, *Gender and the Politics of Welfare Reform: Mothers' Pensions in Chicago, 1911–1929* (Chicago: University of Chicago Press, 1997).

2. Mary Louise Roberts, "Gender, Consumption, and Commodity Culture," *American Historical Review* Vol. 103 (1998): 817–844; Roland Marchand, *Advertising the American Dream: Making Way for Modernity, 1920–1940* (Berkeley: University of California Press, 1985); Andrew Heinze, "From Scarcity to Abundance: The Immigrant as Consumer," in *Consumer Society in American History: A Reader*, ed. Lawrence B. Glickman (Ithaca, NY: Cornell University Press, 1999).

3. Duke Ad Access, http://library.duke.edu/digitalcollections/adaccess.

4. Shelley Stamp, *Movie-struck Girls: Women and Motion Picture Culture after the Nickelodeon* (Princeton, NJ: Princeton University Press, 2000).

5. Robert and Helen Merrell Lynd, *Middletown: A Study in Modern American Culture* (New York: Harcourt Brace and World, 1929).

6. Ruth Schwartz Cowan, *More Work for Mother: The Ironies of Household Technology from the Open Hearth to the Microwave* (New York: Basic Books, 1983).

7. Ruth Bordin, *Frances Willard: A Biography* (Chapel Hill: University of North Carolina Press, 2000).

8. Nan Enstad, *Ladies of Labor, Girls of Adventure: Working Women, Popular Culture, and Labor Politics at the Turn of the Century* (New York: Columbia University Press, 1999).

9. Mary P. Ryan, *Cradle of the Middle Class: The Family in Oneida County, New York, 1790–1865* (New York: Cambridge University Press, 1983).

10. Carl Bernstein, *A Woman in Charge: The Life of Hillary Rodham Clinton* (New York: Alfred A. Knopf, 2007).

11. Ann Hulbert, *Raising America: Experts, Parents, and a Century of Advice about Children* (New York: Knopf, 2003); Julia Grant, *Raising Baby by the Book: The Education of American Mothers* (New Haven: Yale University Press, 1998).

12. Janice Williams Rutherford, *Selling Mrs. Consumer: Christine Frederick & the Rise of Household Efficiency* (Athens: University of Georgia Press, 2003); Sarah Stage and Virginia Bramble, *Rethinking Home Economics: Women and the History of a Profession* (Ithaca, NY: Cornell University Press, 1997).

13. Mary S. Hoffschwelle, "The Science of Domesticity: Home Economics at George Peabody College for Teachers, 1914–1939," *Journal of Southern History* Vol. 57 (1991): 667.

14. Stage and Bramble, *Rethinking Home Economics.*

15. Stephanie Coontz, *The Way We Never Were: American Families and the Nostalgia Trap* (New York: Basic Books, 1993), 391; Susan Strasser, *Never Done: A History of American Housework* (New York: Henry Holt, 2000); Cowan, *More Work for Mother.*

16. Jacquelyn Jones, *Labor of Love, Labor of Sorrow: Black Women, Work, and the Family from Slavery to the Present* (New York: Vintage, 1985), 123; also see S. J. Kleinberg, "Technology and Women's Work: The Lives of Working-Class Women in Pittsburgh, 1870–1910," *Labor History* Vol. 17 (1976): 58–72.

17. Ross Wetzsteon, *Republic of Dreams: Greenwich Village: The American Bohemia, 1910–1960* (New York: Simon and Schuster, 2003), 191–201.

18. Strasser, *Never Done,* 93.

19. Oliver Zunz, *Making America Corporate, 1870–1920* (Chicago: University of Chicago Press, 1990); Lawrence B. Glickman, *A Living Wage: American Workers and the Making of Consumer Society* (Ithaca, NY: Cornell University Press, 1999).

20. Donna R. Gabaccia, *From the Other Side: Women, Gender, and Immigrant Life in the U.S., 1820–1990* (Bloomington: Indiana University Press, 1994); Judith Smith, *Family Connections: A History of Italian and Jewish Immigrant Lives in Providence, Rhode Island, 1900–1940* (Albany, NY: SUNY Press, 1985); Kathy Peiss, *Cheap Amusements: Working Women and Leisure in Turn-of-the-Century New York* (Philadelphia: Temple University Press, 1986), 68.

21. Karen Manners Smith, "New Paths to Power, 1890–1920," in Nancy F. Cott, *No Small Courage: A History of Women in the United States* (New York: Oxford University Press, 2000), 368.

22. Peiss, *Cheap Amusements,* 69, 102, 187.

23. Peiss, *Cheap Amusements,* 187; see also Daniel Delis Hill, *Advertising to the American Woman, 1900–1999* (Columbus: Ohio State University Press, 2002); Lisa Botshon and Meredith Goldsmith, eds., *Middlebrow Moderns: Popular American Women Writers of the 1920s* (Boston: Northeastern University Press, 2003).

24. John D'Emilio and Estelle B. Freedman, *Intimate Matters: A History of Sexuality in America* (Chicago: University of Chicago Press, 1998), 241.

25. Linda Gordon, *The Moral Property of Women: A History of Birth Control Politics in America* (Urbana: University of Illinois Press, 2007), 243.

26. Judith Walzer Leavitt, *Brought to Bed: Child Bearing in America, 1750–1950* (New York: Oxford University Press, 1985).

27. Michael Haines, "Fertility and Mortality," http://eh.net/encyclopedia/article/haines.demography.

28. Lynd and Lynd, *Middletown,* 150–151.

29. Kathleen M. Blee, *Women and the Klan: Racism and Gender in the 1920s* (Berkeley: University of California Press, 1991).

30. Kraft Foods still provides the recipe for the pie at http://www.kraftfoods.com/kf/recipes/ritz-mock-apple-pie-53709.aspx. James Agee, and Walker Evans, *Let Us Now Praise Famous Men: Three Tenant Families* (New York: Houghton Mifflin, 1960); Elizabeth Partridge, *Restless Spirit: The Life and Work of Dorothea Lange* (New York: Penguin, 2001); Pierre Borhan, *Dorothea Lange: The Heart and Mind of a Photographer* (Boston: Little, Brown, 2002); Robert L. Reid et al., *Chicago and Downstate: Illinois as Seen by the Farm Security Administration Photographers, 1936–1943*

(Urbana: University of Illinois Press, 1989); Charles Hagen, *American Photographers of the Depression: Farm Security Administration Photographs, 1935–1942* (New York: Pantheon Books, 1985).

31. Linda Gordon, *Heroes of Their Own Lives: The Politics and History of Family Violence: Boston, 1880–1960* (Urbana: University of Illinois Press, 2002).

32. Elizabeth Rose, *A Mother's Job: The History of Day Care, 1890–1960* (New York: Oxford University Press, 2003); Sarah Deutsch, "From Ballots to Breadlines, 1920–1940," in Cott, *No Small Courage*, 474.

33. David M. Kennedy, *Freedom from Fear: The American People in Depression and War, 1929–1945* (New York: Oxford University Press, 2001), 249–287.

34. Peter H. Irons, *Justice at War: The Story of the Japanese-American Internment Cases* (Berkeley: University of California, 1993).

35. Emily Yellin, *Our Mothers' War: American Women at Home and at the Front During World War II* (New York: Simon and Schuster, 2004).

36. The birth rate per woman continued to decline during the century overall. James W. Hughes, and Joseph J. Seneca, eds., *America's Demographic Tapestry: Baseline for the New Millennium* (New Brunswick, NJ: Rutgers University Press, 1999); Lizabeth Cohen, *A Consumer's Republic: The Politics of Mass Consumption in Postwar America* (New York: Knopf, 2003).

37. Joanne Meyerowitz. *Not June Cleaver: Women and Gender in Postwar America, 1945–1960* (Philadelphia: Temple University Press, 1994).

38. Mary P. Ryan, *Womanhood in America* (New York: Franklin Watts, 1983), 201.

39. Betty Friedan, *The Feminine Mystique* (New York: Norton, 1963). See also Daniel Horowitz, *Betty Friedan and the Making of the Feminine Mystique: The American Left, the Cold War, and Modern Feminism* (Amherst: University of Massachusetts Press, 2000).

40. Elaine Tyler May, *Homeward Bound: American Families in the Cold War Era* (New York: Basic Books, 1999); Brett Harvey, *The Fifties: A Women's Oral History* (New York: HarperCollins, 1993).

41. Karal Ann Marling, *As Seen on TV: The Visual Culture of Everyday Life in the 1950s* (Cambridge, MA: Harvard University Press, 1996).

42. Harvey, *The Fifties*.

43. Marcia M. Gallo, *Different Daughters: A History of the Daughters of Bilitis and the Rise of the Lesbian Rights Movement* (Berkeley, CA: Seal Press, 2007); Lillian Faderman, *Odd Girls and Twilight Lovers: A History of Lesbian Life in Twentieth-Century America* (New York: Columbia University Press, 1991); Vern L. Bullough, *Before Stonewall: Activists for Gay and Lesbian Rights in Historical Context* (Philadelphia: Haworth Press, 2002).

44. Steven Sanders Coyne and Tom Gilbert, *Desilu: The Story of Lucille Ball and Desi Arnaz* (New York: William Morrow & Company, 1993).

45. Amy Swerdlow, *Women Strike for Peace: Traditional Motherhood and Radical Politics in the 1960s* (Chicago: University of Chicago Press, 1993).

46. Nena O'Neill and George O'Neill, *Open Marriage: A New Life Style for Couples* (Blue Ridge Summit, PA: M. Evans, 1972).

47. Susan Jeanne Douglas, *Where the Girls Are: Growing Up Female with the Mass Media* (New York: Times Books, 1994).

48. Ella L. Bell et al., *Our Separate Ways: Black and White Women and the Struggle for Professional Identity* (Cambridge, MA: Harvard Business Press, 2003); Myra Marx Ferree et al., *Revisioning Gender* (Thousand Oaks, CA: Sage, 1998).

3

Women and Popular Culture and the Arts

Lillian Russell, four times married and the companion of Diamond Jim Brady, performed before adoring audiences in turn-of-the-century New York. Voluptuous, with the perfect hourglass figure, Russell sang such favorites as "Come Down Ma Evening Star" to packed houses before eventually leaving the stage to write columns, advocate women's suffrage, and travel to Europe on behalf of President Warren G. Harding.

Nearly a century later, another tightly corseted performer sang lustily to eager audiences filling stadiums, concert halls, and arenas. Madonna, once Madonna Louise Ciccone of suburban Detroit, Michigan, transformed herself into the world's richest female popular performer by mixing sex, seduction, femininity, and scandal. Much like Russell, Madonna manipulated popular interests and anxieties. Both simultaneously utilized and subverted popular conceptions of women's sexuality and beauty to become major stars.

Women played many different roles in the creation and evolution of American culture during the twentieth century. As artists, writers, musicians, actors, and in many other positions, women contributed to the full expression of national cultural life and sometimes also constructed art that was distinctly female. At the same time, many women challenged the limitations of gender as performers or audiences and opened a wide variety of opportunities for achievement, expression, and enjoyment.

Women's role as consumers of culture also shaped national life in ways that historians have only recently begun to document. As manufacturers and advertisers focused on female audiences and purchasers through the century, women shaped choices, from what was consumed in the home to the types of homes and cars Americans purchased. Women played an equally central role in politicizing consumption in housewives' boycotts to a growing consumers' movement. It has been contended that in the second half of the twentieth century, consumer culture reshaped the politics of a prosperous nation, and slowly ideas of consumption and citizenship merged. The consequences in the "consumers' republic" extended from political campaigns increasingly driven by television advertising to new ideas of entitlement based on purchases and consumption.[1]

The concept of "culture" itself continues to be an important topic for debate among scholars. Although to some degree the components of what makes up "culture" might seem obvious to a casual observer, many academics suggest different definitions or emphasize particular aspects of what culture might be or how it operates. One scholar ventured the notion that culture included "the sharing and transmission of memory, ideology, emotions, life-style, scholarly and artistic works, and other symbols." English critic Raymond Williams very famously suggested that the notion of culture evolved to include all of those features and the consideration of how they interact. In the most basic ways, people all inhabit, participate in, resist, and recreate the society in which they live. While they do, they make art, from scribbled pictures that grace mothers' refrigerators to complex works in galleries; they make music in raunchy bar songs or in symphonies; they laugh or cry at plays, movies, or school shows; each act constitutes creation and reinforcement—or possibly subversion—of culture. Scholars have distinguished between "high" and "popular" culture and written at great lengths about the many ways in which culture shapes life. Yet most agree today that culture includes not only classic works of art or music, but quilts made by Alabama women and even the once-popular crocheted poodle toilet paper holders.[2]

Situating women within the context of American culture in the twentieth century requires a multifaceted approach, in which women can be viewed as creators, consumers, and objects of change. Examining the shifting notions of beauty, for example, reveals that women had many different roles in the emerging cosmetics industry. Women entrepreneurs such as Elizabeth Arden founded companies; women wore cosmetics; women served as models to entice other women to consume; women informally used or rejected some types of cosmetics based on their notions of what was appropriate. The "beauty culture" reflected women's interests, while manufacturers and advertisers responded to and manipulated women's desires. While some critics of cosmetics in 1910 or in 1975 sought to condemn makeup as simply a commercial exploitation, women have been seen to use cosmetics in more complex ways. Makeup allowed women to "put on a face" while entering public life, for example, or to become more playfully glamorous. Women wearing Revlon's fire-engine red lipstick in the 1940s made it clear that even in coveralls, they were female; young women in the 1990s painted their nails green or black to reject conventional beauty culture.[3]

While historians have been alert to shifts in practices that constitute the frameworks of culture, the questions surrounding the formation of culture remain, for some, an unresolved problem. Scholars working with theories of poststructuralism and deconstruction have argued that meanings, symbols, and language itself were not fixed or static, but could be interpreted and understood in differing ways. One could not write a precise history that would absolutely reflect the past, in other words, only an interpretation of that history. The word "gay," for example, meant in 1933 that the heroine of the film *The Gay Divorcee* was happy, not homosexual. By the 1970s, "gay" appeared as an accepted alternative definition for male homosexuals, and older lyrics of earlier decades suddenly seemed risible. That idea that culture is not static, and that meanings may shift, remains particularly useful in exploring the ways in which women participated in and shaped twentieth century American culture.[4]

THE GIBSON GIRL AND THE NEW WOMAN

In 1900, most Americans still lived on farms, traveled by horse and buggy, and many adults had, at best, an eighth-grade education. Houses and homesteads ranged from solid brick structures for single families to tenement buildings in eastern cities and sod houses on the Great Plains. In New York City, electricity lit the streets and some homes; in places such as rural Tennessee, the prospect of electric appliances remained two decades away. Regional differences persisted despite the nationalizing forces of railroads and politics. The vast territory of the United States held a diverse array of peoples, lives, and prospects.

Two companies promised to level these differences by sending almost three million catalogs to American families. The Sears Roebuck's "wish book" and Montgomery Ward's equally massive volume contained everything from opera glasses and horse harnesses to plows and clothing. For a little less than two dollars, any woman could order shoes; any man could decide which rifle and which hat best suited him. The advent of rural postal routes in 1898, or "rural free delivery," made it simple for any customer with money to make purchases. The catalogs served customers without regard to race or class and made the same goods accessible to rural purchasers throughout the nation.

The housewife who shopped by using the Sears catalog could find many of the items that once consumed a large part of her grandmother's time. Finished clothing for all members of the family, down to baby's moccasins, meant less sewing, although those who wished could purchase patterns and fabric. The icebox, wringer washer, and carpet sweeper might make her labor more pleasant, if not less intense. Yet the majority of women outside of the most advantaged circles still cooked and baked, preserved foods, and did most, if not all, of their own cleaning. Even in those homes with domestic servants, the amount of time spent in house-work did not decline with new technology.[5] What did change significantly with the new century were the connections among manufacturers, adver-tisers, and audiences, as makers of soaps, vacuums, and a plethora of other housewares focused on the female consumer.

The development of mass media also contributed to the growing em-phasis on women as consumers. Mass market newspapers and magazines, facilitated by improving printing technologies, allowed writers and adver-tisers to reach an expanding number of readers. By 1890, American mag-azines reached a total circulation of nearly eighteen million volumes; successful publications such as *Scribner's*, the *Saturday Evening Post*, *Life*, *Collier's*, and *Atlantic Monthly* became the reading fare of middle-class families nationwide. After the turn of the century, color advertisements became affordable to publishers and advertisers, making publications more appealing. By 1911, over a billion periodicals went into homes through the postal service.[6] Women's magazines also entered the era of mass circulation, with *Ladies' Home Journal* and *Good Housekeeping* emerging as the most popular among white, middle-class readers.

The advertisements of *Ladies' Home Journal* featured national brands such as Quaker Oats, Jell-o, Kodak, Kellogg's, and Ivory. With ads depict-ing a young and fair white woman enjoying the pleasures of home life, be it cleaning or feeding her children, the *Journal* reassured women that even in the most difficult times or trying personal circumstances, reliable products meant order, security, and confidence. Historians suggest that the *Journal* and similar periodicals placed feature stories to reinforce that message, tying consumer fantasies to both experiences and ideals. By 1930, according to one historian, the *Journal* had constructed a consumer culture around the "story of a common woman, the 'average' woman, the 'American' woman."[7]

That average woman, as depicted by *Journal* editors and writers, linked her heritage back to America's idyllic *Mayflower* past; immigrant and African American women portrayed in the magazine remained subordi-nate recipients of benevolence or patronizing concern. The *Journal*'s ideal woman married happily, or worked to achieve a good marriage with her husband, but her greatest contentment and fulfillment implicitly lay in consumption. The *Journal* woman was a consumer, not a producer, rel-ishing a role that gave her some leisure and seeming control over a vast array of goods and products.

The construction of women as consumers also received impetus from department stores, which created a special environment of luxury and fantasy for the purchaser. The thousands of "palatial giants of urban retail" had, by the 1900s, developed numerous strategies to entice buyers, from seasonal themes to color schemes and spaces designed for leisurely shopping. The savvy department store owner encouraged service, which ranged from the odd addition of a library outlet in New York's Macy's to restaurants, tearooms, and auditoriums for fashion shows. The woman who entered found herself subtly directed to the women's spaces, with decors meant to flatter the purchaser and the merchandise. By 1915, the success of the department store and other lures to female consumption was evident in the involvement of women in purchases; women bought nearly 85 percent of consumer goods in the United States. Diaries also revealed the growing significance of shopping in women's lives; one woman's notations of her nearly daily purchases from New York stores mirrored an enthusiasm shared by others.[8]

In the first decades of the twentieth century, women gradually became defined as consumers, a role in which they were not entirely passive. From the National Consumers' League, organized to use middle-class and advantaged women's positions as consumers as a form of political leverage in the interests of working women, to the choices women made in daily purchases, female shoppers exercised a particular form of power. Styles and quality of clothing had long marked status and class among women, but the expansion of options encouraged young women to "put on style." Working women adopted more colorful and dramatic fashions, sometimes deferring other needs for a particularly fetching hat or more elegant skirt. During the 1909 New York textile strike, working women dressed in hats sporting feathers and artificial fruit, French heels, and carried fur muffs, to dignify their claims and themselves. More restrained settlement house workers voiced concern over the lavish displays among young female workers in their neighborhoods; Lillian Wald of the Henry Street Settlement in New York complained about the absence of a "pronounced modesty in dress." Historians note that fashion became a way for young working-class women to explore identity, particularly for those of immigrant backgrounds.[9]

Style defined feminine types with increasing frequency. The Gibson Girl, popularized by illustrator Charles Dana Gibson, captured the fantasies of men and women at the turn of the century in drawings of a tall, slender, elegant young woman. In drawings for the nation's leading magazines such as *Collier's*, *Harper's*, and *Life*, Gibson featured his "girls" in activities ranging from sunbathing to golf. While the Gibson Girl suggested a more worldly and active ideal than many of the maternal images dominant in the late nineteenth century, however, she remained decidedly

Charles Dana Gibson's illustration "The Weaker Sex," circa 1903, provided a popular image of female beauty as well as a continuing commentary on gender roles. Courtesy of the Library of Congress.

feminine. Gibson's women still displayed tightly corseted bodies; they looked fragile and delicate, with long thin necks, and large heads balancing a mass of hair. Gibson also parodied other women, particularly older ones, as full and frumpy. Torn between his profitable work as an illustrator and a belief that his trade represented an inferior form of art, Gibson sometimes infused his "girls" with a taunting, disdainful quality; in one illustration, a bevy of smug-looking Gibson girls dissect a tiny man. Similar pictures convey a dour outlook on society and women, with the "Gibson Girl " regally distant and unmoved by those around her.

Gibson's image contrasted with other emerging images of women, from the "New Woman" of suffrage, reform, and temperance crusades to the increasingly popular heroines of working class film serials. In 1912, *The Ladies' World* joined with the Edison Company to produce a story series in combination with serialized films, *What Happened to Mary*? Both the stories and the films proved enormously popular with young working women, and the magazine reached over one million subscriptions as the films drew an estimated two million viewers. Mary, and other serials which followed featuring the *Hazards of Helen*, *Dollie of the Dailies*, and the *Adventures of Kathryn*, presented a young woman in "the city" (usually New York), who maintained dignity and respectability while challenging robbers, defeating workplace fraud, and other exciting feats. Mary found her identity by going "bravely into a new world where it was possible to be happy by becoming what one might become." The heroines rejected romance, as did viewers and readers; when producers and publisher planned a second series, *Who Will Marry Mary?* it failed to win fans. It has been suggested that although the series and films originated as an attempt to profit from an expanding audience of young working women, female viewers welcomed the adventures. The heroines struggled for respectability and the right to define themselves, as did young women who enjoyed the fantasies and the possibility of independence.[10]

The activities of working-class urban youth contributed to other shifts that resonated throughout American culture. From Coney Island to Palisades Amusement Park in New Jersey, Kennywood Park in Pittsburgh, and Cedar Point in Ohio, the amusement park at the turn of the century promised young working-class couples thrills and a chance to explore new physical boundaries in courtship. The rides featured opportunities for "accidentally" touching, from the Tunnel of Love, which forced the supposedly frightened woman into her male companion's reassuring arms, to the Razzle-Dazzle, with a tipping surface to throw riders together. Similar opportunities could arise at the nickelodeons, patronized primarily by working-class Americans until the 1920s. In the darkened theater, young men could easily sneak a covert squeeze of a hand, while young women found opportunities to lay their heads on a male companion's willing shoulder. The result, according to one historian, was an "expressive heterosocial culture."

Women's presence in areas once closed to them became literal as well as figurative. A pioneering few took to the air. Harriet Quimby, Matilde Moisant, Ruth Law, and Katherine Stinson defied arguments that women lacked the technical sense to fly a plane. Bessie Coleman, the world's first licensed African American pilot, challenged the widespread assumption that race also limited an individual's ability to master the complexities of flight. Some male observers greeted the growing popularity of the automobile with similar concerns over women's mechanical capabilities, but well-publicized transcontinental trips by Alice Huyler Ramsey, Blanche Stuart Scott, and Emily Post proved the durability of both cars and female drivers. Although some women disliked the difficult hand crank used to start cars prior to 1920, most handled it with ease. Women in rural areas especially welcomed the opportunities to drive, which provided relief from isolation. Ironically, in many families, men assumed the prerogative for driving during family outings, but even in the 1920s automobile manufacturers dedicated some of their advertising appeal to potential female customers.[11]

World War I opened other avenues for women to explore. During the war, working women found jobs in manufacturing, as police officers, and as railway conductors. Other women sold war bonds, worked for the Red Cross, or volunteered as nurses and drivers in the war effort. At war's end, the upheavals of 1919, with strikes throughout the nation and a well-publicized Red Scare, signaled what a historian has called a "pervasive sense of newness."[12] Prohibition and the achievement of votes for women appeared as victories for social change.

Fashion revealed the shift in attitude. The corseted S-figure of the early century gave way to looser, more flexible forms; by the early 1920s, skirts began to rise as the fitted bodice disappeared. Manufacturers continued to promote undergarments to restrain unwanted jiggles and suggested that refined women still needed the sophisticated firmness of a "scientific" design. Many young women preferred the freedom of the longer-waisted dresses, no corset, and the movement possible with shorter hemlines. With a cloche hat and bobbed hair, the fashionable woman became a "flapper," the symbol of the era.

The flapper image represented difference and controversy. The evident change in women's style from regulated bodies, ornate hair, and yards of fabric to the sleek, neat look of the 1920s indicated other new behaviors for women. Sexuality became more open, and couples courted beyond the chaperoning eyes of family or friends. "Dates" with one man replaced group outings, and the sexual foreplay deemed permissible by virtuous women more frequently included what came to be called "necking" and "petting." As the works of Freud, Havelock Ellis, and other psychologists began to circulate in popular forms, the idea of a vital female sexuality became commonplace, replacing far older concepts of "passionlessness" or an innate womanly reserve. The new media, from radio to movies and pulp magazines, also celebrated sexuality if not sex. Perhaps most important, young women and their male companions separated themselves into a peer-defined culture, a society of the young free from the rigid strictures encountered by their parents' generation.[13]

Educators and pundits worried in print over the "wild young people" and fretted about the consequences for civilization. Yet young women challenged the stereotype of undisciplined abandon; one college student from Illinois insisted that the flapper was "the independent, a 'pally' young woman, a typical American product."[14] What mattered in this formulation was youth; it remained an important quality of the flapper and increasingly distinguished women as workers, consumers, and citizens. The older woman did not find herself included in the bold new culture of cosmetics, college, and new mores; fashion divided the older matron from her daughter as a growing array of products promised the illusion of youth. The dominant image of women in the nineteenth century had been that of a mother with her children; in the twentieth century it became the young, beautiful, unmarried woman. Advertisers utilized the importance of youth and the fear of age to sell cosmetics, soaps, and other products. Losing one's youthful appearance might endanger marriage, social connections, and even motherhood. One advertisement for Palmolive soap in 1927 made it clear that "every daughter [wished] ... for her mother to retain, *above all things,* her youthful allure."[15] Lacking the necessary glamour, the earlier reformers and suffragists of the Progressive era in the 1920s appeared stuffy and drab. Younger women rejected the politics of equal rights in asserting what appeared to be a social and cultural liberation. At the same time, however, age emerged as yet another substantial division among women, as younger women took advantage of the greater possibilities for mobility, sexuality, education, and consumption.

Young women smoked, drank in speakeasies, and danced with abandon to jazz. They appeared at the seashore in scanty bathing costumes covering only their torsos, and competed for the new title of Miss America in 1921. The "modern" young woman also competed with her female friends for the most desirable acquisition, the appropriate young man. The homosocial culture of shared connections and friendships between women slowly eroded in the 1920s and thirties; the networks that tied the New Deal's female reformers together, for example, seemed outmoded to a younger generation.

Films and novels instead encouraged the prospect of women fighting over men; in 1928's *Our Dancing Daughters,* heroine Joan Crawford battled against the scheming man-stealing gold digger Anita Page. A year later, Crawford and Page took similar roles in *Our Modern Maidens.* F. W. Murnau's *Sunrise* in 1927 featured a duplicitous woman plotting to kill her lover's wife. The competitive struggle over men informed advertisements as well; Hi-Ja Hair Fix warned women about those who might "take a fancy to your sweetheart." Palmolive soap continued to alert women to lurking dangers, using competition with other women to increase feminine insecurities. "Would your husband marry you again?" one ad inquired, while another asked women to wonder if "others he meets outrival you in natural charm."[16] One historian suggests that "at the very moment when women no longer seemed to need marriage on economic or political grounds," older types of support, especially those among women, eroded.[17] Instead, a competitive individualism emerged, with sexuality, consumption, and insecurity as key elements.

The body, beauty, and physical appearance became a central focus of anxiety and the search for perfection. Women learned from any number of media sources that blemishes, size, and physical characteristics could be transformed with the right aid. Straight hair could be processed or heated for curls; curly hair could be straightened. Dark skin needed whiteners; pale skin required tanning. The smart woman knew the right products and treatments to ensure success. Before the 1920s, young women "rarely mentioned their bodies in terms of strategies for self-improvement." As the twentieth century progressed, concern over physical flaws became more commonplace, with a series of attendant problems from eating disorders to dependency on plastic surgery.[18]

By the close of the 1920s, the image of the American woman had evolved from "a serious-minded college (or working) woman to a carefree, scantily clad 'flapper' who existed to wear modern clothes, have fun, and ultimately catch a man who would support her," one historian wrote. The reality remained something different, however. Increasingly, women attempted to combine marriage with work, at least until the arrival of children; the number of married professional women doubled between 1910 and 1930. Dorothy Dunbar Bromley wrote in *Harper's* of the "new style" feminist, who attempted "a full life" of marriage and career.[19] For African American women and Latino women, migration to better jobs often meant dividing family responsibilities with spouses in another area or efforts to restructure family supports. The popular depiction of the young, frivolous urban woman failed to reflect the lives of rural farm women as well, whose lives combined the chores familiar to the nineteenth-century housewife with new techniques for tending crops and livestock.

One popular shift affected a great number of women, however. The emphasis on female sexuality and the message of female responsiveness from physicians, birth control planners, and magazines led many couples to a new attitude about marital sexuality. One historian suggests that "middle-class married women were the unsung sexual revolutionaries of the twentieth century." A study of sexual practices in 1918 by Katherine Bement Davis of over two thousand female respondents found that younger women expected sexual pleasure within marriage. By 1926, birth control advocate Margaret Sanger wrote a manual for *Happiness in Marriage*, which depicted marital partners finding "the complete fulfillment of love through the expression of sex."[20] Middle-class women expected to be partners; unlike nineteenth-century wives who occupied a "separate sphere" of domestic influence, the new wife of the 1920s insisted on companionship, pleasure, and participation in her husband's life. When Robert and Helen Merrell Lynd surveyed couples in Muncie, Indiana, for their study *Middletown*, they discovered that middle-class wives commonly used contraceptives and some sought time alone with their husbands, even at the expense of social obligations.

As many women in the 1920s asserted a new sexuality, however, sexual politics also took forms that harmed individuals and communities. In the South, the use of lynching as a means to control local protest or politics and to assert white domination became more widespread. Often, accusations of sexual impropriety or rape would precede the jailing of a young African American, whose death by hanging or torture signaled the limits of social justice. Laws limiting marriage between partners defined as belonging to different races also flourished. In New Mexico, for example, one couple with similar backgrounds found themselves barred from wedding because of their supposed racial heritages.[21]

The creation of "red light" districts in American towns and cities, and the stigma placed on women engaging in sex for pay, also marked another part of this early sexual revolution. During the Progressive era, reformers focused on "white slavery" and the possibility that young women arriving in large cities would find themselves entrapped by predatory entrepreneurs, who would force them into prostitution. Laws and police enforcement increasingly limited women in the sex trade to districts within cities or blocks within towns. Growing public disapproval dovetailed with another twentieth century development, the tendency to use social science to construct new categories of identity and personalities.

Notions of expertise, the development of new disciplines such as psychology and sociology, and emphasis on individual flaws and strengths contributed to new concepts of personality types. Historians note that behaviors became linked to identity, particularly in the discussion of homosexuality. A man who had sexual encounters with other men might not be labeled as homosexual in the nineteenth century; as the twentieth century developed, psychologist defined the "sexual invert" as deviant. The evolving concept of lesbian relations, as it was portrayed by social scientists, undermined the innocence attached to the romantic friendships between women in the nineteenth century. Historian Lillian Faderman argues that "sexologists were certainly the first to construct the conception of the lesbian," defining intimacy between women as aberrant and dangerous. Women who were attracted to or in love with other women no longer had the safety of community approval for "Boston marriages" or homosocial networks. Gradually, a lesbian subculture developed, with social sites, literature, and new networks. By the 1950s, the possibility of identity merged with politics, as the Daughters of Bilitis formed in San Francisco.[22]

A more open sexuality infused developing forms of music. Jazz and blues gained in popularity with each decade of the new century, and by the 1920s each drew audiences to clubs, dance halls, and other venues. Frequently raw, always imbued with energy and innovation, the new music provided opportunities for a generation of talented female singers and composers to reach audiences. Gertrude "Ma" Rainey, "mother of the blues," became the first woman to tour as a blues performer, while Mamie Smith made the first jazz recording by a female vocalist in 1921. Some singers such as Ethel Waters, who recorded "Stormy Weather" and "I Can't Stop You from Loving Me," reached popular music fans. Lil Hardin, who eventually became the second wife of musician Louis Armstrong, played piano and composed.

Jazz and blues served to bring African American women performers to prominence as exceptional interpreters of music and culture. Bessie Smith dominated the blues in the 1920s with a distinctive, true voice and gutsy, sexual style. The lyrics of Smith's songs could frequently be full of double-entendres, such as "Put It Right Here (Or Keep It Out There)," and "Empty Bed Blues." Billie Holiday, who began her career in the 1920s, continued to command large audiences through the 1930s. Holiday joined the bands of Count Basie, and later Artie Shaw, becoming one of the first African American singers to perform with white orchestras. By the late 1930s, her repertoire included the controversial "Strange Fruit," a blues song explicitly about the lynching of black men. Her musical choices made Holiday a favorite performer for intellectuals and critics. Equally famous would be the young Ella Fitzgerald, who won a 1934 Apollo Theater contest and quickly established herself as a major jazz performer. Hattie McDaniel, the first African American performer to win an Academy Award, also started her performing career as a blues singer. McDaniel left music for more lucrative roles in film, but despite her Oscar in 1939, she continued to play the parts available to African American women in Hollywood, those of maids, nannies, and nurses.[23]

African American women influenced American culture through literature as well during the 1920s, as a movement of writers, poets, and journalists flourished in the Harlem Renaissance. The "flowering of Negro literature," according to National Association for the Advancement of Colored People (NAACP) head James Weldon Johnson, provided impetus for a uniquely African American perspective in theater, novels, and verse. Jessie Redmon Fauset, the first female African American Phi Beta Kappa graduate, finished her studies at Cornell University and joined the staff of the NAACP in 1912. Novels followed, from *There Is Confusion* (1924), the study of African American family life, to *Plum Bun* (1929) and *The Chinaberry Tree* (1931). Zora Neale Hurston, an anthropologist, worked to organize the journal *Fire!!*, and produced a study of folk culture, *Mules and Men*, as well as a novel, *Their Eyes Were Watching God*. Nella Larsen, another novelist, wrote *Quicksand* in 1928 and *Passing* in 1929, which considered the experiences of racial identity. From Washington, DC, Georgia Douglas Johnson organized a salon for writers, and contributed her own poetry, from *The Heart of a Woman* in 1918 to *Bronze* (1922) and *An Autumn Love Cycle* (1928). Alice Dunbar-Nelson, whose literary career began in the 1890s, continued to write extensively through the 1920s in association with other Harlem writers, and Angelina Grimke Weld also maintained deep connections within the circle of writers. Her 1920 play *Rachel* vigorously attacked lynching. Other writers such as Anne Spencer, Gwendolyn Bennett, and Helene Johnson, and composer Nora Douglas Holt, would later seem overshadowed by the fame of

Hurston and male contributors. The robust creativity of this period nevertheless brought a distinctive African American female voice more fully into American literature.

By the end of the 1920s, Americans knew that daily life seemed quite different from the routines and conventions that occupied citizens before World War I. Media innovations represented one of the most obvious changes. Radio stations began commercial broadcasts in 1920, and through the decade, Americans listened to sports, speeches, and bands. Movies drew more patrons as well. Mary Pickford and Lillian Gish appeared typically as virtuous women struggling against adversity, while sexuality and innuendo defined Greta Garbo, the "vamp" Theda Bara, and Norma Talmadge. Latin American actress Dolores del Rio and the "It" girl, Clara Bow, attracted viewers with distinctive images of beauty and vitality. The advent of sound in 1927 with *The Jazz Singer* signaled an end to the careers of female performers unable to speak in attractive feminine tones, but many made the transition successfully to speaking roles. By 1929, sound films were quickly replacing the silents, and a new generation of women arrived in film.

The Great Depression of the 1930s brought a new austerity to the lives of many Americans. For some, it meant the loss of opportunities for education, advancement in jobs, or the end of financial security. For others, the Depression created a struggle for economic survival, no employment, and increasing desperation. The frivolity that characterized one aspect of the 1920s disappeared, replaced by new worries over work and making ends meet. Despite the economic crisis, however, emphasis on consumption continued, as both government agencies and individuals reconceptualized the role of the consumer.[24]

Even in the face of the nation's crisis, advertisers continued to promote products through appeals based on fear and desire. Cosmetics companies still used ads that threatened women with old age, the loss of a husband, or social ostracism. Ivory soap also added the potential of seeming "mannish" in 1937, when rough hands might suggest more than dishwashing. Some advertisers offered readers escapist fantasies based on trips, royalty, or economic advantage, while others promoted the cost of their product. Proctor and Gamble declared that Ivory soap, at its "lowest price in seventeen years," could be used for baths, dishwashing, and cleaning rugs, teeth, and furniture. It might even cure depression, promising that if a customer was "feeling blue," a good bath would wash away worries. Advertisers abandoned many of the images of carefree (and careless) women that had been prominent in the previous decade. College women now "lead the way" to innovations such as tampons, rather than partying. Women in advertisements shared concerns such as "my budget's pretty tight," and engaged in vigorous activities from tennis to swimming.

A similar image appeared on screen. The heroines of movies in the 1930s became more assertive and adventurous than those of the 1920s. New stars such as Katherine Hepburn, Jean Harlow, Bette Davis, and Carole Lombard became spunky characters in films such as *Bringing Up Baby*, *It Happened One Night*, and *Design for Living*. Davis made *The Little Foxes*, *Jezebel*, and *The Old Maid*, upsetting notions that a major female star could not become a villain. Mae West challenged sexual conventions directly, using innuendo with a new enthusiasm in *She Done Him Wrong* and *I'm No Angel*. Gold diggers, young women determined to use their attractiveness to win a man, also became heroines when played by Ginger Rogers in *The Gold Diggers of 1933* or Joan Blondell in *The Gold Diggers of 1937*. The Movie Production Code of 1934, instituted by the industry to calm critics of a supposedly lax morality, brought new restrictions and limited depictions of sexuality. Despite the Code's provision that immoral acts required a moral resolution, however, even the popular crime films of the decade used imaginative methods to circumvent some of the code's limits. Dorothy Arzner, one of Hollywood's first female directors, made *Dance, Girl, Dance* in 1940, featuring Lucille Ball as a performer capable of symbolically lighting men's cigars.

In the arts, women found new support through New Deal programs such as the Works Progress Administration, which funded a wide variety of endeavors. Writers such as Meridel Le Sueur, Tillie Olsen, Margaret Walker, and Anzia Yezierska found temporary support through the agency. In theater, experimental efforts received backing from the Federal Theater Project's director, Hallie Flanagan. Photographers such as Margaret Bourke-White, Dorothea Lange, and Marion Post Wolcott worked for the Farm Security Administration, capturing the life of workers throughout the country; their images remain among the most vivid commentaries on the depths of the Depression. Imogene Cunningham, already an established photographer, joined the studio of Ansel Adams, while Berenice Abbott focused her work on the buildings of New York in the 1930s.

Cunningham became best known for the *Vogue* cover featuring dancer Martha Graham in 1932, six years after Graham had started her own company. Graham revolutionized dance from the late 1920s onward, changing its forms and presentation. Her works featured strong, spare movements and dramatic emotion, with costuming to enhance the forms created by her dancers. Agnes de Mille, a close friend of Graham's, brought a similar energy and intelligence to use of dance in theater. Following her debut piece, *Rodeo*, in 1942, de Mille choreographed a sequence in the musical *Oklahoma*. Her infusion of modern elements of dance into theater transformed both. Graham and de Mille served as the pioneers for successive generations of American dancers, from Alvin Ailey and Merce Cunningham to Paul Taylor and Jose Limon.

Women also challenged notions of female limitations in sports. Since the inception of physical education courses for women at colleges and universities in the late nineteenth century, Americans had gradually accepted women's participation in "appropriate" athletic activities. The first women to compete in the modern Olympics, four years after the Games began in 1896, were restricted to golf, tennis, and croquet. American Margaret Abbott earned Olympic gold by winning the ladies' nine-hole golf contest. Attempts to participate or to hold separate women's events led the International Olympic Committee to increase women's sports in 1928. By then, women had already proved their talents in tennis, baseball, and basketball. May Sutton, for example, won the Wimbledon women's singles championship in 1905 and in 1907. Women's baseball teams, called "bloomer teams" by many, took to the field in the late nineteenth century, using names such as the Chicago Ladies' Base Ball Club and the Western Bloomers. Hampered by the difficult costume, female players shed the cumbersome outfit for pants after 1900. Teams toured to play "pick nine" games with local teams or among their members. Managers promised that the sport offered viewers "a high class, moral amusement," and some teams even traveled with bands. African American female teams also flourished, forced to play separately because of segregation. Women at colleges played, and informal baseball games among women continued to be popular throughout the nation. By 1943, with men's minor leagues unable to field strong teams due to the war, the All-American Girls' Professional Baseball League was created by Philip Wrigley, owner of the Chicago Cubs. Teams such as the Racine Belles and the Rockford Peaches toured throughout the Midwest until 1954, when audiences grew too small to sustain the League. Women excelled in basketball as well, although with rules modified to limit running and competition.

In other sports, from figure skating to boxing and field hockey, female athletes played, performed exhibitions, and competed, slowly erasing doubts and obstacles. Eleanor "Babe" Didrikson of Texas seemed to excel at any sport she tried. The 5'5" dynamo played basketball and baseball, starred in track, and won Olympic gold for the javelin and hurdles in 1932. After marrying wrestler George Zaharias, Didrikson became a golfer and a founder of the Ladies Professional Golf Association in 1949. As the first American woman to win the British Amateur title, she continued to play and amass tournament wins until her death from colon cancer in 1956. She continues to be routinely listed as the most outstanding female athlete of the twentieth century by sports authorities.

The idea that women could take on any challenge motivated the legendary attempt of Amelia Earhart to fly around the world. Earhart, who learned to fly in 1921, teamed with pilot Wilmer Stultz and copilot Louis Gordon, in a trans-Atlantic flight that captured international attention.

Mildred "Babe" Didrikson excelled at track, baseball, and golf. Pictured here in 1932 at the beginning of her career, Didrikson would be heralded later as one of the great female athletes of the twentieth century. AP photo.

Publicist G. P. Putnam, who would become her husband, used Earhart's fame to get commercial endorsements and further publicity, and Earhart rapidly became a public favorite. President Herbert Hoover received her at the White House, and Earhart served on the boards on early airlines such as TWA and Northeast. She also worked to live up to her reputation as a pilot, crossing the American continent solo in 1928 as the first woman to make the flight. In 1932, she made the first trans-Atlantic flight by a woman, following it with a solo flight from Hawaii to California. In 1937, Earhart began a well-publicized attempt to fly around the world, traveling with navigator Fred Noonan. After completing 22,000 miles of the flight, with only 7,000 remaining, Earhart flew the last leg of the flight over the Pacific Ocean. Somewhere near Howland Island, her plane disappeared. An extensive search by the U.S. Navy, followed by a private investigation by Putnam, turned up no traces of the plane or its crew.

Earhart's popularity reflected the emphasis on gutsy, determined women during the Depression. Even in fiction, heroines confronted and overcame obstacles. Scarlett O'Hara, the protagonist of Margaret Mitchell's Civil War novel *Gone with the Wind*, epitomized the resilient spirit of the decade. Movie heroines from Rosalind Russell in "His Girl Friday" to Jean Arthur in "Mr. Deeds Goes to Town" or "Mr. Smith Goes to Washington" used their wits to secure justice, or at least the right result. Even on the comic pages in newspapers, "girl reporter" Brenda Star began a glamorous career, challenging the ever-popular Blondie's claim on female wisdom.

By the end of the 1930s, an observer attempting to define American women would have been stymied by the variety of achievements and possibilities in women's lives. From activist Eleanor Roosevelt to the eager young performer Shirley Temple, women and girls defied any quick summary of what they did—or couldn't do. Despite their accomplishments, however, women continued to face numerous barriers based on gender. The possibility that some of these limitations could be erased quickly became apparent as the nation entered World War II.

FROM ROSIE TO ROCK

As children, Americans in the first part of the twentieth century learned that certain jobs belonged to men. Women could not rightfully operate heavy machinery, work on construction, or do the difficult tasks involved in steel production. Manufacturers such as Henry Ford barred women from production lines; women found they were unwelcome in mines, as steel workers, or as welders making ships. Some work was men's work, almost naturally.

That message disappeared as the United States entered the most dangerous year of World War II. In 1942, the nation needed to accelerate production of war materials and enlist millions of men as soldiers. The slack in manufacturing would have to be taken up by available laborers, and that meant women. The War Advertising Council and the Office of War Information publicized the need for women to take defense industry jobs. Propaganda focused on women laboring in industries while maintaining their feminine appeal. "The girl he left behind ... she's still a WOW!" declared on 1943 poster of a woman holding a wrench. "Good work, sister!" proclaimed a 1944 poster featuring an older male worker speaking to a younger woman. "We never figured you could do a man-sized job!" Another declared, "The more women at work the sooner we win!" Commercial advertisers told women that they could remain attractive while serving military duty. Elizabeth Arden featured a permanent for hair that was "designed for the military Miss or Mrs." Arden also promoted "burnt sugar" lipstick as "most effective with khaki," while "redwood" worked well with "uniforms of blue." Coty displayed a G.I. being kissed by an elderly man and woman liberated in Paris in 1944 as the company celebrated the return of French fashion; Evening in Paris cosmetics promised their products would "storm the heart of any devil-may-care hero."[25] Women's devotion to their country would enhance their appeal, and beauty could lift the spirit of the most fatigued soldier.

Sexuality became noticeably more public during the war years. Servicemen enjoyed pin ups of movie stars such as the young Marilyn Monroe and Betty Grable; fighter pilots used depictions of women on their planes. Touring USO teams brought attractive women to their shows, and few seemed to question the propriety of raising "the boys" morale. For couples, the wartime emergency also meant rethinking a quick marriage or premarital sex, and for gays and lesbians, war mobilization strengthened the emergence of a gay identity.[26]

Once the war ended, the period of reconversion to a civilian economy allowed employers to rehire male workers. Some did not, leaving a lower-waged female labor force in place, but both patriotism and the availability of male labor led most to resume job divisions based on gender. Advertisements served to advise women of their role in this transition to the prewar gender divisions in work. Greyhound bus lines ran a series of advertisements in 1945 celebrating the return of the soldier, emphasizing his happiness to reunite with his wife or wake up to a breakfast in bed cooked by his mother. Ivory soap featured a returning serviceman holding up a baby while exclaiming, "Happy New Year! I'm your Dad!" Dad went on to explain, "Dads like me want kids like you to grow up happy, strong, and gay!"[27]

Movies reflected the tone of reconversion as well. The advent of *film noir*, a style of film making that featured strong contrasts of light and dark, the use of shadows, and an emphasis on morality and betrayal, brought stories of duplicitous women to the screen. In *Double Indemnity*, Barbara Stanwyck plotted her husband's death; in *The Postman Always Rings Twice*, Lana Turner planned her husband's murder with a seductive stranger. Even films meant to appeal to women, such as *Mildred Pierce*, managed to convey the damage caused by women's work and their failure to sustain passive domestic roles.[28]

True happiness, women learned, came from domesticity. As the nation shifted to a postwar economy, that domesticity meant opportunities to enjoy an increasing prosperity and a mounting array of consumer goods.

Even nuclear fears paled before an expanding array of merchandise and appliances. While Americans worried about the atomic bomb's potential, the Civil Defense Administration calmed fears with plans for family fall-out shelters plentifully stocked with food and other postnuclear necessities. Children learned to "duck and cover" at school, while songs and jokes circulated about the new atomic age. Anxiety and fear over potential destruction would be reduced by the stability and order of family life.

By the later 1940s, the emphasis on domesticity and the family seemed widespread. President Harry S. Truman declared, "children and dogs are as necessary to the welfare of this country as is Wall Street and the railroads." Male college students reported to an interviewer that they hoped for a wife "like Grace Kelley" who would be "centered in the home." There she would command the vast array of new appliances and master recipes using all the latest convenience foods from commercially frozen vegetables to instant pudding. Developments such as New York's Levittown sprouted, as suburban populations doubled from 1950 to 1970. The ranch house favored by many in the middle class stood isolated by a yard from neighbors, but its inhabitants could easily feel connected to the national culture through the ever-more popular television.[29]

Television, increasingly affordable for most families, featured new versions of radio soap operas from *Father Knows Best* to *Leave it to Beaver*. Even shows centered on female stars such as Donna Reed used stories with fathers and husbands as the main authority figure. A subversive subtext appeared in some shows, however; scholars point to *I Love Lucy* as an example of mixed messages about domesticity. In many episodes of the popular show, the character of Lucy attempts to leave her domestic role to join her husband Ricky at his job. Inevitably, Lucy must be rescued by Ricky, and returns to the chores of a happy housewife—until the next week's adventure. As many observers note, Lucy remains persistent in her efforts to abandon domesticity. Perhaps equally important, Lucille Ball, whose role of Lucy carried her through the 1950s into the 1970s, founded Desilu Studies with husband Desi Arnaz. Even as audiences delighted at Lucy's mistakes, most viewers knew that the hair-brained antics held little semblance to Ball's real power as a creative entrepreneur.

Other television wives of the 1950s appeared more docile and content with deferring to a husband's authority. Unlike later situation comedies in which male roles became as comedic, the male head of the family in 1950s television remained clearly in control. One popular exception was *The Honeymooners*, which began as part of 1951's *Cavalcade of Stars* and later became a sit-com before resuming the short format after 1956. In *The Honeymooners*, Jackie Gleason played a sewer worker with frequent misadventures. His acerbic wife Alice, played by Audrey Meadows on television, responded to insults with robust retorts.

The possibility of unhappy housewives also emerged in domestic fiction. Grace Metalious's 1956 novel *Peyton Place* offered readers incest, adultery, and domestic discontent; the book remained on the New York Times' best seller list for over a year. By 1963, Smith graduate Betty Friedan summarized domestic discontent as "the problem that has no name" in *The Feminine Mystique*. The image of happy housewives began to fade as the developing Women's Movement of the 1960s raised questions about women's secondary status. Yet even in the 1950s, domesticity did not disguise the obvious variety of women's roles and issues. When African American students won legal victories for desegregation in *Brown* v. *Board*, or when Rosa Parks refused to move to the back of the bus, or when Althea Gibson won the Women's Singles championship for tennis at Wimbledon in 1957, it was clear that the dominant image of domesticity had limits. Ironically, too, as media focused on home life, women were heading into the labor force in increasing numbers.

Two iconic images of the 1950s clarified the shift from domesticity. Actress Marilyn Monroe epitomized female sensuality and vulnerability, yet her very public marriages to baseball player Joe DiMaggio and writer Arthur Miller suggested something deeper. After her death in 1963 at the age of thirty-six, Monroe gained even greater popularity as a film star; commentators and scholars deconstructed, critiqued, and pondered her cultural importance. Barbie, a doll initially marketed in 1959, had even greater popularity and staying power. Designed by Ruth Handler, the original Barbie offered girls the opportunity to play with fashion rather than babies. The glowering and busty Barbie acquired new costumes and accessories rapidly, adding a boyfriend, Ken, in 1961. The doll became one of the most popular toys ever sold in the United States, and the topic of scholarly discussion, ribald jokes, and collectors' bidding. In her many incarnations, Barbie transformed from the very adult original version to a model with a more demure and friendly appearance. The doll also allowed Mattel to create an extensive line of "Barbie's friends," different versions of Barbie and Ken, from the "Earring Magic" dolls of the early 1990s to talking and posable models. Barbie signaled a shift in ideas about women, as girls put aside "baby dolls" to dress Barbie, marry her to Ken, and then plan her career. While early Barbie was limited to jobs such as nursing or teaching, later Barbies had options for becoming a doctor, an astronaut, or an international traveler.

By the early 1960s, the popular images of women reflected a movement from domesticity to college, careers, and independence. As the children born after World War II, the historic "baby boom," became adults, many headed to college, and some rebelled against the domesticity and consumerism of the fifties. One historian suggests that "frustrated women and exhausted men provided ambiguous role models" of "discontent" with home life and stress at work.[30] Other signals of the shift from the

Wilma Rudolph became the first American woman to win three gold medals in track and field during the 1960 Rome Olympics. The "Tennessee Tornado" is featured here running in 1961 with teammate Vivian Brown in a relay event in England. AP photo.

conventions of the 1950s came in the growing popularity of magazines such as *Playboy* and *Cosmopolitan*, which celebrated single life and the possibility of premarital sex. The advent of oral contraceptives in the early 1960s meant that pleasure and procreation could be separate and pregnancy avoided. Films depicted women in ever more sexually explicit formulas, from the young unwed mother played by Sandra Dee in *A Summer Place* in 1959 to Shirley MacLaine's adulterous heroine in 1960's *The Apartment*. The Motion Picture Code, which had regulated the depiction of sex, no longer determined the content of all films; by the late 1950s, directors such as Billy Wilder and Alfred Hitchcock openly rejected compliance for their movies. Helen Gurley Brown, editor of *Cosmopolitan* magazine, seemed to convey approval for women's adventurous sexuality when her book *Sex and the Single Girl* covered premarital encounters.[31]

The Civil Rights movement also made questions of personal freedoms more relevant and provided a powerful impetus for women to challenge gender barriers. Even before an organized women's movement emerged, the conventions defining women through home and family had been upset by politics, war, and youthful rebellion. Women Strike for Peace in

1961 presented a public portrait of mothers as activists; students joining the Students for a Democratic Society formed in 1962 articulated a "yearning to believe that there *is* an alternative to the present."[32]

What became known as the "counterculture," evident in language, music, art, and fashion and sexual attitudes, developed as an apparent rebellion against the status quo. Depicted in the mainstream media as hippies wearing beads and bell-bottomed jeans, the counterculture embraced a variety of people and ideas. Singer Phil Ochs described the inchoate movement as "a change in the wind, a split in the road." Young women joined in work against the Vietnam War, in attempts to establish communes, and in the celebration of "free love" and freedom. Photographer Lisa Law captured the spirit of discovery as she and her husband moved to San Francisco's Haight Ashbury district in 1967. In what became known as the "Summer of Love," students, protestors, drug enthusiasts, and musicians shared in a sense of revelry and experimentation. From the "Human Be-In" to a "Love In" in Malibu, celebrants of the counterculture rejected conventions of monogamy, family structure, and repression.[33]

Ironically, for many the spirit of rebellion soon gave way to conformity and consumerism. Manufacturers and advertisers adapted to countercultural choices and marketed the music, clothes, and other goods that defined alternatives. The group Strawberry Alarm Clock appeared in a Sony ad; the soft drink 7-Up promised purchasers that they would stay "wild because you're you." By 1969, the Woodstock musical festival at Bethel, New York, drew half a million listeners to hear thirty-two musical groups play; the concert illustrated the vanishing line between commercialism and the aspirations of many to remake social values. Even with commercial cooptation of the counterculture, however, the movement shifted ideas and attitudes away from conformity and toward the possibility of many points of view.

Women's options widened through the challenges of the counterculture, the activities of the Civil Rights movement, and the growing feminist movement. Fashion, for example, changed from the mandates of designers and marketers to more comfortable choices. In the early 1960s, women's hair required straightening or curling, odd flips and "teasing," or exaggerating the hair's volume. Within a few years, many women shifted to more natural styles, from Afros for African American women to frizzy or straight long hair for others. Undergarments became more natural, and by the end of the decade, a young woman could wear jeans, long skirts, or mini skirts rather than the ubiquitous knee-length skirt. Pantyhose eliminated the need for cumbersome garters and ungainly stockings. Styles adapted from other cultures coexisted with the "mod look" from Britain.[34]

Tennis champ Billie Jean King changed women's sports through her athletic prowess and her politics, insisting on equal pay with male players. At Wimbledon in 1965, King failed to win the single's title, but the following year she emerged as the dominant female player in the game. AP photo.

Through the late 1960s and into the 1970s, women challenged many of the restrictions that had limited their lives. The title of "Ms" appeared as an alternative to "Miss" or "Mrs," embraced by many young women who argued that, like men, they did not need to show their marital status. Conscious-raising groups attracted women interested in exploring feminism; the National Organization of Women appealed to those who wanted to secure legal and political change. Even in the small details of daily life, women questioned conventions that depicted them as subordinate. The automatic adoption of a husband's last name after marriage, or language that failed to include women, such as "chairman," "fireman," or "Congressman," were challenged as feminists suggested new options which acknowledged women's individuality.

In music, women also played key roles in the expansion of options. In the early 1960s, folk music grew popular through the works of Joan Baez, Bob Dylan, The Kingston Trio, and Peter, Paul, and Mary. As some folk artists began to develop music in opposition to the Vietnam War, folk choices split, with "old time music" increasingly identified and performed with Country Music. Performers such as Loretta Lynn, Dolly Parton, Tammy Wynette, and Brenda Lee adopted the "Nashville sound," which distinguished country music. The legacy of previous performers such as the Carter Family and Patsy Cline drew women into bluegrass, blues, or popular music.

Rock music provided opportunities for other female performers in the 1960s. Grace Slick of the Jefferson Airplane and Janis Joplin with Big Brother and the Holding Company proved that women with extraordinary voices could move to the forefront of rock. Other women came to prominence from different styles of music. African American women, who remained marginalized in a business that continued to separate black and white artists until the 1960s, topped the charts in groups such as The Supremes, The Marvelettes, and Gladys Knight and the Pips. Increasingly through the 1960s, musical styles began to "cross over" to new audiences, and performers experimented with adapting other styles and forms. Emmy Lou Harris, for example, began as a rock performer who eventually became identified more substantively with Country Music; Canadian Joni Mitchell moved from folk to rock to jazz-infused songs.

In the movies, the depiction of women's roles underwent a similar shift. Jane Fonda, daughter of screen legend Henry Fonda, began her rise to stardom in the early 1960s in sexual comedies, such as *Sunday in New York* and *Barefoot in the Park*. As *Barbarella* in 1968, Fonda took on a more satirical, sexual role, but soon emerged as a leading performer, nominated for Academy Awards for *They Shoot Horses, Don't They* in 1969 and *Klute* in 1970. Fonda would be best remembered not for her Academy Award winning role in the anti-war drama *Coming Home*, however, but for a famous trip to North Vietnam in 1972. Nonetheless, Fonda's professionalism as an actor and her political involvement indicated a new direction for women performers. In the generations of female film actors (no longer called "actresses") that followed the 1960s, women such as Meryl Streep, Julie Christie, Susan Sarandon, Shirley MacLaine, and Diane Keaton focused on serious performance. As earlier film actors such as Bette Davis and Katherine Hepburn had, a new generation of women film actors demanded respect and independence, and publicly criticized the smaller number of major roles for women. Female directors and producers would also claim a place in the film industry by the end of the century. In 1980, Sherry Lansing became the first female head of a major motion picture studio, Twentieth Century Fox. She later moved to Paramount, where she headed the motion picture division from 1992 to 2004. Women producers such as Nora Ephron, Kathleen Kennedy, and Cathy Schulman won awards and box-office records for their films, while women directors found it easier to win picture approval and jobs. In an

Janis Joplin pioneered the image of a tough, strong female rocker. Joplin died of a heroin overdose in 1970. AP photo.

industry once reluctant to give women control of significant film projects, women finally found more open doors.

Films reflected many of the social changes in women's roles. Movies such as *Alice Doesn't Live Here Anymore, Norma Rae,* and *Thelma and Louise* depicted women characters fighting to achieve independence; *Million Dollar Baby* focused on a female boxer. Careers for women no longer seemed suspect or unusual, and the possibility of a female superhero, from the X-men's Jean Grey or Storm to Invisible Woman and Isis, became a commercial reality. Yet a significant number of films continued to portray women in passive or negative roles, as less intelligent, compliant, or merely as sexual symbols. Box office hits such as *Pretty Woman* and *Fatal Attraction* featured female characters in stereotypical roles, as a prostitute or a murderous "other woman." The top grossing American films in the past two decades have remained dominated by implicitly subordinate images of women.[35]

Women in television fared somewhat better from the 1970s. The *Mary Tyler Moore* show provided a positive image of a single career woman, featuring stories that did not denigrate women's work or desire to be likeable. Other shows followed. *Maud*, portrayed by Beatrice Arthur, focused on an explicitly feminist heroine; *All That Glitters*, which attempted to show women as leaders and men as subordinate, lasted only one season in 1977. Far more successful ventures placed adventurous or strong women in a context that reinforced femininity. *Charlie's Angels*, for example, used three beautiful women working for a male boss to temper the ability of the heroines to solve crimes and beat up bad guys. *Cagney and Lacey*, which followed, abandoned the glamour to focus on two female police officers and their personal lives. Initially cancelled after its first year in 1982, fan letters encouraged the CBS network to resume the show, which later won Emmy awards for feature performers Tyne Daly and Sharon Gless. Television continued to use "jiggle" and sex to win audiences, however, despite more liberal roles for women. As commentators have noted, viewers might easily believe that prostitution ranks after housework as women's major occupation in the United States.

The mixed message on women's roles in film and television persisted past the end of the century. In films such as *Working Girl*, *The Hand that Rocks the Cradle*, and *Sleepless in Seattle*, the major female characters work and still must be made whole by men. Even films that offered supposedly independent female protagonists end with women finding happiness through a male partner. Television shows tended to emphasis a similar resolution; the popular *Thirtysomething* of the 1980s focused on couples with unhappy working wives, while even the resolute *Murphy Brown* remained unfulfilled without a husband.

The growth of pornography as a business also indicated a mixed message about women's sexual equality. Although *Deep Throat* became a middle-class phenomenon in the 1970s by luring new audiences to see a sexually explicit film, most pornographic films remain relegated to specialized venues. The arrival of the Internet made pornography more available, and the home use of films and recording materials allowed for more private viewing options. As a result, pornography in the United States has emerged as a major part of the film industry, with profits regularly over $10 billion per year after 2000. Debate over the sex trade, free speech, and regulation of performance continues but has had little economic impact on the profitability of sexually explicit material.[36]

Even fashion conveyed contradictory ideas about women's roles. Writing in the *New York Times* in 1989, Constance Rosenblum complained that the images of working women with "drop-dead suits, their burnished briefcases and their understated Perragamo pumps" had little to do with the balancing act of career and family encountered by many women. The sexy working woman became a stable of modern media, however. Maidenform ran a series of ads in the 1980s featuring working women clad only in underwear; Samsung featured a cell phone flung over a pair of high heeled shoes, leaving viewers to wonder what kind of woman the ad implied. Television shows such as *House* and *CSI* offered major female characters as working women with plunging necklines and skin-tight skirts, while the popular *Sex and the City* made women crave shoes by Manolo Blahnik with very high heels. Despite the declining number of housewives on television, the working woman still seemed to be outfitted for a date rather than a corporate meeting.

The rise of hip hop as a musical form has created an equally vociferous debate about the sexual depiction of women. Although women played an important role in the beginnings of hip hop, and some female rappers such as Queen Latifah and Roxanne Shanti became stars, the persistence of negative images of women has led some female performers to critique the aggressively masculine tone created by male rappers. The first female group to record a rap hit, Salt-N-Peppa, openly challenged the sexually charged lyrics of male rappers; Shazzy rapped in 1990 that "no man control me." Even with such declarations, gangsta rap and the assertions of male control continued, with performers such as Ice-T asserting a right to be "bitch killers." By 2007, a Congressional hearing on rap lyrics concluded with a continuation of debates over the problems of free speech, artistic license, and explicit songs.[37]

Hip hop remains a small but vital part of the cultural contributions of African American women by the end of the twentieth century. In the decades after the Civil Rights movement, African American women faced continued obstacles to achievement, but barriers that once appeared immovable began to crumble. In 2001, Halle Berry won an Academy Award for Best Actress, a first for African American women. Venus and Serena Williams dominated women's tennis after 1995, winning at Wimbledon, the U.S. Open, and other major championships. By far the most successful and influential African American woman in American history, Oprah Winfrey turned her career as a talk show host into a major business, Harpo, producing films, a magazine, and a Broadway play. Winfrey became one of the wealthiest entertainers in the nation as well, influential in publishing as well as film and television.

As a new century began, cultural messages about women, and women's responses to them, contained many contradictory elements. Depictions of women as fearless in films such as *The Brave One*, in which Oscar winning actress Jodi Foster's character aggressively sought revenge against her boyfriend's killers, contrasted with standard slasher fare with female victims, such as Lindsey Lohan's *I Know Who Killed Me*. "Chic lit" grew more popular with female readers, who enjoyed romantic stories of consumption and female networks. Novels such as Candace Bushnell's *Sex and the City* became films, attracting eager audiences of female viewers. On television, female broadcasters might have grown older, but stars such as Diane Sawyer and Katie Couric refused to look their ages, as cosmetic treatments and plastic surgery became more popular. The possibility of a woman who lacked a desirable sense of fashion became the subject of television situation comedies such as "Ugly Betty" and movies such as *The Devil Wears Prada.*

Actress Meryl Streep, considered by many film scholars and fans to be one of the great female performers of the twentieth century, chose a film course that illustrated the contradiction of the twenty-first century. Streep played a fashion mogul in *The Devil Wears Prada*, a singing ex-diva in *Mamma Mia!*, a serious journalist in *Lions for Lambs,* and the evil political mother in a remake of *The Manchurian Candidate.* Silly and serious, sexy and sober, Streep's characterizations offered few clues to identifying any one American ideal for women.

Perhaps the most salient clues to the evolving concepts of womanhood emerged from the responses to the two leading female political candidates, Hillary Clinton and Sarah Palin. As Clinton ran for the presidency, and Palin became the Republican pick for the Vice Presidency, voters debated their qualifications, domestic responsibilities, and positions of concerns such as reproductive rights, marriage, and women's work. Clinton's supporters and Palin's fans heralded the "toughness" of each woman, while Clinton's tears on the campaign trail and Palin's young infant son cemented their femininity. Neither could assume the mantle of the "Iron Lady" of Great Britain, Margaret Thatcher, who as Prime Minister rarely bowed to feminine conventions. As the campaigns demonstrated, Americans seemed not yet ready to entirely redefine women's roles.

NOTES

1. Lizabeth Cohen, *A Consumers' Republic: The Politics of Mass Consumption in Postwar America* (New York: Alfred A. Knopf, 2003).

2. Akira Iriye, "Culture," *Journal of American History* Vol. 77, No. 1 (1990), 99–107; Raymond Williams, *Culture and Society, 1780–1950* (New York: Columbia University Press, 1983).

3. Kathy Peiss, *Hope in a Jar: The Making of America's Beauty Culture* (New York: Metropolitan Books, 1998).

4. See Joan W. Scott, "Deconstructing Equality-versus-Difference: Or, the Uses of Poststructuralist Theory for Feminism," *Feminist Studies* Vol. 14, No. 1 (1988): 33–50; Joan W. Scott, "Gender: A Useful Category of Historical Analysis," *American Historical Review* Vol. 91, No. 5 (1986): 1053–1075; Stephan Fuchs and Steven Ward, "What is Deconstruction, and Where and When Does It Take Place? Making Facts in Science, Building Cases in Law," *American Sociological Review* Vol. 59, No. 4 (1994): 481–500.

5. Angela H. Creager et al., *Feminism in Twentieth-Century Science, Technology, and Medicine* (Chicago: University of Chicago Press, 2001); Ruth Schwartz Cowan,

More Work for Mother: The Ironies of Household Technology from the Open Hearth to the Microwave (New York: Basic Books, 1983).

6. James R. Beniger, "Communication and the Control Revolution," *OAH Magazine of History* Vol. 6, No. 4 (1992), http://www.oah.org/pubs/magazine/communication/Beniger.html.

7. Jennifer Scanlon, *Inarticulate Longings: The Ladies' Home Journal, Gender, and the Promises of Consumer Culture* (New York: Routledge, 1995), 5.

8. William R. Leach, *Land of Desire: Merchants, Power, and the Rise of a New American Culture* (New York: Pantheon Books, 1993).

9. Kathy Peiss, *Cheap Amusements: Working Women and Leisure in Turn-of-the-Century New York* (Philadelphia: Temple University Press, 1986); Nan Enstad, *Ladies of Labor, Girls of Adventure: Working Women, Popular Culture, and Labor Politics at the Turn of the Century* (New York: Columbia University Press, 1999).

10. Enstad, *Ladies of Labor.*

11. Mark Aldridge, "Determinants of Mortality among New England Cotton Mill Workers During the Progressive Era," *Journal of Economic History* Vol. 42, No. 4 (1982): 847–863.

12. Sarah Jane Deutsch, "From Ballots to Breadlines, 1920–1940," in Nancy F. Cott, *No Small Courage: A History of Women in the United States* (New York: Oxford University Press, 2000), 413.

13. Beth L. Bailey, *From Front Porch to Back Seat: Courtship in Twentieth-Century America* (Baltimore: Johns Hopkins University Press), 1988.

14. Paula Fass, *The Beautiful and the Damned: American Youth in the 1920s* (New York: Oxford University Press, 1975).

15. Duke Ad Access, http://library.duke.edu/digitalcollections/adaccess.

16. Lori Landay, *Madcaps, Screwballs, and Con Women: The Female Trickster in American Culture* (Philadelphia: University of Pennsylvania Press, 1998).

17. Deutsch, "From Ballots to Breadlines," 439.

18. Carolyn Kitch, *The Girl on the Magazine Cover: The Origins of Visual Stereotypes in American Mass Media* (Chapel Hill: University of North Carolina Press, 2001).

19. Nancy Woloch, *Women and the American Experience* (New York: McGraw Hill, 2006), 391–392.

20. Ibid., 399, 409.

21. Peggy Pascoe, "Miscegenation Law, Court Cases, and Ideologies of 'Race' in Twentieth-Century America," *Journal of American History* Vol. 82, No. 1 (1996): 44–69.

22. Lillian Faderman, *Odd Girls and Twilight Lovers: A History of Lesbian Life in Twentieth-Century America* (New York: Columbia University Press, 1991).

23. Hattie McDaniel, *Black Ambition, White Hollywood* (New York: HarperCollins, 2005).

24. Cohen, *A Consumers' Republic.*

25. Duke Ad Access.

26. Allen Berube, *Coming Out under Fire: The History of Gay Men and Women in World War II* (New York: Simon and Schuster, 2000).

27. Library of Congress, "Rosie Pictures: Select Images Relating to American Women Workers During World War II," http://www.loc.gov/rr/print/list/126_rosi.html.

28. Molly Haskell, *From Reverence to Rape: The Treatment of Women in the Movies* (Chicago: University of Chicago Press, 1987); Andrea S. Walsh, *Women's Film and Female Experience, 1940–1950* (New York: Praeger, 1984).

29. Mary Ryan, *Womanhood in America* (New York: New Viewpoints, 1975), 232.

30. Elaine Tyler May, *Homeward Bound: American Families in the Cold War Era* (New York: Basic Books, 1999), 217.

31. Helen Gurley Brown, *Sex and the Single Girl* (New York: Bernard Geis, 1962).

32. The Port Huron Statement, http://www2.iath.virginia.edu/sixties/HTML_docs/Resources/Primary/Manifestos/SDS_Port_Huron.html.

33. Avital H. Bloch and Lauri Umansky, *Impossible to Hold: Women and Culture in the 1960's* (New York: New York University Press, 2005); Richard Crawford, *America's Musical Life: A History* (New York: W.W. Norton, 2001), 812–836.

34. Douglas Owram, *Born at the Right Time: A History of the Baby-boom Generation* (Toronto: University of Toronto Press, 1996), 192–194.

35. Harry M. Benshoff and Sean Griffin, *America on Film: Representing Race, Class, Gender, and Sexuality at the Movies* (Boston: Blackwell, 2004), 201–244.

36. Gwendolyn D. Pough, *Check It While I Wreck It: Black Womanhood, Hip-Hop Culture, and the Public Sphere* (Lebanon, NH: Northeastern University Press, 2004); George Lipsitz, "Diasporic Noise: History, Hip-Hop, and the Post-Colonial Politics of Sound," in *Popular Culture: Production and Consumption*, ed. C. Lee Harrington and Denise D. Bielby (Boston: Blackwell, 2001), 180–200.

37. Martin Cloonan and Reebee Garofalo, eds., *Policing Pop* (Philadelphia: Temple University Press, 2003).

4

⸺⊸∞⊷⸺

Women and Education

In 2007, Drew Gilpin Faust became President of Harvard University. The inauguration of a female historian to head one of the nation's elite educational institutions marked a dramatic moment in the history of women and education. In an interview, Faust recalled her mother's admonitions as she was growing up in rural Virginia that "it's a man's world, sweetie." Instead, Faust earned a PhD at the University of Pennsylvania, directed a Women's Studies program, and served as the first Dean of the Radcliffe Institute, an internationally renowned center of research. Faust noted that as a girl, she could not have imagined such possibilities. Her extraordinary career reflected the changing opportunities for women in education, clearly an area of women's most significant advances in the twentieth century. In many ways, Faust's remarkable story remains an exemplar of women's accomplishments.

Changes in women's education characteristically mirror larger changes throughout American society. In the first years of the new nation, arguments for "Republican mothers" who would educate their citizen children proved new legitimacy for girls' schooling. Public education originated in Massachusetts, which mandated free schools in every community of over five hundred residents. High schools also developed first in the Bay State; English High School in Boston, which opened in 1821 with a counterpart for girls created in 1825, offered an "advanced" curriculum. The need for teacher training led school advocate Horace Mann to champion "normal" schools; the concept of institutions devoted to teacher training spread from Massachusetts to Illinois, Michigan, and other states. By 1840, the

Female students leaving Mary Lyon Hall at Mount Holyoke College in 1908. Courtesy of the Library of Congress.

first graduates of normal schools entered classrooms. The first kindergarten, created by Elizabeth Peabody to follow the ideas of German educator Frederich Froebel, began in Boston in 1860. Teachers' associations also evolved, with the organization that would later become the National Education Association starting as the National Teachers Association (NTA) in Philadelphia in 1857.

For young women who wanted to secure an education beyond high school and normal school, the options in early nineteenth-century American institutions of higher education remained more limited. Most early colleges did not accept female applicants at all; the first female academies served as alternatives. Sarah Pierce opened the Litchfield Academy in Connecticut in 1791, for example, offering a curriculum that emphasized "female arts" rather than the more rigorous Greek and mathematics of Yale. Emma Willard's Troy Seminary in New York moved closer to the type of courses offered at colleges, and when Mary Lyon founded Mount Holyoke in 1837, she mandated that women use the same texts utilized by male students. Oberlin College, opened in 1833, accepted women in 1837. Four graduated in 1841 and became the first women to receive undergraduate (AB) degrees.

It has been suggested that by midcentury, three forces drew an increasing number of women into higher education. The growing availability of public education paralleled the slow onset of industrialization. Middle-class and advantaged Americans embraced the notion of childhood as a time of innocence and training instead of work. Advancement in life also benefited from better (and more prestigious) education, many thought. Finally, the American Civil War drew young women out of the home, either as part of the war effort or in response to the absence of men.[1]

After 1865, women's education opportunities expanded substantially with the growth of public education, the creation of public universities, and construction of private colleges for women. A key component of access for less advantaged women was the Morrill Act of 1862, which established land-grant universities and provided for funding. Ostensively for scientific, mechanical, and scientific study, the Morrill institutions responded to demands for women's education. Although debates were frequent, universities such as Cornell, the University of Wisconsin, the University of Illinois, and Michigan State University moved to admit women to undergraduate classes and to graduate schools. By 1900, over one hundred colleges and universities allowed female admissions and served as the primary source of advanced education for women.

Private colleges for women also offered new prospects. Vassar College opened in Poughkeepsie, New York, in 1861, with a curriculum comparable to those of the best colleges for men. The other "Seven Sisters" followed; Wellesley and Smith welcomed their first students in 1875, and Bryn Mawr in 1884. Barnard, affiliated with Columbia University, started classes in 1889, and Radcliffe, Harvard's counterpart, began as the "Harvard annex" in 1879. Religious groups also founded colleges that admitted women, from the coeducational Swarthmore, begun in 1864 by Hicksite Quakers, to Antioch College in Ohio and Bates College in Maine. When Boston University accepted its first class in 1873, women were among those selected. In the South, Spelman College began in 1881 and granted its first college degrees in 1901.[2]

Female college students faced a variety of challenges, even after surmounting the hurdles of admission. Many medical experts continued to cite women's intellectual exertions as a potential harm to reproductive capacities, and colleges such as Vassar instituted physical education programs to combat possible damage. The experiences of the first generations of college women have been described as "markedly different" from their undergraduate brothers. "Constant supervision by teachers, rules governing the actions of every hour, and twice-daily periods of silent devotion" ensured that women remained appropriately circumspect and ladylike. Under M. Carey Thomas, Bryn Mawr began to break from these traditions by allowing a greater independence and community and insisting on the highest academic standards. The most ambitious of women's colleges modeled excellence on the standards equivalent to those applied to men.[3]

As the number of colleges and normal schools expanded, however, women found few options for careers. The Association of Collegiate Alumnae, founded in 1872, attracted a growing number of women attempting to sustain their networks; the organization eventually became the American Association of University Women. Women graduates shared concerns about the difficulties of utilizing their education fully; one Radcliffe graduate described the "void midway between two spheres" of home and profession.[4] College-educated women in these first generations frequently married later than male counterparts or other women in a period when over 90 percent of women eventually wed. Ironically, perhaps, the development of home economics as a field of study emerged by the end of the century; by 1908, the American Home Economics Association served as the professional organization for college instructors and administrators working in the new discipline.

Education remained an important outlet for women's talents, and by 1870, nearly 90 percent of teachers were women.[5] For the next century, teaching continued to be an overwhelmingly female occupation, although supervisors and directors continued to be predominantly male. The typical teacher in the late nineteenth century was a young woman with surprisingly little education herself; most left (or were fired) at marriage. Many teachers stayed on fewer than five years, although the average length for a teacher's career in Boston by the end of the twentieth century was nineteen years.[6] A few who persisted might become principals of elementary schools, yet men continued to dominate positions in high school administrations.

School reform became a major concern throughout the United States as the twentieth century began. Reformer John Dewey campaigned vigorously for new approaches to teaching and learning, arguing that a focus on children's experiences should inform teaching practice. Parents became increasingly involved in parent-teacher organizations as well. Local officials asserted more control through school boards and professional superintendents; consolidation of smaller schools into larger centralized ones promised lower costs and expanded, rigorous coursework. Efforts to professionalize gained momentum at century's end, and the idea of licensing or certifying teachers became more widespread. The first state to require some type of teacher accreditation was Pennsylvania, which instituted testing in reading, writing, and mathematics in 1834. By 1900, New York, Rhode Island, and the territory of Arizona maintained a state criterion for teacher performance. Thirty-eight states had established teaching regulations by the 1930s. Some historians have suggested that the establishment of teaching standards reflected a process of deskilling, in which curriculum became the province of male administrators and politicians. Greater regulation of teachers also increased the number of middle-class daughters in the occupation. As superintendents gained the ability to hire district teachers, and to demand a normal school education and certification, the numbers of working-class women as teachers declined.

Teachers responded to the process of professionalization in a variety of ways. Large city schools tended to make the transition to a managed curriculum first, and teacher organizations emerged in New York, Chicago, and other cities. Two associations dominated; the National Educational Association developed from the NTA, founded in 1857. In its first years, the relatively small association lobbied for a national Department of Education and transformed itself into an organization that included male and female members. The NTA became the National Education Association (NEA) in 1870, and by 1907 claimed nearly six thousand members. A reorganization of the association in 1917 clarified its organizational structure and its purpose, with a focus on the professionalization of education. To a significant degree, that emphasis emerged from a challenge mounted by Chicago teachers, who in 1902 organized as a trade union. Within four years, teachers created 174 locals, and in 1916, the American Federation of Teachers (AFT) began, recognized by the American Federation of Labor. AFT members accepted a premise that teachers were workers, with the right to bargain, strike, and organize for better working conditions and wages. This notion appalled some NEA members, who viewed teaching as a career and a profession, not a job. The leaders of the NEA, all male, broadened an appeal to female teachers by positioning the association as pro-American, in direct opposition to the more controversial and potentially radical AFT. The strategy worked; by 1931, NEA membership had grown to almost a quarter of a million teachers, while the AFT soldiered on with fewer than five thousand.[7]

The Progressive era from the late nineteenth century until the 1920s became a period of female activism. College-educated women such as Jane Addams, Sophonisba Breckinridge, and Florence Kelley applied their training in social settlements and reform associations and created a new role for women in civic life.[8] The women's suffrage movement also opened new doors for engagement and encouraged new avenues for women's achievements. The female college graduates of the late nineteenth century demonstrated that women's intellectual achievements, their political skills, and their understanding of society could change both their lives and others'.

For African American women, however, access to education and advancement in education remained restricted by a pervasive racism. During Reconstruction, white missionary societies, the federal Freedman's Bureau, and African American community groups worked together to establish schools and advance education. With the end of Reconstruction, the segregated schools of the South operated with few resources, shorter days, and poorer conditions for black students. Gradually, an all-black teaching force served both rural and urban schools, as teacher pay declined for the separate black institutions. By the 1880s, even the African Methodist Episcopal Church argued that black teachers should educate black children as a matter of community control. While this meant that African American teachers could instill some pride in students, even in an increasingly hostile South, it also allowed white political leaders to abandon black schools. By the height of Jim Crow legislation at the turn of the nineteenth century, disenfranchisement further reduced the ability of black voters to effect improvements. By 1910, only 123 high schools served all the African American students in the historic Confederacy and border states.[9]

Private schools and academies became one solution to the declining quality of public schools. By the first years of the twentieth century, hundreds of schools started by black educators offered instruction. Mary McCleod Bethune's Daytona Educational and Industrial Training School for Negro Girls provided both academic courses and lessons in household arts such as cleaning, sewing, and care of small farm animals. Much like Booker T. Washington, Bethune insisted that education should reflect "the life and needs of the people." Bethune vigorously promoted the

Classes for women at Hampton Institute included training in cooking and domestic service. Courtesy of the Library of Congress.

school among vacationing northerners, and convinced James Gamble, of Proctor and Gamble, to head the school's Board of Visitors. In 1923, the school joined with Cookman School, an academy for young men, to become the Bethune-Cookman College. Bethune became the first African American woman to head an institution of higher learning.[10]

By the 1920s, the idea for the "little Tuskegee's" declined. Demands for teacher certification by states, coupled with efforts by some schools to become colleges, led others into debt and closures. In reality, the black public schools in the South continued to need donations from their communities and philanthropists such as Julius Rosenwald, who funded the building of nearly five thousand schools. In the North and Midwest, the segregation of public schools also increased in this period, the result of the "Great Migration" of blacks to industrial cities outside of the South. In Springfield, Ohio, for example, the establishment of separate schools for African American students followed the growth of the local black population and riots in 1904, 1906, and 1921. The move to segregated schools split Springfield's black community, with prominent ministers supporting exclusive schools and the local National Association for the Advancement of Colored People (NAACP) leaders opposing it. In the ensuing controversy, which included the revelation that two school board members belonged to the Ku Klux Klan, the opponents took their case to the courts. Although they won an injunction barring the school board from implementing racial restrictions, in practice white parents transferred their children to all-white public schools. The school board denied transfers for African American children, and by 1936, Springfield's schools were effectively segregated.[11]

Opportunities for higher education also suffered from racial barriers. Prior to 1865, fewer than fifty African American men or women had graduated from colleges. After the Civil War, while Oberlin and Boston University allowed African American women students, other colleges barred black applicants. Hortense Parker earned a degree from Mount Holyoke in 1883, and Harriet Alleyne Rice received her degree from Wellesley in 1887. The other Seven Sisters remained reluctant to accept female black applicants. When Anita Hemmings finished Vassar in 1897, the college unenthusiastically agreed to award her degree after discovering that she was African American. The next black Vassar graduate, Beatrix McCleary, received a degree in 1940. Bryn Mawr's first African American undergraduate to earn a degree, Enid Cook of the Class of 1931, was not allowed to live in the college dormitories. A similar story emerged from other elite colleges; Colby and Middlebury admitted black women before the twentieth century, but colleges such as Swarthmore and Haverford retained barriers until the second half of the century. By 1964, as the Civil Rights movement shook campuses nationwide, Mount Holyoke could claim only thirty-nine African American graduates.[12]

The 1890 Morrill Act, which expanded the original Morrill act, required that states admit African American students or establish separate public colleges for them. In the South, states responded by creating over seventy institutions for black students. In Alabama, for example, the Huntsville Normal School opened in 1875. Funding from northern philanthropists through the Peabody Fund and the Slater Fund allowed for expansion. Under the Morrill Act, the college became the State Agricultural and Mechanical School for Negroes. In 1939, the school offered undergraduate degrees and extended those credentials to all graduates since 1920; in 1969, the university became Alabama Agricultural and Mechanical University. North Carolina Agricultural and Technical University in Greensboro began directly as a result of the Morrill Act.[13] A different process shaped another historically black college, Morgan State University in Maryland. There, what originated as a private college for African American men evolved by 1939 into a state college for both men and women.[14]

Colleges for African American women also developed after the Civil War. Scotia College in North Carolina, for example, began in 1867 as Scotia Seminary, founded by Presbyterians; Hartshorn College opened in 1883 in Richmond, Virginia, funded by the American Baptist Home Missionary Society. Spelman College in Atlanta had a similar beginning in 1881; the next year, John D. Rockefeller began contributing to its development. The college dropped its original name of Atlanta Female Baptist Seminary to adopt "Spelman" in honor of Laura Spelman Rockefeller and her parents.

Similar obstacles appeared for other women defined by a minority status. Colleges maintained quotas for Jewish students, for example, from the 1920s until, in some cases, the 1960s. Some determined to follow the examples set by elite institutions such as Harvard and Yale, which created a variety of methods to reduce the numbers of Jewish students. Quotas, the use of applicant interviews, and the establishment of legacy preferences served to block Jewish students. Exclusionary practices have been documented at Cornell, Barnard, Pennsylvania State, and the Universities of Minnesota, Kansas, and Washington, among others. Female Jewish students faced segregation in the dormitories at Ohio State, while Syracuse University allowed a Ku Klux Klan chapter on campus. Sarah Lawrence restricted the number of Jewish admissions, much like brother colleges in the Ivy League. Jewish scholars faced an equally solid barrier in academic employment; many universities and colleges retained a "Jewish quota" for faculty.[15]

The nation's educational systems also faced challenges with the influx of over twenty-five million immigrants, many from Southern and Eastern Europe, between 1880 and 1914. The children of immigrant families changed the public schools in a myriad of ways, from the growing use of allegiance pledges to "Americanize" the new arrivals to the need for school nurses to ensure health standards. In New York City, where enrollment in public schools jumped by 60 percent between 1900 and 1914, Superintendent William H. Maxwell instituted language classes and remedial education for those children who needed to learn English. Maxwell also challenged the application of grades for immigrant children, insisting that not all needed to start in the "first" grade. Despite his efforts, fewer than 10 percent of immigrant children entered high school, and by 1913, critics complained about overcrowded classes and truancy. Teachers in cities as different as New York City and Schenectady, New York sometimes had as many as seventy or more students in their classrooms.[16]

Girls' experiences differed from those of boys in the public schools because of the general assumptions about women's roles. Courses in vocational training allowed boys to study rudimentary engineering, while girls took classes on sewing, art, and housekeeping. Girls also learned the "American" diet in cooking classes, as well as advice on fresh air, infant care, and household budgeting. According to one historian, immigrant daughters found out the importance of "creamed vegetables" and expert advice.[17] In comparison, Chicago schools at the turn of the century emphasized boys' education as a prerequisite for jobs and economic advancement. Girls instead typically received less encouragement, despite the possibility that a significant number would enter the workforce. Laws for compulsory attendance, which became standard throughout the states by 1920, also kept some girls out of the labor market, and in school, longer than some families desired.[18] By the 1920s, vocational education for girls usually included typing and stenography, and at the end of the decade, one in six public high school students took some form of business training.[19]

Another aspect of education frequently ignored emerged from the social settlements and immigrant organizations. Immigrant adults sought education, from language courses to readings in political economy. Through the settlements, older immigrant women received courses in childcare, cooking, and housekeeping, usually presented from the viewpoint of middle-class reformers who preferred "American" standards over European customs. Although Mary Kingsbury Simkovitch praised the "tomato pies" of Italian cooks, few settlement workers shared her enthusiasm for the folkways arriving with immigrant women in American cities. Reformers sought to educate immigrant women "not so much as citizens but as mothers who needed help to raise American children."[20] By World War I, the numbers of immigrants into the United States slowed, and the imposition of immigration restrictions in the 1920s gradually reduced the impact of many diverse cultures in the classroom. The second generation, the children of immigrants, came to school more eager for the "cultural capital" of American schools and the advantages of education. In New Haven, Connecticut, for example, the children of Italian immigrants became more likely to remain in school in the years between 1910 and 1930, although many still cited family need as a reason for leaving.[21]

Schools for Native American children originated in attempts to assimilate and "civilize" them. Richard Henry Pratt, who established the Carlisle School in Pennsylvania in 1879, declared that his goal was "immersing the Indians in our civilization and when we get them under holding them there until they are thoroughly soaked." Children taken from their Native homes in the Dakota Territory faced strict discipline and the abolition of their culture. Forbidden to wear Native dress or speak their languages, the Carlisle children were segregated by age and gender into dormitories and then classrooms. They received a vocational education determined by gender, with girls in domestic service courses and the boys in industrial arts. Other schools, such as the Phoenix School, maintained a similar discipline and provided students with few options other than service labor after graduation. In 1928, the Meriam Report for the Department of the Interior proposed the end to nonreservation schools. Through the twentieth century, reservation schools continued to provide for thousands of students. In 1975, the Indian Self-Determination Education Assistance Act eliminated practices that diminished Native cultures and established better funding for the remaining reservation systems.[22]

By the 1920s, women could find vocational courses to prepare themselves for the workforce, home economics classes to perfect their domestic skills, and colleges to study a growing array of subjects. At the same time, however, women's educational opportunities eroded slightly during the decade. Despite gains in the numbers of women entering colleges and universities between 1910 and 1920, in the next ten years female admissions slowed. The exceptions would be women enrolling in Catholic colleges, which increased in number, and African American women, who found easier admissions policies in place. It appeared as if women's achievements in higher education slowed as well, as the number of doctorates received by women remained relatively stagnant from 15.1 percent in 1920 to 15.4 percent in 1930. While the number of women faculty members grew slightly, fewer women entered graduate schools from 1920 to 1930. Some women became discouraged or were blocked by new campus quotas designed to keep female enrollments from expanding. Historians have also suggested that the powerful networks created by women in previous decades failed to work effectively in education during this decade, mirroring a similar pattern in women's politics.[23]

The Great Depression in 1929 significantly altered teaching and access to education for many American women. As the economic crisis deepened in the next few years, school districts lacked the monies to pay teacher salaries. By 1933, Chicago had been unable to pay months of teachers' wages, while Alabama owed nearly $7,000,000 in back pay. Those areas that could keep schools open and maintain personnel still cut programs, from night programs in Detroit to summer classes in Indianapolis. One way to save money was eliminating teachers, however, and in 1931, three-fourths of school districts implemented policies for firing married teachers. At the same time that schools confronted shortages, enrollments increased, as the nation's youth headed to school rather than the job market. By 1940, most American teenagers completed high school. At the same time, the Depression reduced the ability of women and men to attend college; during the decade, college admissions in both public and private institutions fell.[24]

The New Deal programs between 1933 and 1938 provided funds for schools to resume, for students to have additional opportunities, and for communities to restore decaying buildings and hopes. The Works Progress Administration created nursery school programs and paid for school lunches; the National Youth Administration (NYA) offered work-study jobs. Nearly 50 percent of the NYA student aid went to women students, allowing for women to continue their educations. The Wagner Act of 1935 provided for collective bargaining rights, and in Chicago, a new teachers' union revitalized the AFT. The Chicago Teachers Union, formed in 1937, militated for better wages and improved working conditions, revitalizing the organization.[25]

World War II brought new opportunities for women's education. As men entered military service, women discovered that access to colleges and universities became easier. Women constituted a third of master's degree recipients by 1940; by 1945, they received 57 percent.[26] Universities that had barred women opened doors slightly or significantly;

An eager student attended class in a one-room school in Ojo Sarco, New Mexico, in 1943. The school's two teachers taught courses primarily in Spanish for the region's children and adults. Courtesy of the Library of Congress.

Harvard, for example, allowed women from Radcliffe to attend classes. By 1947, Harvard formalized its "joint" relationship with Radcliffe, but limited women undergraduates to Saturday afternoons at Harvard's well-stocked undergraduate library. Women's enrollment in science courses also increased, and Columbia University and Rensalear Polytechnic Institute accepted female engineering students for the first time.[27] African American women found new choices as well; nursing schools expanded programs, for example, to meet wartime needs.

In public schools, the war allowed for consolidation of some gains by teachers, such as eliminating pay differences between elementary and secondary teachers, ending marriage bans, and raising salaries. Teacher shortages also allowed teachers to assume more prestige and status.[28] Far more significant for public schools, the Cold War that emerged after 1946 made the education of American children a critical aspect of challenging national enemies. At the same time, schools coped with the explosion of children arriving in classrooms, as the baby boom children entered schools. As school officials planned for the increase, they clarified new elements they hoped to add, from improved training on global issues to the encouragement of student government. Consumer courses would be necessary, one writer insisted, while all included the increased importance of teaching values to the citizens of a victorious nation. Racial differences and the lower quality of rural schools disturbed some commentators, due in part to the poor overall educational level of America's wartime troops. In World War I, white enlistees typically had less than a high school education; only 9 percent had one year or more. In 1940, improvement still seemed to indicate the need for better education; only 40 percent of the nation's young men had attained some high school education.[29]

If educators argued for the necessity of education, the G.I. Bill (officially called the Serviceman's Readjustment Act) of 1944 seemed like a good solution. Returning veterans received guarantees of unemployment compensation and funds to attend college or vocational schools. Ultimately, over seven million veterans used some form of the benefits, from housing assistance to tuition relief. For women, however, the G.I. Bill became a doubled problem. First, some female veterans failed to understand fully how the legislation applied to them. Others believed it was a "male" prerogative, repayment for the sacrifices born especially by soldiers. With women only 2 percent of the military forces during the war, the impact on women would inevitably be less than that on men. Even with relative small numbers eligible, however, only 132,000 women took advantage of the programs available.[30]

The G.I. Bill created another kind of dilemma as well. Servicemen using benefits eagerly went to college, and college administrations willingly displaced women students to accommodate them. Cornell University reduced the number of admission slots open to women; the University of Wisconsin stopped accepting applications from out-of-state female applicants. By 1947, half of all college students were ex-G.I.s. Their enrollment meant changes in college life, from new policies allowing married students to new housing for couples. At the same time, however, the government stipend didn't allow for dependents, and student wives typically filled in the gap by working. "Putting hubby through" became commonplace at Stanford, where two-thirds of student wives worked, and at the University of Michigan, where half did.[31]

Women's access to higher education slowed for other reasons connected to the postwar culture. A reassertion of domesticity filled advertisements and political speeches; even college presidents chimed in. Mills College President Lynn White, Jr. spoke glowingly of female students learning to make paella; psychologists Marynia Farnham and Frederick Lundberg asserted in their book *The Modern Woman: A Lost Sex* that domesticity reordered troubled women. The origins of Cold War domesticity continue to intrigue scholars, who have cited male anxieties, changing consumption patterns, and the growing hegemony of middle class values as sources. Yet women of the period frequently shared a desire to center their lives around home, husband, and family. The extraordinary stresses of the Great Depression and World War II demanded sacrifice and public service. When the war ended, many couples perceived themselves taking time for their needs, establishing homes and raising children. The expanding economy allowed many families to attain a level of material prosperity unknown to their parents. For some women, the ability to work within their families seemed an almost contradictory freedom. That choice remains obscured by the vehement public prescriptions underwriting women's household roles and makes it more difficult to determine female preferences.[32]

If domesticity may have been a choice for some women in the 1950s, for other women it became a rationale for restricting their advancement. The number of women earning advanced degrees plummeted, and by 1947, women made up less than a third of students receiving master's degree. Openings for female college faculty mirrored the decline, and by the mid-1950s, fewer than one in four professors were women. Some college administrators simply concluded that women lacked the abilities to work as effective academics. A sociological study of university hiring declared that because women remained outside of the academic mainstream, they remained less useful to ambitious students. Such circular reasoning effectively relegated female academics to the "second tier" of university and college life.[33]

The expansion of women's labor force participation in the late 1940s and through the 1950s had another, less obvious, impact on women's educational possibilities. Increasing numbers of married white women with older children joined the workforce. This population would be less likely to attend college and had usually finished with high school. In the postwar period, however, another option held new prospects for their participation. Junior colleges, which provided two-year degrees, expanded dramatically to meet the demand for some higher education. In 1920, only 52 colleges existed nationwide, with fewer than 9,000 students. By 1940, over five hundred had started, attracting nearly a quarter of a million students. Increasingly, these junior colleges were public institutions funded through state budgets. In 1947, the President's Commission on Higher Education called for more "community colleges" to serve both younger college students and returning adults.

If the late 1940s and early 1950s appeared to be what one historian has termed the "dark hour" of women's education, major changes lay ahead. The first came in the desegregation of schools. For Mexican Americans, segregation in schools ended through local challenges and in 1946's Supreme Court decision, *Mendez* v. *Westminster,* curtailing segregation in Orange County, California. The landmark Supreme Court decision *Brown* v. *Board* in 1954 ordered the end to racial segregation in the nation's schools with "all deliberate speed." While some Southern whites and southern legislatures attempted to block African Americans from entering all-white schools, in the years that followed legal challenges and changing attitudes slowly ensured access. The achievement came in painful steps, however, from Rudy Bridge's solitary year in a New Orleans public school to angry reaction at Central High School in Little Rock, the University of Mississippi, and the University of Alabama. It has been suggested that the focus on school desegregation, rather than less controversial areas of segregation involving adult interaction, prompted the frequently violent response of white southerners. The reaction finally led the federal government to (sometimes reluctantly) enforce *Brown*, and led to protections in the Civil Rights Act of 1964 and the Voting Rights Act of 1965.[34] Student organizations became critical in this achievement, and women played important roles in the creation and work of the Student Non-Violent Coordinating Committee (SNCC), as well as the sit-in movement and the NAACP. Colleges became a center for activism because of the involvement of young women and men.

The Civil Rights movement energized other claims for access, and in part, the developing women's movement of the 1960s benefited from women's activism. At the same time that schools struggled with desegregation, the baby boomers born in the wake of World War II filled schools and began to enter colleges. Their sheer numbers as the largest generation in American history worked to solidify changes already underway and to create new pressures for educational reform and access.

In 1961 Charlayne Hunter became the first African American woman to attend
the University of Georgia. AP photo.

By midcentury, school curricula had already become far more child
centered than it had previously. Teachers used new techniques to encourage discussion, reflection, and dialog in classes. Cold War concerns refo-
cused attention on science and math for both girls and boys. Prosperity
also meant that more children came from families of some means,
although by 1960, 20 percent of Americans continued to live in poverty.
Relative affluence meant that more families could devote funds to toys,
children's activities, camps, and sports. For girls, these elements of childhood development remained largely gender-determined, as did school
courses. Girls continued to be directed toward home economics and to
read that in the world of *Dick and Jane*, an elementary reader used in 46
percent of American schools by 1946, Jane and sister Sally played with
dolls. At the same time, however, more families aspired to send daughters
to college and encouraged intellectual achievement. Many Americans
began to associate higher education with career mobility.[35] For the first
time, working-class families could think of college as an option. By 1965,
the Higher Education Act made that more affordable by providing access
to federal loans for college.

When the baby boom went to college, they were most likely to choose
a public college or university. At major research universities, the arrival of
G.I. Bill recipients and baby boomers changed the types of students who

achieved success, as working-class Americans with diverse ethnic and religious backgrounds earned undergraduate and graduate degrees. As some
scholars note, American education "democratized," providing a new generation with access and voice. For women, the change transformed what
they experienced and expected. Women's enrollments began to increase
steadily, rising from 32 percent of college students in 1950 to 42 percent
in 1970. Over the next decades, women would surpass men in their college attendance; by 2005, 59 percent of American women had at least
some college training, while only 51 percent of men did. Enrollments
from older women provided for a growing segment of this change.

Student activism flourished on campuses during the 1960s, as Americans grew more concerned with individual rights and liberties. The Civil
Rights movement allowed some to gain experience in organization and advocacy, and at the same time, a free speech movement at Berkeley and the
emerging Students for a Democratic Society raised new questions about
student rights. Women's organizations developed in this politically fertile
environment; in 1964, for example, SNCC members Casey Hayden and
Mary King disputed the treatment of women in the organization. Their
complaints mirrored other objections to women's domesticity raised by
authors such as Betty Friedan in her best-selling book *The Feminine Mystique.* The women's liberation movement shared many origins in this period, including the work of college women and faculty who began
"conscious-raising" groups and initiated new investigations of the nature
of gender bias. By the end of the decade, a new scholarship on gender had
appeared, and women's activists created women's centers on campuses.
Women faculty who had been experimenting with new material in courses,
from the addition of more writings by women to additional readings about
women, secured a spot for the first "women's studies" courses on college
campuses, from the University of California at San Diego to Goucher and
Cornell. San Diego State University offered the first women's studies program in 1970, and through the next two decades, similar programs offering
majors or minors developed throughout the nation. By 1975, 112 women's
studies programs could be counted, with over nine hundred women's studies courses offered during the year nationwide.[36]

The most significant change for women's education came in the 1970s,
as female activists began to demand better access to programs and challenge restrictions and sexual stereotypes. In public school curricula,
teachers increasingly argued against readings that reinforced only one
view of women, or excluded girls and women from view at all. The passage of Title IX of the Educational Amendments of 1972 added weight to
this effort, prohibiting sexual discrimination in educational institutions
receiving federal funding. By 1997, Title IX covered over fourteen million
college students and nearly fifty-two million elementary and secondary

students. The additional clarity of Title IX substantiated changes that had been made, often enthusiastically, by colleges and universities in admitting women. For example, by the late 1960s, the elite colleges that had excluded women began to open admissions. Yale allowed women into the undergraduate schools in 1969, as did Princeton, Trinity College, and Georgetown University. In the next year, Williams, the University of Virginia, Boston College, and Johns Hopkins accepted women. Harvard, Bowdoin, Brown, Dartmouth, and Davidson were among the other institutions that followed, but some remained unwilling to allow female undergraduates access until later. Haverford, for example, finally admitted women in 1980, and Washington and Lee did so in 1985. Vassar College moved in the opposite direction by allowing men admission in 1969, as officials worried that its students would decamp for the previously male Ivy League. By the end of the century, more women in the United States earned college degrees than any other nation in the world, with 23 percent under age 34 receiving a baccalaureate degree.[37]

Both legal changes and more active unions also provided new protections for teachers. The Pregnancy Discrimination Act of 1979 allowed teachers to continue in their jobs, for example, and by the 1980s, pregnant teachers were no longer an anomaly in the classroom. Unions asserted demands for better pensions, workplace protections, and more teacher control over the education process in the 1960s. The American Federation of Teachers' New York City member union, the United Federation of Teachers, organized a citywide strike in 1968 to assert community control in a centralized system.[38] In the wake of this and similar actions by teachers' unions nationwide, membership grew; by century's end, nearly four million teachers were represented by the American Federation of Teachers or the National Education Association. The tumult of the sixties had transformed the NEA into a less "professional" and more activist organization, as it merged with the historically black American Teachers' Association in 1966 and took on new challenges. Through the next three decades, teachers battled for the right to strike, to establish secure pension funds, and to have a voice in local educational reforms.

A major challenge to that developed through the 1970s, as conservative political organizations and associations began to criticize educational administration and teaching. Sex education, available in some form in American public schools since the 1930s, irritated some who cited explicit demonstrations or valueless curricula as damaging to children. Republican politicians increasingly cited the interference of teachers' unions as a factor in supposedly lower educational standards. Still others from the religious right challenged the teaching of evolution and proposed alternatives; by the 1990s, "creationism" appeared as a formalized expression of a divine construction of life and advocates pushed its inclusion in schools.

Another concern drew educators' attentions in the 1980s, however. Debate over gender equality in the classroom originated with the Project on the Status and Education of Women funded by the Association of American Colleges and Universities. Researchers Roberta Hall and Bernice Sandler published "The Classroom Climate: A Chilly One for Women?" in 1982, spurring debate and similar studies. Hall and Sandler identified verbal and physical behaviors in the classroom that conveyed messages of women's implicit inferiority. For example, women students received less praise for comments, while men tended to dominate discussions for longer periods of time. These behaviors originated in unequal treatment of boys and girls, the authors suggested, and received reinforcement by teachers and professors unaware of their subtle effects.[39]

Other authors and associations responded by investigating the extent of gender differences in the classroom. The American Association of University Women sponsored a major study, *How Schools Stereotype Girls*, in 1992 that validated Sandler and Hall's findings. Colleges and universities responded with reviews of the treatment of women on campuses and in classrooms. Institutions as diverse as the University of Michigan, Purdue University, Stanford, and Southern Illinois University offered systematic examinations of women's experiences from undergraduate differences to tenure and promotion and faculty. Concerns about the impact of parenting on women faculty also increased, as researchers identified greater obstacles in tenure and promotion for female professors than for men.[40] By 2003, female faculty in colleges and universities made up 38 percent of all faculty, but a salary gap persisted, with women earning 80 percent of what male colleagues did. Women also continued to be underrepresented at senior levels, with 41 percent of male professors and only 20 percent of women ranked as "full" professors.

Other educational concerns in the 1990s included the growing numbers of students with diagnosed learning and physical differences and mental health challenges. The Americans with Disabilities Act expanded the protections of section 504 of the Rehabilitation Act of 1973. Both ensured that students could receive an equivalent education to that offered to other students. For both girls and boys, these acts meant that a growing number of students with special needs could proceed through school successfully, and for some, continue to college.

Concern over the quality of education also emerged in the 1990s as a political issue. Studies indicating that American students did not compare favorably with those from other nations in mathematics or science encouraged new criticisms of public schools. Teachers particularly faced criticism. One solution to the supposed decline of learning that became more and more popular in states was the use of standardized tests. Tests would assess whether children acquired knowledge and skills as they moved to upper grades. Implicitly, the emphasis on testing limited teachers' ability to control the content of their classrooms, as school districts mandated preparation for required tests. This movement led in 2001 to the No Child Left Behind Act, which imposed testing and required penalties for poor results.[41] The NEA pointed to the need for improvements in teacher preparation programs to ensure that those in the classroom could provide the results demanded by tests.

As controversy continued, women could point to dramatic gains by the end of the twentieth century. The numbers of women in colleges and universities stood at a historic high; women had also succeeded in professional schools and graduate education. Remarkably, when former Harvard President Lawrence Summers raised the question in January 2005 of why few women entered into science and mathematics, the Harvard Faculty of Arts and Sciences passed a "no confidence" resolution in objection. Summers resigned a year later, and Drew Faust was chosen as the university's next president.

NOTES

1. Barbara Solomon, *In the Company of Educated Women: A History of Women and Higher Education* (New Haven, CT: Yale University Press, 1986); Michelle M. Tokarczyk and Elizabeth A. Fay, *Working-Class Women in the Academy: Laborers in the Knowledge Factory* (Amherst: University of Massachusetts Press, 1993).

2. David Tyack and Elisabeth Hansot, *Learning Together: A History of Coeducation in American Public Schools* (New York: Russell Sage, 1990).

3. Helen Lefkowitz Horowitz, *Alma Mater: Design and Experience in Women's Colleges from their Nineteenth Century Beginnings to the 1930s* (Boston: Beacon Press, 1984), 4.

4. Nancy Woloch, *Women and the American Experience* (New York: McGraw Hill, 2006), 279.

5. Ibid., 245.

6. William J. Reese, *America's Public Schools: From the Common School to "No Child Left Behind"* (Baltimore: Johns Hopkins University Press, 2005).

7. Wayne J. Urban, *Gender, Race and the National Education Association: Professionalism and Its Limitations* (New York: Taylor & Francis, 2000); American Federation of Teachers, "History," http://www.aft.org/about/history/index.htm; Marjorie Murphy, *Blackboard Unions: The AFT and the NEA, 1900–1980* (Ithaca, NY: Cornell University Press, 1990).

8. Seth Koven and Sonya Michel, "Womanly Duties: Maternalist Politics and the Origins of Welfare States in France, Germany, Great Britain, and the United States, 1880–1920," *American Historical Review* Vol. 95, No. 4 (1990): 1076–1108. See also Victoria Bissell Brown, "The Fear of Feminization: Los Angeles High Schools in the Progressive Era," *Feminist Studies* Vol. 16, No. 3 (1990): 493–518.

9. Davidson M. Douglas, *Jim Crow Moves North: The Battle over Northern School Segregation, 1865–1954* (New York: Cambridge University Press, 2005); Adam Fairclough, *A Class of Their Own: Black Teachers in the Segregated South* (Cambridge, MA: Harvard University Press, 2007).

10. Henry Louis Gates, Jr., and Cornel West, *The African American Century: How Black Americans Have Shaped Our Century* (New York: Simon and Schuster, 2002), 42–46; Mary McLeod Bethune et al., *Building a Better World: Essays and Selected Documents* (Bloomington: Indiana University Press, 2002).

11. Fairclough, *A Class of Their Own;* August Meier and Elliott Rudwick, "Early Boycotts of Segregated Schools: The Case of Springfield, Ohio, 1922–1923," in *Education in American History: Readings on the Social Issues,* ed. Michael B. Katz (Westport, CT: Praeger, 1973), 290–312.

12. Journal of Blacks in Higher Education Foundation, *Journal of Blacks in Higher Education,* No. 38 (2002–2003): 104–109.

13. Henry N. Drewry, Humphrey Doermann, and Susan H. Anderson, *Stand and Prosper: Private Black Colleges and Their Students* (Princeton, NJ: Princeton University Press, 2001).

14. "A Brief History of Morgan State University," http://www.morgan.edu/about-msu/history.asp.

15. Jerome Karabel, *The Chosen: The Hidden History of Admission and Exclusion at Harvard, Yale, and Princeton* (New York: Houghton Mifflin, 2006); Leonard Dinnerstein, *Antisemitism in America* (New York: Houghton Mifflin, 2006), 85–88.

16. Robert R. Pascucci, *Electric City Immigrants: Italians and Poles of Schenectady, N.Y., 1880–1930* (State University of New York at Albany, Department of History, 1984), http://www.schenectadyhistory.org/resources/pascucci/6.html.

17. Donna R. Gabaccia, *From the Other Side: Women, Gender, and Immigrant Life in the U.S., 1820–1990* (Bloomington: Indiana University Press, 1994), 116.

18. S. N. Robinson, *History of Immigrant Female Students in Chicago Public Schools, 1900–1950* (New York: Peter Lang, 2004); Pamela Barnhouse Walters and Philip J. O'Connell, "The Family Economy, Work, and Educational Participation in the United States, 1890–1940," *American Journal of Sociology* Vol. 93, No. 5 (1988): 1116–1152.

19. John L. Rury, *Education and Social Change: Themes in the History of American Schooling* (New York: Routledge, 2005); see also Rury, "Vocationalism for Home and Work: Women's Education in the United States, 1880–1930," *History of Education Quarterly* (1984): 21–44.

20. Gabaccia, *From the Other Side,* 117.

21. Stephen A. Lassonde, "Should I Go, or Should I Stay?: Adolescence, School Attainment, and Parent-Child Relations in Italian Immigrant Families of New Haven, 1900–1940," *History of Education Quarterly* Vol. 38, No. 1 (1998): 37–60.

22. Michael C. Coleman, *American Indians, the Irish, and Government Schooling: A Comparative Study* (Lincoln: University of Nebraska Press, 2007); Barbara Landis, "Carlisle Indian Industrial School," http://home.epix.net/~landis/index.html.

23. Morton Keller, *Regulating a New Society: Public Policy and Social Change in America, 1900–1933* (Cambridge, MA: Harvard University Press, 1994); Paula Fass, *The Beautiful and the Damned: American Youth in the 1920's* (New York: Oxford University Press, 1975).

24. Langdon Eunice, "The Teacher Faces the Depression," *The Nation,* August 16, 1933; Kathleen Weiler, "Women and Rural School Reform: California, 1900–1940," *History of Education Quarterly* Vol. 34, No. 1 (1994): 25–47.

25. Clarence J. Karier, *The Individual, Society, and Education: A History of American Educational Ideas* (Urbana: University of Illinois Press, 1986); Suzanne Mettler,

Divided Citizens: Gender and Federalism in New Deal Public Policy (Ithaca, NY: Cornell University Press, 1998).

26. Linda Eisenmann, *Higher Education for Women in Postwar America, 1945–1965* (Baltimore: Johns Hopkins University Press, 2006), 58; Matthew Gaffney, "Curriculum Planning for Postwar Education," *School Review* Vol. 53, No. 4 (1945): 212–217.

27. Susan M. Hartmann, *The Home Front and Beyond: American Women in the 1940s* (Boston: Twayne, 1982), 105.

28. Earl W. Eliassen, "Teacher Supply and Demand Reported in 1945," *Anderson Educational Research Bulletin* Vol. 25, No. 4 (April 10, 1946): 98–112; Newton Edwards, "Problems of Equality of Opportunity in Education," *Review of Educational Research* Vol. 16, No. 1 (1946): 46–49; Kersey Vierling, "City Schools Face Problems of Postwar Education," *Journal of Educational Sociology* Vol. 18, No. 2 (1944): 96–101.

29. Lamar Johnson, "Junior-College Trends," *School Review* Vol. 52, No. 10 (1944): 606–610.

30. Hartmann, *The Home Front and Beyond*, 106; Suzanne Mettler, *Soldiers to Citizens: The G.I. Bill and the Making of the Greatest Generation* (New York: Oxford University Press, 2005).

31. Hartmann, *The Home Front and Beyond*.

32. Elaine Tyler May, *Homeward Bound: American Families in the Cold War Era* (New York: Basic Books, 1999).

33. Eisenmann, *Higher Education*, 61.

34. Michael J. Klarman, *Jim Crow to Civil Rights: The Supreme Court and the Struggle for Racial Equality* (New York: Oxford University Press, 2006), 147; See also Pierrett Hondagneu-Sotelo, *Gendered Transitions: Mexican Experiences of Immigration* (Berkeley: University of California Press, 1994); Vicki L. Ruiz, *From Out of the Shadows: Mexican Women in Twentieth-Century America* (New York: Oxford University Press, 1998).

35. William R. Beer, *American Stepfamilies* (Edison, NJ: Transactions Publishers, 1992), 188.

36. Florence Howe and Mari Jo Buhle, *The Politics of Women's Studies: Testimony from Thirty Founding Mothers* (New York: Feminist Press, 2000); Liza Fiol-Matta et al., *Looking Back, Moving Forward: Twenty-Five Years of Women's Studies History* (New York: Feminist Press, 1997).

37. Daniel Golden, *The Price of Admission: How America's Ruling Class Buys Its Way into Elite Colleges—and Who Gets Left Outside the Gates* (New York: Crown Publishers, 2006); Jerome Karable, *The Chosen: The Hidden History of Admission and Exclusion at Harvard, Yale, and Princeton* (New York: Houghton Mifflin, 2005).

38. The 1968 New York teachers strike hinged on issues of teacher control and created significant racial tension as white teachers bargained about their role in largely African American schools.

39. Melissa Marie Deckman, *School Board Battles: The Christian Right in Local Politics* (Washington, DC: Georgetown University Press, 2004); Myra and David Sandler, *Failing in Fairness: How America's Schools Shortchange Girls* (New York: Scribner's, 1994); Roberta Hall et al., *The Classroom Climate: A Chilly One for Women* (Washington, DC: Association of American Colleges, 1982).

40. See, for example, the American Association of University Professor's *Statement on Family Responsibilities and Academic Work,* http://www.aaup.org/AAUP/pubsres/ policydocs/contents/workfam-stmt.htm.

41. Wilson Smith and Thomas Bender, *American Higher Education Transformed, 1940–2005: Documenting the National Discourse* (Baltimore: Johns Hopkins University Press, 2008); Robert L. Osgood, *The History of Special Education: A Struggle for Equality in American Public Schools* (Westport, CT: Praeger, 2007); John R. Thelin, *A History of American Higher Education* (Baltimore: Johns Hopkins University Press, 2004).

5

---∞∞∞---

Women and Government

At the beginning of the twentieth century, most American women could not vote. By the end of the century, women had held major positions in the federal government, as Justices on the U.S. Supreme Court, as Secretaries of State, governors, and senators. By 2008, a viable female candidate for the Presidency became reality. To any observer, it would seem as if women's achievements in government and politics were nothing short of remarkable, and that in this arena at least, women made significant strides toward equality.

The history of women's roles in American government reveals a more qualified success story, and it brings to light unresolved issues still challenging women as politicians and citizens. Those issues have deep roots in women's political roles from the nation's colonial foundations. Scholars have noted that as the American colonies became a republic, the rights and obligations of Americans became, and remained, a matter of continual discussion and struggle. At the nation's beginning, the vote belonged only to white men who owned property; some Americans were counted, as slaves, part of that property. As rights gradually widened to include men without holdings, and then freed male slaves, a small minority of women demanded the vote.

Voting rights became the most famous element in nineteenth-century women's politics, and the extraordinary personalities of Elizabeth Cady Stanton and Susan B. Anthony, the most famous pioneers of that movement, continued to inspire new generations of women. The campaign for the vote has frequently obscured other critical developments in women's political activism, however. The eventual suffrage victory in 1920 fit neatly into the kind of tale Americans prefer, that of the underdog working against the odds and eventually winning. Historians sometimes note that this is "linear history," a progression from bad to good, which often overlooks any number of contradictory examples in the interest of a compelling account.[1]

As Anthony and Stanton worked to gain the vote, in fact, other women throughout the nineteenth century pursued different political avenues to exercise the rights of citizenship. Women's associations, from Female Moral Reform Associations in the 1830s, to the powerful General Federation of Women's Clubs in the 1890s, used moral suasion, petition drives, and community pressures to exert influence on government. Women in the Sanitary Commission of the Civil War achieved another type of governmental role, convincing President Abraham Lincoln to recognize officially their medical relief efforts as part of the Union's services. Women's understanding of citizenship included volunteer work as "carpetbagger" teachers and as church women in African Methodist Episcopal churches establishing charities for newly freed families in the Reconstruction south. Temperance crusades, too, engaged women in championing abstinence and confronting saloon keepers and liquor businesses in order to improve their communities. Throughout the nineteenth century, women found avenues to assert a political voice outside of the decidedly male sphere of party politics.

Women also shouldered the burdens and obligations of citizenship. During the Civil War, approximately five hundred women donned uniforms and posed as men in both Confederate and Union armies.[2] Women paid school taxes and estate taxes, despite protests by some that this constituted "taxation without representation."[3] Victoria Woodhull, a suffragist and critic of nineteenth-century marital restrictions, appeared before the U.S. House Judiciary Committee in January 1871, and argued that men had no more right to deny women's rights than women might to object to men's "free, public, political, expression."[4] Yet even if women were citizens, the Supreme Court held in its 1874 ruling in *Minor* v. *Happersett*, states could bar women from voting. The Justices unanimously agreed somewhat blithely that although women were indeed citizens with "privileges and immunities," voting remained a privilege to be granted by states, rather than a right protected by the Constitution.[5] Women continued to be excluded from the activities that defined electoral politics. When parades for political candidates occurred, women remained in their homes to cheer on their marching men. The political meetings in saloons or the infamous "smoke-filled back room" operated in spaces that discouraged or denied women entrance.

The course of women's rights and the "woman movement" of the nineteenth century made it clear that gender remained a critical dividing line in American politics and government. Women stood in a different relationship to their governments than their male kinsmen did, whether that meant voting for state electors or serving as local sheriff. Unlike their husbands and brothers, women at the beginning of the twentieth century did not have the same ability to participate in the civic life of their communities, states, or nation because of their gender. Some women accepted their particular roles and leveraged them to achieve influence in their homes and communities. Others fought to remove notions of inherent inequality. To a significant degree, the strategies and analyses of politics that evolved appeared to place women at odds with each other over tactics and goals. In the suffrage movement, for example, some women demanded the vote as a natural right of every adult citizen, while others began to claim it on the basis of women's interests in home and morality. As important, some women rejected the notions of women's public participation in politics and argued forcefully that female activism would undermine home and family life. Women who insisted on equality sometimes overlooked or ignored the importance that other women ascribed to the ideals of femininity and womanly virtue. New Yorker Emily Bisell, an opponent of women's suffrage, contended that the vote would limit women's "place and her own duty to the family."[6] Other women remained as outspoken about the dangers of voting to domestic order and civility, or to efforts for social reforms such as temperance. The differences among women also involved issues of class and race, with some, such as Helen Kendrick Johnson, founder of New York's antisuffrage Guidon Club, proclaiming that "without the ballot none but the best women will take interest in political affairs."[7]

Women debated their political role through many guises. Clubwomen discussed the type of activism they should undertake; suffragists argued about strategy. Organizations that attempted to join working-class and advantaged women together in efforts to improve social conditions, such as the National Consumers' League and the Women's Trade Union League (WTUL), also tackled the questions of how to appeal to potential members and legislators. After winning the vote in 1920, women's organizations would continue to grapple with the same fundamental questions in fights over protection legislation for working women and support for the Equal Rights Amendment (ERA). Even in the Women's Movement of the 1960s and 1970s, the issues of equality and difference separated advocates and analysts. At the center of these debates, two questions remained unresolved. First, should women act and argue for their rights as citizens to be treated without reference to gender? Or did something make gender an essential component of women's political persona, in a way that it might not affect men?

An equally important question raised by historians focuses on the nature of women's political involvement. Women's organizations tackled a

Belva Lockwood (left), the first female attorney to argue a case before the U.S. Supreme Court, and Olympia Brown, the first American woman to complete a divinity degree, remained firm advocates of women's suffrage. Courtesy of the Library of Congress.

range of concerns throughout the century. It is relatively easy to determine that a woman's book club in which members simply meet to share discussions of literature has only a remote political character, if any. What of clubs that discuss literature and begin to provide literacy classes, however? Through the first years of the twentieth century, organizations that began as social clubs did take on social service work. Whether intentionally or not, members made up for the lack of public services and assumed what could be seen as a quasi-political function. At times, women's organizations became more explicitly political, petitioning for school improvements or supporting suffrage. The exclusion of women from the political mainstream meant that women often utilized indirect or informal politics, sometimes couched in seemingly nonconfrontational forms, to attain civic goals.

These questions about the political role of women remained connected to larger issues about gender, the social order, and identity. Advocates for women's rights pointed to the common disadvantages shared by all female citizens. While American women typically understood the similarities that linked them regardless of location, class, or race, aspects of identity other than gender frequently seemed more important. Would a female member of the Ku Klux Klan in Muncie, Indiana, of the 1920s perceive her interests as connected to those of a poor African American wife in a sharecropping family? Would either recognize what united them in any common cause with a young Jewish working woman in New Jersey or New York? In the twentieth century, the size and diversity of the population of American women lessened the chances that women could unify as a political bloc, or act, as radical feminists hoped, as a class with shared interests.[8]

At times, however, shared interests did bring women together despite dissimilarities. In the final push to win the vote, suffragists accommodated many of the divisions among women, and the new movement for women's rights in the late twentieth century attracted women of color and working-class women to new considerations of work and justice. The successes have allowed historians to examine the type of political appeals women activists made to widen civic opportunities. Differences in political style, new forms of organization, and old barriers play equal parts in that history.

THE PROGRESSIVE ERA ACTIVIST AND
THE "NEW WOMAN"

In the fall of 1889, two well-connected young women moved their belongings into a large old mansion at the corner of Halsted and Polk Streets in Chicago's notoriously poor nineteenth ward. Surrounded by immigrants from Italy, Russia, Bohemia, Ireland, and Germany, Jane Addams and Ellen Gates Starr leased the somewhat dilapidated house in order to live and work among the poor. "We have been accustomed for many generations to think of woman's place as being entirely within the walls of her own household," Addams later said. Now, as "society grows more complicated it is necessary that woman shall extend her sense of responsibility to many things outside of her own home, if only in order to preserve the home in its entirety."[9]

Jane Addams soon became one of the most visible public women in the nation, an activist, reformer, and advocate. The social settlement that she and Starr established, Hull House, would be one of hundreds of similar efforts initiated in the next twenty years. As Starr and Addams unpacked their silver and saw to the arrangement of the leather chairs and sideboard in September of 1889, they perceived to some degree the significance of their endeavor. They had solicited donations carefully, drawing upon Starr's connections to her famous aunt, artist Eliza Allen Starr, and Addams had visited Toynbee Hall, the forerunner of American settlements, in London. This would be "an experimental effort" to address some of the social and industrial problems of city life. Little did they realize, as they opened their doors to their neighbors, how large an impact Hull House and its residents would have in its community or on its city.

Nor could they imagine, in 1889, the changes in women's political roles over the next two decades.

Like most Americans in the late 1880s, Addams and Starr recognized how much had reshaped American life in the last half century. Businesses such as Pullman Coach, Carnegie Steel, McCormick Reaper, and the secretive Standard Oil had grown into extraordinary enterprises of unprecedented size. Labor unrest, too, increased. Violent strikes resulting in the deaths of workers or police officers, the development of socialism and anarchism, and the appearance of two national movements of protest, the Knights of Labor and the Farmers' Alliance, showed the depth of dissatisfactions with what labor termed the "haves and have nots." When a middle-class American picked up a newspaper with her morning coffee in 1889, it must have seemed as if the nation could fall apart anew.

Behind much of the protest and discontent lay the emergence of what historians would later term "Big Business," the modern hierarchical firm. Cut-throat competition led employers to slash wages in order to remain competitive, and many shared the sentiments of one who said that the way to deal with workers was to "hit 'em over the head." As businesses concentrated into large national concerns serving national markets, the dominant entrepreneurs would stand at the helms of enterprises unprecedented in size and influence. Monopoly seemed epidemic, and few business leaders demonstrated sustained concern about the social conditions around them.[10] Congress, too, was populated by men who had been won by lobbies and financial incentives. City governments appeared equally corrupted by machine politics and graft.

The movement of Americans to cities, at once appealing and disconcerting, generated new challenges. The population of the nation's urban areas expanded from ten million in 1870 to over fifty-four million by 1920. Most of this growth prior to 1910 came with little planning, as haphazard development through informal patterns. Adding to the resulting chaos, a new wave of immigrants, predominantly from Eastern and Southern Europe, flooded to America after the 1870s, most bound for the cities. It was no accident that Addams and Starr opened Hull House in the midst of such apparent social instability.

Historians continue to debate which convergence of factors sparked the reforming impulse shared by Addams, Starr, and many other women and men at the end of the nineteenth century. The "Progressive Era" movement for reform between 1890 and 1920 was not, as the name implies, a unified, organized, or cohesive approach to tackling societal problems. Rather, Progressivism signified a confluence of efforts by predominantly middle-class men and women, many involved in a number of different organizations. The Progressive movement included the political work for eliminating machine governments, adopting the referendum, recall, and initiative on state ballots, and suffrage changes. Progressives proposed a new juvenile justice system, parks and playgrounds for cities, argued for kindergartens, proposed old-age insurance, and won new public health care. Progressives championed ideas of efficiency, social justice, and the necessity of scientific study. It has been suggested that Progressive reform remained full of paradox, from moral exhortations to an emphasis on the secularism of study and analysis, from frequent inclinations toward managerialism and rationality to the enthusiastic embrace of democracy. Throughout this generalized movement ran a concern for social welfare, be it the amelioration of existing conditions of poverty, an end to child labor, or the improvement of city conditions.[11]

Progressive reformers would find their way from local reforms to advocating change on a national scale. As they increasingly understood the issues that shaped poverty, low wages, and other challenges in neighborhoods or cities, they began to envision a different relationship between citizen and government. It has been argued that Progressives viewed government as the agency best suited to protect those in need, to guarantee justice or safety. The women involved in Progressive reform, such as Jane Addams, brought their uniquely feminine views to reform, attitudes shaped in response to their era and articulated in ways that both promoted and contested prevailing notions of womanhood. Assuming new importance in public policy, Progressive women reformers played a profound role in the evolving notions of government for the coming century.[12]

A quick look at Hull House offers an insight into the progression of reform in its early years. At first, the settlement offered little of immediate assistance to poorer neighbors; classes on Shakespeare or bookbinding would not put food on the table, cure the sick baby, or improve working conditions. But the new residents quickly realized that those services fell short if workingmen earned inadequate pay, if children starved, or if seven-year-olds died in industrial accidents. They began to campaign for legislative reforms and won a child labor law and improved factory inspection in Illinois. Hull House attracted other middle-class women who would be instrumental in reshaping the nation's social safety net: Julia Lathrop, the first head of the federal Bureau of Labor's Children's Bureau; Louise DeKoven Bowen, who founded the Juvenile Protective Association; Florence Kelley, later head of the National Consumers' League; Margaret Dreier Robbins, future head of the National Women's Trade Union League; and others who would become prominent sociologists, social workers, reformers, and suffragists.[13]

Hull House, along with Greenwich House, Rivington Street House, and the Henry Street Settlement in New York, Denison House in Boston, and hundreds of other settlements, gave women new opportunities for activism. They represented, in the words of one settlement resident, the chance to experience life at its richest and fullest, and provided an important avenue for middle-class women to exercise their intelligence and expertise. By the 1890s, a generation of college-educated women had developed skills yet found little opportunity to utilize them in professions traditionally dominated by men. Social services seemed to be a "natural" outlet for women defined as innately nurturing and giving, and thousands entered into social welfare work.

Many believed that they could bring their talents for cleaning up to the cities, and their "conscience into the general movements for social amelioration," as Jane Addams put it.[14] This idea, which historians have labeled "municipal housekeeping," meant more than simply bringing female training in household tasks into policy and social service work. The connection women made between their customary obligations in the home and the ones they now assumed in the civic life of the nation drew upon women's historically defined instincts of caring, nurture, and motherly virtue. Empowered by a new legitimacy to enter into arenas previously closed to them, however, female activists forged new avenues for their own independence, achievement, and expression. Many found their opportunities exhilarating. Work among the poor allowed women to travel freely throughout the city; reformer Mary Simkovitch recalled how the settlement workers got to enter into city life at its most intense.

The idea of municipal housekeeping became a complex vehicle for women's entry into a larger role in public life. For example, it endowed women reformers with virtue and the assumption of correct values. Some middle-class reformers believed wholeheartedly in the superiority of certain practices and attitudes over others, whether that was the importance of baking bread at home (a middle-class preference) to purchasing it (often a working-class necessity), or decorum in dancing. Historians continue to debate the Progressive reformers' inclinations toward social control, regulation, and social engineering. Some scholars view Progressive mandates for middle-class norms, imposed in legislation, policy, prescriptions from social workers, and surveys, as a central and deliberate feature of Progressive efforts. In fact, some settlement workers commented on the "Lady Bountiful" attitude held by others among them. Mary McDowell recalled that in her early years she often "sailed . . . into a house and told [the poor family] to 'clean up' in a most righteous manner."[15]

Historians' disputes about social control often obscure the significance of gender in the development of Progressive social reform. A dramatically new attitude about poverty appeared within the social settlements and other "social welfare" groups, as reformers constructed an analysis based on fact and observation. The use of social survey, pioneered in places such as Hull House in the 1890s with *Hull House Maps and Papers*, a block-by-block analysis of local living and working conditions, allowed reformers to reject the overt moralism of nineteenth-century charity workers. Most of the poor, they argued, worked hard for inadequate wages and lived in harsh conditions. Their poverty stemmed not from a lack of virtue but from incomes too small to support families, unsafe conditions in jobs and housing, and a lack of health care. Such poverty was environmental and could be remedied not by exhortation and moral suasion but by social action, legislation, governmental involvement, and proper analysis.

It remains difficult to sort through Progressives' many impulses. The settlement workers openly objected to the less sympathetic and "unscientific" approach of the Charity Organization Societies and their friendly visitors, whose methods remained decidedly moralistic until after 1900. Leaders such as Addams and McDowell spoke frequently about democracy and fondly about immigrant neighbors. Perhaps most revealing, women reformers had knowingly shifted their claims in civic life from those based on their natural rights as citizens to those based in maternal instincts. This transition allowed women a broad claim, as citizens and reformers, to protect and be protected. The maternal argument challenged the control of men *as men*, and offered instead defense by the state and courts, against abusive husbands, greedy employers, and crafty landlords. It became commonplace for both male and female reformers to refer to "the emerging welfare state in the feminine gender."[16]

The connection between female reformers, who brought municipal housekeeping and a new maternalism into the public sphere, "exerted a powerful influence" in the construction of these emerging governmental forms of the twentieth century.[17] Within both the federal and state governments, new agencies such as the Children's Bureau, Public Health departments, and the Women's Bureau provided formal mechanisms of influence. As historians have noted, informal or extra-governmental avenues of influence became an even more important, and arguably more subtle, means of reform. For example, Florence Kelley, the head of the National Consumers' League from 1899, worked to establish minimum wages for women workers by creating alliances between women of means and laborers. Her influence resonated through the Progressive community. She would join Josephine Goldmark in drafting what would become the "Brandeis Brief" in the Supreme Court's decision in *Muller* v. *Oregon*, upholding limited hours for women workers. The brief, a compilation of information about women's working conditions, substantiated arguments about the detrimental effects of long unregulated hours. In 1909, Kelley helped to found the National Child Labor Committee and the National Association for the Advancement of Colored People (NAACP). Through work outside of governmental agencies, women reformers such as Kelley exercised a powerful influence on policy. This type of role, in adjunct or extra-governmental capacities, began to create more innovative social programs. At Hull House, settlement residents focused on improving the opportunities of the neighborhood through services such as a day nursery for babies; the Jane Club, a residence for young single women; and meeting places for local societies, associations, and political groups to gather.

The largely middle-class reformers of settlement houses and charities were not the only female activists of the era who pressured for governmental changes. Working-class women in the WTUL, formed in 1903 as an alliance of middle-class reformers and working women, initially focused on working conditions. Increasingly, the League's more advantaged "allies" argued for governmental action, such as minimum wages for women, and prominent members such as Leonora O'Reilly and Mary Kenney O'Sullivan found themselves straddling the differences between labor and protective legislation. When allies such as Margaret Drier Robbins insisted that minimum wage laws were the best guarantee of adequate pay for women workers, O'Reilly defended the position of the American Federation of Labor (AFL) opposing wages established outside of union negotiation. Ultimately, the allies won, with younger women activists such as Rose Schneiderman advocating change for working women. Schneiderman argued, "the government can be made to be our government, that we can do what we want with it, make legislation that we want."[18] With few union options for women beyond the vigorous International Ladies Garment Workers, and with the AFL continuing to allow member unions to prohibit female membership, many working women joined in the belief that government protections remained their best leverage against employers.

As middle- and working-class women developed new arguments for governmental protections and guarantees, two other groups of female activists remained uniquely positioned outside of the changing sphere of the liberal state. Women drawn to the more radical politics of the Socialist Party, anarchism, or the Industrial Workers of the World (IWW), such as Emma Goldman, Elizabeth Gurley Flynn, and Mary Harris "Mother" Jones, believed in revolution to transform American capitalism. This political stance initially subsumed demands for women's rights, but by 1908 the Socialist Party appointed a Women's National Committee to Campaign for the Suffrage. Activities such as parades for International Women's Day also meant increased public visibility for women's equality. The women in the IWW faced a more difficult challenge from many male members, who argued at times for better wages for men, or who joked about domesticity. One IWW woman writer responded to such jibes by noting "that is just what we are trying to escape; being obligated to marry you for a home." Despite such vocal rejections of men's privileges, the IWW hired only three female organizers prior to 1920. Some men continued to view women's activism as problematic, suggesting that women "agitate in a quiet way."[19]

African American women also occupied a distinct position in the political movements of the Progressive era. The majority of African Americans at the turn of the century continued to live in the South, where Jim Crow laws segregating blacks and whites relegated blacks to increasingly limited social spaces and opportunities. Between 1890 and the 1920s, Southern legislatures constructed legal barriers to African American voting, and nationally, racial barriers and prejudice limited African American access to education, housing, and jobs.[20] Many white women's organizations refused black women membership or participation. Josephine St. Pierre Ruffin and Mary Church Terrell, leaders of the black women's club movement, were denied seats to the General Federation of Women's Clubs convention in 1900, and the National Association of Women Suffrage allowed Southern suffrage leagues to remain white only. The Young Women's Christian Association, too, allowed chapters to separate black and white members. Eva Bowles became the first "secretary for colored work" in 1913; eight years later, the Y appointed its first African American national board member, Charlotte Hawkins Brown.[21] Acknowledging how race and gender posed obstacles to equality, African American women activists understood the multifaceted significance of black women's clubs and settlements. As the founder of Boston's Women's Era Club in 1895, Ruffin believed that African American clubwomen would have to "teach an ignorant and suspicious world that our aims and interests are identical with those of all aspiring women." The National Association of Colored Women (NACW), formed in 1896, used the motto "Lifting as We Climb" to define the goals of personal advancement and public service, each implicitly a challenge to a persistently segregated society. Mary Church Terrell, president of the NACW, told other members in 1897 that "our peculiar status in this country . . . seems to demand that we stand by ourselves."[22]

The development of African American women's clubs illustrated the difficult nature of this challenge. Some clubwomen came from the African American elite and hoped that their organizations would validate their gentility. The NACW periodical *Woman's Era* promoted the refinement and abilities of African American women, for example, and asserted the NACW goals of "harmony and cooperation among all women" in elevating "home, moral and civic life."[23] Laying claim to the same domesticity that white women championed meant a unique subversion of race, however, African American women's insistence on their place as ladies undermined the notions held by many whites that all black women were inferior, childlike, or promiscuous, and constituted a special demand for equality.[24]

African American women also used clubs to provide social services for less advantaged African Americans. These efforts retained a dual purpose, serving to reinforce class differences among blacks yet also establishing needed institutions within the African American community. Mary

Church Terrell, for instance, demanded that organizations "go down among the lowly, the illiterate, and even the vicious."[25] Advantaged black women had less distance between them and poorer African American families, however, either in terms of economic background or geography, because of discrimination and segregation. African American activists understood as well that many of the needed institutions for education, medical care, and advancement would not appear unless they built them. Efforts centered during this period on improving opportunities for children and sustaining women in need. The NACW funded a kindergarten in St. Louis in 1900 and subsequently supported others in Montgomery, Alabama; Charleston, South Carolina; Philadelphia, and other cities.[26] Mothers' Clubs to teach women proper childcare became equally popular, as did day nurseries and homes for the elderly. Clubs such as New York's Women's Loyal League spawned settlements; founder Victoria Earle Matthews established the White Rose Mission in New York in 1897 as a shelter for women, but its mission soon expanded to include mothers' clubs and other supports. Other clubwomen started to advocate direct political reforms, supporting anti-lynching campaigns, petitioning for an end to the convict lease system, and demanding woman suffrage.

The Neighborhood Union (NU) in Atlanta demonstrated the evolution from social club to politics. Begun in 1908 by Lugenia Hope and women in the communities of Atlanta Baptist University (renamed Morehouse College in 1913), and Spelman College, the Neighborhood Union took on social service work and political campaigns. Atlanta public schools offered no vocational training for black students, so the NU women provided courses in millinery, cooking and baking, and dressmaking. The absence of a playground accessible to African American children resulted in the creation of one on the grounds of Morehouse. As the NU grew, its branches in Atlanta organized street cleanings, childrens' clubs, and drives for medical care and tuberculosis treatment. In 1913, the Social Improvement Committee of the NU launched an investigation of public school facilities and programs for Atlanta's African American children. After documenting abysmal conditions, the NU lobbied the mayor, the city council, and other white leaders and philanthropists for improvements, an overtly political result of social work. Even though the schools available to African Americans had only one teacher for every seventy-two children, and teachers had to offer "double sessions" of less than three hours each for students, the city council refused to make substantial changes in the segregated system. The NU would eventually win better (but still low) salaries for teachers and an annex to existing buildings, but white Atlantans funded black education only reluctantly. A similar campaign to force the city to provide better water and garbage services to the segregated African American neighborhoods in 1917 also fell short of its goals. The women in the NU responded to these politics of discrimination by creating an array of new services, from a health center to recreation for soldiers to free milk for the neediest families. African American women created the "social safety net" for their communities, in other words, when white governments purposely failed to do so. Unlike their white counterparts, black female activists believed that service work remained an essential part of the larger battle for equality.[27]

WINNING THE VOTE

The demand for the vote became the lasting legacy of the Seneca Falls convention on women's rights in 1848. Since the American Revolution, women such as Abigail Adams had raised the issue of women's suffrage, presenting the ballot as a logical extension of their citizenship. In 1838, abolitionist Angelina Grimke declared "it is woman's right to have a voice in all the laws and regulations by which she is to be governed."[28] Nonetheless, legislators in the states and in Congress repeatedly rejected the idea that women might have the same claims as men to a political voice. The laws of *coverture*, the English tradition of domestic relations, held that husbands, as the legal heads of their families, represented their wives in most civic matters. A man's vote reflected not only a personal choice, but the family's needs; undermining the male prerogative to make such decisions would damage family order and function, at least according to those opposed to women voting. Throughout the nineteenth century, as suffragists pressed for access to the ballot, critics responded by invoking women's role in family life.

From 1848 onward, a small group of women suffragists persistently pursued the vote as a logical extension of their rights as citizens. During the course of their campaigns before 1890, advocates of women's vote confronted numerous challenges. As Congress moved to ensure the rights of freed slaves after the Civil War, for example, suffragists hoped that the historic change would include women's vote. Instead, the newly formed American Equal Rights Association, created in 1865, faced painful choices when the proposed Fourteenth Amendment pointedly specified voting rights for "men" in Section 2, forcing women advocates to decide whether to support its ratification. The movement split, with Elizabeth Cady Stanton and Susan B. Anthony campaigning against a measure limited to men; they soon formed the National Women's Suffrage Association (NWSA). Supporters of the Fourteenth Amendment formed the American Women's Suffrage Association (AWSA), with Julia Ward Howe and Lucy Stone at the helm. In the decades that followed, the AWSA adhered to a "suffrage only" strategy, working to win the vote in state legislatures. Stanton and Anthony, in contrast, embraced a series of causes and

champions, including the notorious "free love" crusader Victoria Woodhull. In 1871, Woodhull testified before the House Judiciary Committee,
which speedily rejected her calls for voting rights. Woodhull also became
the first female candidate for President, running for the Equal Rights
Party in 1872.

The NWSA in these years utilized a new strategy for the vote based on
the Constitutional changes brought by the Fourteenth Amendment.
Arguing on the basis of the "privileges and immunities" clause, NWSA
members contended that the equal protections guaranteed to all citizens
provided women with the vote. The attempts to prove this point by voting led to arrests, however. In November 1872, Susan B. Anthony cast
her ballot for President Ulysses Grant, but two weeks later faced arrest
for "illegal voting." At trial, Anthony was denied the right to testify, and
after being found guilty, received a $100 fine. Sojourner Truth, who tried
to vote in Battle Creek, Michigan, could not persuade officials to provide
her with a ballot. In Missouri, Virginia Minor also could not register
when she tried to challenge the law. Minor brought suit against Reese
Happersett, and in the resulting 1875 case, *Minor* v. *Happersett*, the
Supreme Court ruled that the states alone set voting standards.

One territory did give women the vote. In 1869, Wyoming surprised
the nation when the twenty-man legislature agreed that women over
twenty-one should vote in all elections. Other states and some municipal-
ities granted women "school suffrage," limiting them to voting for school
boards or at school meetings. Typically, state legislatures restricted wom-
en's votes carefully; New Jersey's school suffrage, approved in 1887, only
allowed rural women to vote at local meetings. Women in New Jersey's
larger towns and cities were still barred from using the ballot in school
elections. By 1900, twenty-seven states allowed women some voice in
school decisions, but still regulated the circumstances of voting narrowly.
States such as California and Massachusetts allowed women to run for
school offices but continued to bar women's voting.

The first proposal for a national suffrage amendment to the Constitution arrived in Congress in 1878. Lawmakers promptly rejected it. Critics
of women's votes continued to argue that full female citizenship would
harm family life; other opponents, such as the influential lobby of liquor
manufacturers and distributors, believed that women voters would overwhelmingly back temperance. Suffragists kept campaigning; between 1870
and 1910, they mounted 480 campaigns in thirty-three states to secure
access to the vote. From these efforts, they gained fifty-five referendums,
but only two would result in the vote for women, in Colorado in 1893
and Idaho in 1896. In the meantime, Wyoming joined the Union as a
state, bringing with it women voters. Utah women won the vote in 1870,
but as Congress debated the territory's admission as a state, suffrage

became a casualty of a greater fear of polygamy. The Utah legislature restored women's voting rights in 1895. American women, at least in a few states, could legally vote in all elections.

The two suffrage organizations also reached a new turning point in 1890, and ending their differences, united to form the National American Women's Suffrage Association (NAWSA). Elizabeth Cady Stanton served as president for the first two years, followed by Susan B. Anthony. Yet the NAWSA would differ from the previous associations, and a new generation of suffragists would soon replace these pioneers. The nation, too, was vastly different in 1890 from the first days of the suffrage movement when Stanton and Anthony began their work. With a population of over sixty-three million, the United States had emerged as a major industrial power. Cities like New York had electricity; streetcars ferried passengers to growing suburbs in places such as Richmond, Virginia, and Boston. Millions of immigrants entered into the country as well, bringing with them new languages and cultures. In this increasingly urban and industrial nation, the issue of women's voting rights would be transformed from an appeal about the rights of citizens to the promises that women could bring special feminine talents to civic life.

The years between 1890 and 1910 would not be easy for suffragists, however. The NAWSA retained many of the old equal rights arguments for the vote even as new assertions about women's public roles developed. Increasingly, as women became active in clubs, in social reform work, and in temperance campaigns, suffragists accepted the claims of municipal housekeeping. The separation among women reformers blurred as the networks of women activists grew. Jane Addams, for example, emerged as a powerful advocate for woman suffrage, arguing for the social benefits when women gained "a natural and legitimate share" in government. Men, she suggested throughout her writings, tended to focus on administration; women could be an "implement" for doing "some of the things which are most fundamental." Not only would they play a key role in cleaning up corrupt government; women remained attuned to the nuances of daily life which men frequently missed. The separation between politics and reform limited the development of democracy, Addams contended. The civilizing aspect of women's innate character would balance the failures of men and, she implied, ensure ethical government.[29]

As women suffragists continued to fight state by state to secure the ballot, the divergent arguments of voting based on equal rights and suffrage because of women's differences continued. Women's historians suggest that the "competing conceptions of gender equality and gender difference" shaped the debates over women's political roles for the rest of the twentieth century. The basis for women's equality would include sexual difference. Such an apparent conundrum aimed "for individual freedoms by mobilizing sex solidarity." Women would acknowledge their commonalities while asserting their diversity. Such a politics, "requires gender consciousness for its basis yet calls for the elimination of prescribed gender roles."[30] Women would straddle the stream while crossing over it.

In the first decade of the century, women's work as social reformers, their organization in clubs and associations, their eagerness for education, and their growing access to public spaces gradually made their political demands less controversial. The suffrage movement still encountered legislative and organizational obstacles, however. The leadership of the NAWSA passed from Stanton, who died in 1902, to Anthony, who died in 1906, briefly to Carrie Chapman Catt and then to Anna Howard Shaw. An ordained Methodist minister and a doctor, Shaw excelled as a speaker rather than as an administrator. Internal battles over strategy and membership troubled the organization, with Southerners, fearing the possibility of integration, insisting on state campaigns and all white membership. Northern women, too, adopted the rhetoric of exclusivity, as some insisted that women's votes would dilute the threat posed by immigrant men. Although Shaw increased the NAWSA's membership, younger women grew frustrated with her methods.

Washington State provided the breakthrough suffragists needed in 1910, and other states in the West moved to grant women the vote. The California suffrage organizations celebrated in 1911 as they achieved victory, and in 1912, Michigan, Kansas, Oregon, and Arizona followed. Illinois's approval of women's voting rights in 1913 represented an important step toward the East, where legislatures proved more reluctant to award the franchise. In 1914, Montana added women to the polls, and in 1917, suffragists claimed Nevada, North Dakota, and Nebraska.

The suffrage movement became more politically astute, more diverse, and more focused after 1910. Women began to adopt the campaigning techniques used by men, holding parades, outdoor meetings, and rallies. New leaders also emerged with more militant ideas drawn from the English suffrage struggle. Harriet Stanton Blatch, the daughter of Elizabeth Cady Stanton, infused suffrage work with plans to organize working women, and the Equality League she had begun in 1907 mounted the largest demonstrations of women's demand for the vote in New York City. Blatch also worked tirelessly to secure the vote for women in New York. The Equality League, renamed the Women's Political Union in 1910, opened suffrage shops, organized parades, lobbied in Albany, began a newspaper, and even made two movies, *The Suffragette and the Man* and *What 8,000,000 Women Want*.

Another independent organization that stressed militant action emerged, the National Woman's Party. Its organizers, Alice Paul and Lucy Burns, ran the NAWSA's Congressional Committee between 1912 and

1913, as the organization began a two-pronged strategy of working for state suffrage and pursuing a federal amendment for the vote. Paul and Burns organized a large suffrage parade in Washington, DC, for the day before the new President Wilson was to take office. Hostile onlookers attacked the marchers, and police quelled the ensuing violence. Undaunted, Paul and Burns hoped to pressure Wilson to support suffrage with other public actions, plans that led them to split from the NAWSA. Operating first as the Congressional Union, and soon as the National Woman's Party, the confrontational suffragists picketed the White House and encouraged civil disobedience. Deeply influenced by work with English suffragists, Alice Paul insisted that the radical tactics would force politicians to accept the Anthony amendment.

Carrie Chapman Catt resumed the leadership of the NAWSA in 1915. After 1904, when she gave up the presidency of the organization, Catt led in the establishment of the International Woman Suffrage Alliance, traveling internationally to promote women's voting rights. By 1912, she returned to New York to push for suffrage. Neither her work nor that of Harriet Stanton Blatch overcame opposition; in 1915, New Yorkers rejected a suffrage referendum. Similar failures occurred in Iowa, South Dakota, and West Virginia. Undaunted, the New York suffragists threw their energy into another referendum, which passed in 1917.

When Catt replaced Shaw as the NAWSA president in 1915 she brought a new political pragmatism to her work. Between 1910 and 1918, voters in twenty-four states gave their opinions of suffrage in referendums, and eleven states decided for women's votes. By 1917, the organization dropped its state by state campaigns. Women now set their sights on passage of the Susan B. Anthony Amendment to the Constitution. When Congress declared war in April, Catt pledged the members of the NAWSA would assist in the war effort. Persistent wooing of President Woodrow Wilson also began to work, as the President started to pressure Congress for the Anthony amendment. Catt's "Winning Plan" meant that she abandoned her pacificism, accepted the racism of elements within the NAWSA membership, and focused solely on suffrage. Despite criticism from inside the organization and from others in the National Women's Party, Catt's single-minded approach worked.

The Anthony Amendment first came to a vote in the House of Representatives in 1915 and failed by 204 to 174. Catt responded by pressuring representatives of suffrage states to push again for an Anthony bill. By September 1917, with President Wilson as a new advocate of women's votes, the House created a Woman Suffrage Committee. On January 10, 1918, the amendment passed the House by 274 to 136, exactly the two-thirds majority needed. The Senate proved more difficult, and Wilson appeared before the body on September 30, 1918, asking for passage. The next day, the Senate turned him down. It took almost nine more months to secure the winning ballots, and on June 4, 1919, the Senate finally approved the Anthony Amendment.

Ratification by the states occurred quickly. Eleven states agreed to the amendment in the first month, and within six months, twenty-two accepted it. By August 1920, suffragists won the last state needed, as Tennessee became the thirty-sixth to ratify the amendment. On August 26, 1920, the Secretary of State certified the addition of the nineteenth amendment to the Constitution, which declared "the right of citizens of the United States to vote shall not be denied or abridged by the United States or by any State on account of sex."

The long battle for the vote had taken seventy-two years from Seneca Falls to Nashville. Yet the vote itself did not mean political equality. Even with the Constitutional protection, African American women in Southern states faced the barriers of other forms of disenfranchisement in Jim Crow laws. Many Southern legislatures resisted ratification symbolically, finally accepting the inevitable generations after the suffrage victory. Other political and legal barriers to an equal civic role persisted as well. Some states refused women the right of jury service, for example, and throughout state and federal governments, gender structured opportunities and obligations differently. By gaining the vote in 1920, women received the opportunity to a direct voice in the political process. The next question would be whether of not it would make a substantial difference.

1920–1950

The term "feminist" became a popular description for a supporter of women's political and social equality sometime after 1910. Adopted by men as well as women, the rapid acceptance of the concept indicated how much women's political roles had changed in two decades. By the time President Wilson endorsed woman suffrage in 1916, Montana had elected the first woman to Congress, Jeanette Rankin. Inside the government, Julia Lathrop served as the head of the Children's Bureau, a division of the Department of Labor. The war had also linked women internationally, as the Women's Peace Party formed in 1915, and its first president, Jane Addams, lobbied the President. The International Women's League for Peace and Freedom, which followed in 1919, maintained headquarters in Geneva for its efforts to promote peace initiatives.

Reformers and women's organizations increasingly focused on political changes as well. After 1910, women reformers successfully championed mothers' pensions in state legislatures, securing small stipends for widows. Despite the many flaws of mother's pensions, from character requirements and household investigations to discrimination in administration, this in-home assistance represented the first governmental aid available to women and children in modern America.[31] Unsuccessful efforts to limit child labor also occupied women, culminating in two overturned laws and a failed constitutional amendment campaign. Temperance reformers advocating an end to the evils of alcohol won their battle, however, with the ratification of the Eighteenth Amendment.

Women in more radical areas, such as socialism and accessible birth control, confronted more skepticism and difficulty. Socialists such as Emma Goldman, Rose Pastor Stokes, and Elizabeth Gurley Flynn attempted to organize women, but as one historian put it, after 1910, women on the left found themselves pulled toward "exotic courses," including experiments with feminism and syndicalism.[32] The Red Scare after World War I led to the deportation of Goldman and other prominent socialists and eventually to the decline of the IWW. Their earlier alliance with Margaret Sanger, a pioneer in publicizing methods of birth control for working-class women, ended by 1914.

Sanger, who enjoyed publicity and rebellion in equal measures, began publishing her own newspaper, *The Woman Rebel*, to promote contraception. Threatened with arrest for advocating anarchy and political assassinations, Sanger avoided prosecution by traveling to England, but returned in 1915. Indicted and facing trial, Sanger prepared for conviction, but the tragic death of her five-year-old daughter Peggy engendered so much public sympathy that New York prosecutors dropped charges. By 1916, Sanger had organized the first birth control clinic in America, which opened in Brooklyn. Nine days later, police raided its offices, arrested the staff, and Sanger was ultimately convicted of violating laws against distributing contraceptive information. When New York appellate courts determined that physicians could legally provide birth control, however, Sanger moved quickly in 1923 to open another clinic, this time run by a physician. Battles within the birth control movement continued, with Sanger adamantly insisting on physician services, and the primacy of her organization, the American Birth Control League formed in 1921. The opposition within the movement, led by Mary Ware Dennett, who had founded the Voluntary Parenthood League in 1915, focused on women-centered services. Dennett and her supporters had long opposed Sanger's tactics and believed that a political campaign to remove language from laws that restricted contraceptive use would allow the broadest access to birth control. Even with this split, the birth control movement in the 1920s became increasingly conservative and professionally oriented.[33]

For many women in political organizations, the 1920s seemed to be a period of less activism. One suffragist suggested, "after we got the vote, the crusade was over. ... we went back to a hundred different causes and tasks that we'd been putting off all those years. We just demobilized."[34]

Despite the apparently diminished intensity, however, women did not retreat from political roles or aspirations and began to exercise their new political rights. More women followed Jeanette Rankin into Congress, for example. Oklahoma elected Alice Mary Robertson in 1921 to serve in the House. A popular farmer and café owner, Robertson opposed woman suffrage and lost her seat by failing to back veterans' bonuses. Other early female Congressional representatives had equally short stints; Winnifred Huck served out her father's term but did not win enough of her Illinois constituents to capture the general election. Mae Ella Nolan became the first wife to fill a husband's seat and won election in 1923, but discovered she disliked the public demands of Washington life. By 1925, Florence Kahn of California, Mary Norton of New Jersey, and Edith Norse Rodgers of Massachusetts entered the House and served multiple terms; Rodgers finally left in 1960. The daughter of three-time presidential candidate and Secretary of State William Jennings Bryan, Ruth Bryan Owen, became a Representative from Florida in 1929.

Appointee Rebecca Latimore Felton of Georgia entered the Senate in 1922, filling a vacant seat for one day. Hattie Wyatt Caraway entered the Senate in similar fashion in 1931 when she was appointed to her husband's seat after his death. She shocked her fellow Arkansas Democrats by announcing that she would run for election; however, few seasoned politicians believed the widow stood a chance. What they did not count

President Calvin Coolidge hosted the Women's National Law Fraternity at the White House in 1924. Courtesy of the Library of Congress.

on was the support of neighboring Senator Huey Long of Louisiana, whose popularity with poor and rural voters extended easily in the South. Long campaigned with Caraway, knowing that allies in the Senate and popularity throughout the South would benefit both. Caraway won and continued in the Senate until 1945. She spoke rarely, joking that she hadn't "the heart to take a minute away from the men. The poor dears love it so." Unfortunately for Long, Caraway also emerged as a solid supporter of Franklin Roosevelt and the New Deal. She also accomplished many firsts for women in Congress's Upper House, as the first woman to chair a committee, the first woman to preside over the Senate, and the first Senior Senator to be a woman. Caraway supported the ERA, but like her Southern counterparts, rejected anti-lynching laws and the prohibition of poll taxes for voting.[35] Election to the Senate continued to prove difficult for women, however; the women who took office did so after the deaths or illnesses of husbands. Margaret Chase Smith of Maine, who served first in the House following her husband's death, won election to the Senate, but Nancy Kassebaum of Kansas became the first woman to win election to the Senate without following a spouse in 1978.

Women also became governors. In 1925, Nellie Tayloe Ross of Wyoming replaced her husband in office; Texan Miriam "Ma" Ferguson won election the same year when her husband was ineligible for another term. Ferguson's inauguration occurred fifteen days after Ross's. Women's representation in state legislatures increased as well; by 1925, almost two hundred women held state positions. Within the federal government, the Women's Bureau and the Children's Bureau, both housed in the Department of Labor, operated under female leaders, Mary Anderson and Julia Lathrop.

In 1921, a coalition of women reformers celebrated a significant legislative victory, the Sheppard Towner Act for Maternal and Infant Health, which provided funding for pregnant mothers and infants. Even with these apparent advances, the persistent questions of difference or equality that informed women's politics remained unresolved. In 1923, Alice Paul of the National Women's Party proposed an amendment to the Constitution that would verify the equal rights of women and men. Rather than uniting women with a new cause, Paul managed to alienate a vast array of political activists. Many women reformers remained committed to preserving protective legislation for women workers, as courts showed increased enthusiasm for dismantling these laws in the 1920s. Reasoning that protective laws were imperfect but necessary, Progressive era reformers such as Florence Kelley and Alice Hamilton rejected Paul's proposal; Women's Bureau head Mary Anderson stood firmly against it. WTUL organizer Elisabeth Christman wrote to WTUL leader Pauline Newman of her wish to make Women's Party members "work at a conveyor belt at some highly speeded up mass production industry."[36] Female opponents to the ERA from progressive organizations worried that such legislation would unravel the work of previous decades, advantage only privileged women, and undermine women's politics.[37]

Paul remained undeterred. Throughout the 1920s, she continued to promote the ERA, even as the National Women's Party membership dwindled from 35,000 to merely 1,000. Paul focused increasingly on the ERA as a legal issue, perceiving the amendment as an important device to eliminate the multitude of laws that still distinguished between men and women in divorce, child custody, jury service, property claims, and other rights. By extension, Paul narrowed the framework of feminism from larger issues of culture and identity to matters of law and rights. The National Women's Party remained uninterested in the issues confronting African American women, for example, debates over birth control, or expanding education for women. Only one women's organization, the Business and Professional Women's Association, endorsed the ERA, and many activist women remained hostile to Paul's ideas.

That divergence, and the strong personalities that sometimes stimulated heated responses, represented a significant loss for women's political options. Some scholars have suggested that women during this period forged more nuanced definitions of female political identity, moving beyond the rights-difference dichotomy to a more compatible blend. What makes this seem less likely than some historians argue are the exchanges among women, which occasionally carry surprisingly vehement heat, and the persistent defense made by female activists for women's unique political qualities. The debates over the ERA continued into the 1940s and 1950s, and women who identified themselves as part of the network of social reformers remained adamant about protective legislation. A reassertion of equality would not find a significant audience until the 1960s, when a new women's movement and changes in American society made those claims resonant with a new generation of women willing to call themselves feminists.

By the end of the 1920s, the failures of women's activism seemed as clear as the limited successes. Sheppard Towner, which had provided services for prenatal and infant care, was not renewed by Congress. African American women's organizations continued to fight segregation and lynching, and although their causes received international support and greater publicity, no laws provided improvements or protection. Women won elections, but the vast majority of the electorate still preferred to have women casting ballots rather than receiving them. Women activists remained at odds over strategies and goals as well, as they debated whether equality meant equal rights with men or something altogether different.

Historians suggest that women received the vote as American politics shifted in form. The traditions of the nineteenth century, of parades, party camaraderie, machine-style organization, and public spectacle gave way to a growing separation between politician and voter, a less-involved electorate, and more "professional" politics. Women's suffrage had been won by utilizing many elements of nineteenth-century politics, but once women had the ballot, they joined an electorate less likely to vote than their predecessors.[38]

All of the nation's politics came to a significant turning point in 1929, as the nation entered the Great Depression. By 1932, Americans grappled with an economy in crisis, with unemployment as high as 90 percent in some manufacturing cities, starvation for the most vulnerable, and no signs of an immediate recovery. Franklin Delano Roosevelt's election in 1932 promised a change, and as he entered the White House in March 1933, Roosevelt began the first stages of the New Deal. One element of Roosevelt's administration would be new opportunities for women in the administration of federal programs. By 1939, women constituted 44.4 percent of the employees in seven New Deal agencies. Women also found jobs in the Departments of State, Interior, and Labor, and made up over a third of workers there by the end of the decade. In some older divisions, however, from the Department of War to the Post Office, women never became more than 15 percent of the employees.[39] The key to the advances women did make in the New Deal lay in networks forged in previous decades. At a dinner honoring women administrators in the New Deal in 1940, the seventy women seated at the head table shared connections through social welfare work and, as important, Eleanor Roosevelt.

Roosevelt arguably became the single most important political woman of the twentieth century, a person whose influence would open up jobs, create new opportunities, and challenge existing prejudices. During her years in the White House, Roosevelt devoted her energies to expanding opportunities for women, holding press conferences for women journalists only, writing columns, and creating access to her husband, the President. Roosevelt understood the significance of presenting herself publicly as a capable political person, becoming a role model as well as an advocate. She also facilitated networking among political women, serving as a point of connection by the late 1920s.

Many of the women who assumed leadership roles in the New Deal came from reform organizations such as the WTUL, the National Consumers' League, or social work. Francis Perkins, the first woman Cabinet official as Secretary of Labor, began her political career in the National Consumers' League and served under Roosevelt in New York as the state's Industrial Commissioner. Mary Dewson, know as "Molly" to a vast community of women activists, also worked in the National Consumers' League before heading the Women's Division of the Democratic National Committee. Dewson used her position to lobby for appointments for women in federal agencies, a role she played with success in the selection of Perkins, Ruth Bryant Owen as Minister to Denmark, and WTUL activist Rose Schneiderman to the National Labor Relations Labor Advisory Board. Ellen Sullivan Woodward, too, in the Women's Division of the Federal Emergency Relief Agency, and Sue Shelton White in the Consumer's Advisory Board of the National Recovery Administration, were protégés of Roosevelt and Dewson.

Historians have debated the consequences of women's participation in New Deal programs. Many female activists shared Eleanor Roosevelt's belief that social programs should support women in their family roles and not undermine domestic life, and legislation for measures from Social Security to relief treated men and women differently. New Deal programs retained an implicit assumption that single women might work, and that married women should remain at home. At the same time, the New Deal's female administrators did attempt to create opportunities for women and to increase assistance available for them. Women administrators tried to expand female jobs in the Civilian Works Administration under the Federal Emergency Relief Act, for example, and in the Works Progress Administration that followed. Many of these jobs required women to work at stereotypical chores such as sewing, but supporters contended that at the least, they provided work, pay, and quieted critics.[40] The limits of the New Deal for women can clearly be seen in efforts to establish the equivalent of the Civilian Conservation Corps (CCC), a jobs program created for young men between the ages of eighteen and twenty-five. Hilda Smith, as an administrator in the Federal Emergency Relief Agency, drew up plans for a similar program for young women by the end of 1933. The following year, experimental camps opened, serving 1,800 specially selected women. Unlike their male counterparts in the CCC, however, the women did not receive pay or jobs training. By 1937, the program was dismantled, and Smith wrote, "the boys get the breaks, the girls are neglected."[41] The Social Security Act, passed in 1935, established equally troublesome distinctions between men and women. Even when reformers tried to amend its earliest provisions to provide for wives and widows, the results were almost comical. Testifying at a Social Security hearing in 1938, one administrator assured his audience that "it is more costly for a single man to live than for the single woman...," as women could "look after" themselves more successfully.[42]

The other critical limitation of the New Deal, both within government and in the formulation of programs, lay in the persistence of racial segregation. Mary McLeod Bethune, in charge of the Office of Minority Affairs in the National Youth Administration, also became the leader of the informal "Black Cabinet" advising the President. Even with the strong support of Eleanor Roosevelt, however, Bethune remained outside the women's networks that constituted such an important part of New Deal reform, and she won few lasting victories against recalcitrant segregationists either in Washington or in the South. New Deal programs separated recipients by race or allowed states to adjust funds according to local customs. As in the case with programs that treated men and women differently, disadvantages could be ambiguous. Works Progress Administration (WPA) programs provided new schools for African American students, for example, which were a vast improvement over the ramshackle buildings students had used. Even in new buildings, however, students still used old textbooks, teachers earned lower pay, and segregation prevailed. Programs in the WPA to train young women for jobs in the South also frequently limited African Americans to courses in housekeeping and domestic service.

Even with these failures, the New Deal meant more opportunities for women in the face of economic crisis and provided one generation of activists entry into governmental service. Ironically, the female reformers who assumed the offices and responsibilities of New Deal agencies did little to cultivate talented successors. As the 1930s came to an end, leaders such as Mary Dewson retired from public life. Eleanor Roosevelt devoted her attention to the growing crisis in Europe and the dilemmas of racial equality. Even leaders such as Labor Secretary Frances Perkins were no longer able to wield the sort of influence they had held in the first days of the New Deal; Perkins faced calls from conservative Congressmen in 1938 for delaying the deportation of labor radical Harry Bridges. Although some women politicians such as Ellen Woodward remained in New Deal posts, appointments became more difficult to secure. In 1939, the Hatch Act, which prohibited federal employees from public campaigning or partisan activity, further narrowed the opportunities for activists.

World War II resulted in a greater expansion of the federal government, but unlike the New Deal programs, wartime agencies offered fewer openings for women in the upper levels of agencies. The perception that war required male leadership relegated women to support positions and sometimes stymied efforts to improve new programs. For example, the War Manpower Commission, headed by Paul McNutt, maintained responsibility for the labor needs during the war, an obvious area for women's involvement. McNutt rejected efforts to have women on the Commission, and instead, a Women's Advisory Committee with thirteen female members received the right to "recommend" ideas and policies. The WAC members had no salaries, no staff, and no committee budget, and found that their proposals, from split shifts for working mothers to improvements in day care found little sympathy from McNutt.

Unlike the New Deal, when women's participation seemed almost as notable as the agencies in which they worked, during the World War II the national emergency overshadowed individual efforts. Women's political roles and their efforts for the government appeared as patriotic contributions. For example, over 4,500 women served in intelligence through the Office of Strategic Services, and by 1944, 900 worked overseas, including singer Josephine Baker, a young Julia Child, and Virginia Hall, who maintained a secret cover in France. This work remained largely unheralded, as it was for women in the military serving in the Women's Army Corps under Oveta Culp Hobby, or in the WAVES under Mildred McAfee, former president of Wellesley College. The female scientists who collaborated on the Manhattan Project creating America's atomic weapons continued to be equally obscure, despite distinguished later careers for Elda Anderson, present at the Trinity explosion at Los Alamos, or Maria Goeppert Mayer, a future Nobel Prize winner in 1963.

As in the New Deal, Eleanor Roosevelt overturned all previous assumptions about the duties of a First Lady during the war. Roosevelt traveled internationally to visit American troops in the Pacific, promoted the contributions of the Tuskegee Airmen, and lobbied for a postwar international peace agency. Women in Congress shared in war work and also had significant "firsts." Frances Payne Bolton, elected to the House in 1940 from Ohio, secured the 1943 Bolton Act to fund a student nurse corps, equally available to African American and white students. She later became the first woman to lead a Congressional delegation to another country, and the first woman delegate from Congress to the United Nations. In 1954, Bolton used her position to attack South African apartheid. Margaret Chase Smith of Maine secured a position on the House Naval Affairs Committee during her second term in 1943, and by 1946 found her way on to the prestigious Armed Services Committee. In the decade after 1940, twenty-two women won election to Congress, and the majority served at least two terms.

The war also furthered the movement of Native American women into leadership positions within reservations and tribal politics. In 1934, the Indian Reorganization Act restored many rights lost in the late nineteenth century, including the ability to conduct tribal affairs. New constitutions written in the 1930s frequently allowed women positions of authority. In 1944, the National Congress of American Indians formed to lobby on behalf of Native American peoples, and Ruth Muskrat Bronson, a Cherokee, became the organization's executive secretary.[43]

As the war came to an end in 1945, women's politics continued to change in fundamental ways. In 1940, the ERA won endorsement from the Republican Party as part of the party platform. By 1944, the Democratic Party bowed to arguments that it, too, should not thwart symbolic support for equality for women, and so it also added the Amendment to the campaign platform. The older generation of women activists in the Democratic Party, from Eleanor Roosevelt to Mary Dewson, argued against it, and veterans of the older campaign against the Amendment weighed in with their objections. Alice Hamilton wrote that the Amendment would undermine marriage and the family; Mary Anderson of the Women's Bureau insisted that industrial organizations objected. Even in the face of such objections, the Amendment made it to the floor of the Senate in the summer of 1946, where only thirty-eight Senators voted for it, far short of the needed plurality. The ERA came up again in 1950 and 1953, as supporters added a provision that they hoped would answer objections. The "Hayden rider" specified that no protections or privileges enjoyed by women would be eliminated by the Amendment. Although this convinced Senators to pass the provision, the ERA did not win backing in the House, and after 1953, supporters waited for a better opportunity.

The improved chances for the ERA, however, and the alliance that emerged to support it, suggested the new and more complicated nature of women's political roles. The Progressive-New Deal networks of women reformers and the politics of social service that they represented no longer dominated, despite the near-legendary status of Eleanor Roosevelt. The generation of women who arrived in Congress and in federal agencies, or who entered into local politics, typically came of age after suffrage and settlements. Some had worked for the League of Women Voters, others for the Business and Professional Women; many had experience in their respective political parties. Some brought a determination to reform to Washington, but their idea of reform might not necessarily concur with the ideals of the New Deal or previous generations of women activists. Helen Gahagan Douglas, for example, won election from California in 1945 and became a powerful voice for African Americans and labor. Clare Booth Luce, elected from Connecticut in 1943, and Jessie Sumner of Illinois, elected in 1939, entered the House eager to attack the New Deal and Franklin Roosevelt. Luce particularly became a prominent challenger to Roosevelt's wartime policies and gave the keynote address at the 1944 Republican National Convention. Stylish and confident, Luce challenged preconceptions about women's ideas and place in government.

Attacks on women in politics emerged from a new direction in the postwar era. As the war came to an end, a young Vassar graduate named Elizabeth Bentley finally convinced New York FBI agents that she had been part of a Communist spy ring in Washington, DC. As her story unfolded, it led eventually to Whittaker Chambers, an admitted communist, and then to the head of the Carnegie Endowment for Peace, Alger Hiss. Hiss's conviction on perjury charges in the face of Chamber's insistence that Hiss was a Soviet agent fueled a growing anxiety over subversion. The loyalty oaths initiated by President Truman for federal employees were soon copied by state and local governments, and then by employers throughout the country. As anticommunist fears flourished, progressive women found themselves targeted by nervous bosses or ambitious rivals.

What made the Red Scare particularly damaging during the late 1940s and early 1950s for Americans with any sort of liberal past was the broad nature of the accusations leveled against "disloyal" citizens. Some historians have suggested that a tendency to "countersubversive" thought has long characterized one part of national politics. Whether for political gain or from conviction, some Americans have responded to those who are new or different by labeling those groups as dangerous enemies to the purity of a more righteous American character. Outsiders might be Native Americans, slaves, immigrants, or, in the 1950s, Communist spies and sympathizers whose presence threatened to undermine order. Other scholars have noted that gender frequently emerged as a theme in countersubversive literature, with the outsiders depicted as threatening to family, masculinity, and female virtue.[44]

Scholars have noted that one component of postwar anticommunism targeted gay activity or identity as menacing and un-American.[45] A similar message emerged about unruly women and African Americans who did not behave according to conservative standards. A mixed message about women in Cold War investigations has been noted. On one hand, investigators characterized women as dangerous, seductive spies or bossy, overbearing mothers. Tried and convicted for espionage, Ethel Rosenberg, for example, was routinely depicted in reports as her husband Julius's "master." Repeatedly, however, the House Committee on Un-American Activities (HUAC) largely ignored women, believing that any role held by a female would necessarily be secondary and inconsequential.[46]

At the same time, the Red Scare, loyalty oaths, dismissals, blacklists, and occasional criminal penalties made it obvious that supporting progressive causes could be a liability to one's career or one's family. Men and women who had worked alongside the Communist Party in the 1930s to free the Scottsboro men falsely accused of rape, or who served the hungry in a Communist Party soup kitchen, found themselves explaining that connection. Even worse, some found themselves defending their innocence when a family member, friend, or teacher had been the participant or contributor. The famous, such as W. E. B. DuBois or Lillian Hellman, or poorly paid secretaries faced accusations. In her campaign for the Senate in 1950, Helen Gahagan Douglas confronted an eager young Congressman, Richard M. Nixon, who labeled her a "pink lady." Douglas responded by calling Nixon "tricky Dick;" the nickname endured but it did not win her the election or convince voters of her patriotism. Helen Mankin, Sarah Hughes, and Margaret Chase Smith in the House confronted similar claims; only Smith won re-election. In 1950, as Senator Joseph McCarthy accused citizens of being subversives, Dorothy

Kenyon, U.S. Representative to the United Nations Commission on the Status of Women. found herself on McCarthy's list. Although Kenyon cleared her name, her career in foreign service ended, a fate shared by Esther Caukin Brunaeur in the State Department.[47]

The most significant harm to women's politics occurred inside organizations, much as it did in labor organizations. Faced with the prospect of defending some members from charges of connections with communists, the Women's International League for Peace and Freedom rejected those with a questionable past. Other peace associations followed a similar path. For labor organizations, and especially for the Committee for Industrial Organization (CIO), the purge of radical members had a devastating effect on organizing and strategic planning, which never returned to the extraordinary achievements of the 1930s in uniting workers or winning improvements.[48] For women, the politics of the 1950s would be summed up by Business and Professional Women's president Margaret Hickey, who called for a "new feminism" of citizenship rather than women's rights.[49]

The demands of the Cold War and worries over atomic weapons also brought women into a different type of local political position. The Federal Civil Defense Agency urged housewives to volunteer as block wardens and plane spotters for possible nuclear attacks and circulated information on how families needed to prepare for atomic emergencies. The Civil Defense Agency promoted two programs, "Grandma's Pantry" and "Duck and Cover," which highlighted women's special roles as consumers and teachers. Households needed to be stocked, just as "grandma's" was, women learned, as children practiced how best to cover themselves from the nuclear flash and radiation. As some historians have written, the post-atomic age depended on women as consumers and participants in cold war politics. In turn, women's most active role in government seemed increasingly at odds with the small number of visible female leaders.

Margaret Chase Smith of Maine won election to the Senate in 1948, and her challenges to Senator Joseph McCarthy in 1950 led to her name being placed in nomination for the presidency in 1952, the first woman of a major political party to have that distinction. India Edwards championed positions for women as the director of the Women's Division of the Democratic Party from 1948 to 1950 and helped secure slots for Georgia Neese Clark as U.S. Treasurer, Eugenie Anderson as Ambassador to Denmark, and Burnita Sheldon Matthews as the first female judge on a U.S. District Court. Edwards then served for six more years as the Vice-Chair of the Democratic National Committee. During the Eisenhower administration, Oveta Culp Hobby worked to consolidate various governmental agencies into a new Department of Health, Education, and Welfare, and became the Secretary of that Cabinet branch from 1953 to 1955.

A small group of women did try to assert a uniquely nationalistic politics during this period, but one that resulted in prison terms and exile. During the early years of the century, Puerto Ricans gained American citizenship, but Puerto Rico continued to occupy an uncertain position in the nation as a protectorate. Puerto Ricans finally received the right to elect their Governor in 1949, and in 1950 to establish a constitutional Commonwealth. Nationalists who had sought independence responded with a series of actions. The most famous, the 1950 Jayuya uprising, occurred when Puerto Rican Nationalist Party dissidents led by Blanca Canales attacked U.S. installations. Canales read a declaration of Puerto Rican freedom before being taken into custody for the alleged murder of a police officer. Canales served seventeen years in prison before receiving a full pardon from Puerto Rican Governor Roberto Sanchez Vilella in 1967. Four years later, Lolita Lebron acted with another small group of nationalists when they opened fire on those present on the floor of the U.S. House of Representatives. Convicted and sentenced to death, Lebron received a pardon from President Jimmy Carter in 1979 after serving twenty-five years in prison. Lebron continued as an activist in Puerto Rico after her release, advocating an end to U.S. military testing sites in Puerto Rico. Viewed alternately as a heroine of nationalism or a misguided criminal by others, Lebron nevertheless became a unique and largely unrecognized participant in shaping women's political activism.

NEW RIGHTS AND WOMEN'S RIGHTS: POLITICS, 1954–1982

In the twentieth century, one did not have to be an adult or royalty to be politically influential. The struggle for civil rights in the United States depended upon children and teenagers such as Ruby Bridges, Linda Brown, Barbara Rose Johns, and Bernice Johnson Reagon, who played differing yet critical roles in challenging segregation before they reached adulthood. The work to end Jim Crow segregation and find justice took the efforts of women and men, girls and boys willing to risk jail, hardship, and perhaps death to secure equal treatment.

On May 17, 1954, the Supreme Court issued its historic ruling in *Brown v. Board of Education*, overturning the previous 1896 decision upholding segregation if "separate but equal" facilities existed for African Americans. The Brown case represented a victory not only for Linda Brown and her parents, but for the students of Prince Edward County, Virginia, and the case stemming from their 1951 strike for better schools. Frustrated with the absence of a cafeteria, gymnasium, infirmary, teacher restrooms, and overflow classes held in a dilapidated school bus, Barbara Johns and other students at Moton High School in Farmville, Virginia, held a two-week protest. The Richmond branch of the NAACP filed suit on their behalf, and although the U.S. District Court found that the county had not violated the law, the court ordered improvements to the all-black school. The case instead became part of the Brown effort to overturn segregation entirely.

The Brown victory did not eliminate school segregation, however, as students in Prince Edward County learned clearly. Virginia led states in the attempt to avoid integrating schools, and Prince Edward's public schools closed for five years between 1959 to 1964. Other communities resorted to a variety of ploys to block desegregation. The Little Rock Nine in 1957 required the protection of federal troops to integrate Central High School in Little Rock, Arkansas, after near riots by whites blocked their attendance. Ruby Bridges, a six-year-old first grader, became the first student to integrate William Franz Elementary School in New Orleans in 1960. Accompanied by U.S. Federal Marshals, Bridges entered the school as white students and teachers withdrew. For a year Bridges and her teacher, Barbara Henry, remained the only people in class. Similar and less famous incidents played out across the South throughout the years of desegregation, as African American students entered previously all-white schools or classrooms.

In colleges and universities, too, African American students faced violence and hostility. In 1961, Charlayne Hunter and Hamilton Holmes enrolled at the University of Georgia and needed police protection in order to attend classes. Vivian Malone and James Hood faced similar difficulties at the University of Alabama in 1963, when Governor George Wallace declared that the University would not desegregate. Federal intervention ensured their attendance. This was a far more positive result than the experiences of Autherine Lucy. With NAACP support, Lucy filed suit to win admission as a graduate student to the University, and she enrolled in February 1956. When student protest blocked her entrance to class, however, the University expelled Lucy, arguing that she had harshly criticized administrators. (Notably, the university rescinded the expulsion in 1982, and Lucy, now Autherine Lucy Foster, completed a Master's in Elementary Education.) Only gradually would Southern colleges and universities open admissions to African American students. The first African American women students at Virginia Polytechnic University (VPI and SU) entered in 1966, for example; not until the late 1960s and 1970s would college campuses in the South become more fully integrated.

The Brown decision spurred other kinds of action beyond school desegregation during the 1950s. In Montgomery, Alabama, it proved the additional incentive for Rosa Parks to refuse to give up her bus seat to a white rider. Parks' famous determination sparked the Montgomery Bus Boycott from the end of 1955 through 1956, which ended successfully with the integration of the Montgomery bus system, the establishment of the Southern Christian Leadership Conference (SCLC), and the emergence of Rev. Martin Luther King, Jr., as a major leader for Civil Rights. Encouraged by events in Montgomery, the SCLC moved to organize other protests, working with the Congress of Racial Equality (CORE), the National Urban League, and the NAACP. In 1960, as students in Greensboro, North Carolina, started a campaign to desegregate whites-only service at Woolworth's lunch counter, their idea spread to other campuses and communities. SCLC leaders responded by sending organizer Ella Baker to work with the student protestors. A meeting at Shaw University in Raleigh, North Carolina, of students from fifty-eight sit-ins, student organizations ranging from Students for a Democratic Society to the National Student Association, and delegates from southern and northern colleges created the Student Non-Violent Coordinating Committee (SNCC).

Baker came to her work with SNCC with a long history of working with the NAACP in New York and several years with the SCLC. A gifted and insightful organizer, Baker served alongside Howard Zinn as an advisor to the organization until 1962. SNCC emerged as an essential element of the movement, attracting students such as Diane Nash to organize direct action, participating in Freedom Rides to challenge segregation, and collaborating with SCLC to organize the 1963 March on Washington. By 1964, as SNCC moved to organize the Freedom Summer to register black Mississippi voters, Baker aided in establishing the Mississippi Freedom Democratic Party. The members of the "Freedom Democrats" challenged the all-white Democratic delegates at the 1964 Democratic Convention, a deep embarrassment to President Lyndon B. Johnson. While Johnson brokered a deal to seat two of the Freedom delegates and the remainder of the Mississippi party regulars, Fannie Lou Hamer, another Civil Rights activist, protested. Vice Presidential nominee Hubert Humphrey, a longtime advocate of civil rights, appealed to the Freedom Democrats for their agreement, and Hamer demanded that he risk his job to do what was right. If he failed, she said, "you will never be able to do any good for civil rights, for poor people, for peace, or any of those things you talk about."[50] The deal went through without Hamer's consent. Hamer continued to work for civil rights in Mississippi, and Ella Baker left the South to return to New York. By 1965, the Civil Rights Act and the Voting Rights Act guaranteed part of what the Civil Rights movement had sought, legal protections for greater access to civic life.

For the women in SNCC, gender issues emerged as a troubling component of the organization and its activities. African American and white women frequently performed different tasks within the organization. Cynthia Washington recalled a conversation with Casey Hayden about how white female volunteers felt limited to secretarial or menial chores. Other black women in SNCC described their roles as more difficult and less feminine; "we became Amazons, less and more than women," one remembered. Another felt that "white girls came down here for a few months" and then wanted publicity and praise for their courage. African American women were equally aware of the sexual tensions surrounding politics, and the cultural definitions of beauty that continued to define them as less desirable. On both sides, among African American women and among whites, the growing perceptions of these problems would lead in new and different directions.

As the Civil Rights movement reached toward voting rights and legal guarantees of equality, the small number of visible female leaders in government seemed increasingly at odds with shifting political ideologies. In 1961, Esther Peterson, a longtime labor organizer and supporter of John F. Kennedy, convinced the new President to create a committee on women's issues. Peterson herself had been appointed as Assistant Secretary of Labor and Director of the Women's Bureau, but she recognized the growing discontent among prominent women within the Democratic Party. In December, Kennedy named the members of the new President's Commission on the Status of Women, chaired by Eleanor Roosevelt. The Commission, with fifteen female and eleven male members, completed the rounds of testimony, investigation, and deliberations in 1963 (after Roosevelt's death in 1962). They recommended better coverage for women by the Fair Labor Standards Act of 1938, increased support for day care, an end to military quotas for women, and equal pay. The Equal Pay Act of 1963 also became law, requiring employers to give women the same wages that men received for the same jobs. The most important result of the President's Commission lay in the response of state governments. Forty-nine states subsequently established similar committees, and gradually investigators and commission members began to network and share information. The information would become an important foundation for future laws and reforms and a valuable resource for an emerging new women's movement.

In 1964, the Civil Rights Act opened an important historical opportunity for divergent groups of women activists. As Southern Senators worked to undermine legislation to guarantee equal rights for African Americans, Virginia Senator Howard K. Smith added a prohibition against discrimination by sex to Title VII of the bill. When it passed, the Civil Rights Act became a major protection from gender discrimination; Esther Peterson immediately recognized it as "a sudden jump through many stages of history."[51] Between 1964 and 1966, as women activists in labor unions, Democratic and Republican politics, and women's organizations watched the federal response to the new legislation, they grew increasingly frustrated. The Equal Employment Opportunity Commission (EEOC) created by the Equal Pay Act and the Civil Rights Act, failed to penalize employers for discrimination, many argued. Commissioners Aileen Hernandez and Richard Graham voiced particular concern, and by 1966, this discontent surfaced at the third annual conference of commissions on women's status. A small group of participants agreed to create a new organization, the National Organization of Women (NOW). Betty Friedan, whose book *The Feminine Mystique* had been a best-seller in 1963, became the organization's first president.

NOW occupied a philosophical middle ground in the changing political climate of the 1960s. Unwilling to adopt the radical analysis of the left, the militance of the changing Civil Rights movement, or the convoluted politics of the older women's movement, NOW embraced a liberal agenda of reform. The founding statement did not challenge men for "oppressing women," or condemn the American political system, as NOW's leaders asserted that "women can achieve such equality only by accepting to the full the challenges and responsibilities they share with all other people in our society, as part of the decision-making mainstream of American political, economic and social life."[52]

As NOW appeared to place pressure on the political center, other ideas attracted a new generation of activists to a more radical and arguably more personal politics. The new feminism that emerged among young women had its roots in the Civil Rights movement, the antiwar movement, on college campuses, in the cities, within the baby boom and consumer culture, and shifting ideas of American individualism. Historians initially traced much of this feminism to the Civil Rights movement and the supposedly growing dissatisfaction of white female volunteers with subsidiary, menial, and sometimes sexualized work in organizations such as SNCC. More recently, some scholars have suggested that many volunteers did not experience or recognize any real problems; the slow evolution of an awareness of the different status of men and women in American life, they contend, came from a more diffuse recognition of discrimination. What is clear is that a different kind of feminism developed, not centered on organizations and structured meetings but on informal gatherings and shared stories. From these kinds of scattered beginnings, another "women's movement" spread through mimeographed newsletters, radical declarations, and networks of acquaintances. "The Personal Is Political," some young feminists declared, believing that the discussion of life experiences in "consciousness-raising" sessions would provide insights into how gender discrimination affected all areas of society. Much like the radicalizing Civil Rights movement after 1965, this type of feminism addressed politics in its broadest cultural forms, generating political analysis through countercultural dress, sex, language, and art.

Between 1965 and the early 1980s, the Women's Movement in the United States was large, vibrant, influential, and multidimensional.

Participants distinguished themselves through nuanced differences in philosophy, identity, and goals. Some feminists formed groups; others remained part of more free-floating networks of like-mined people. Often feminists of one persuasion might view others of a different philosophy in much the same light as the National Women's Party and social reformers had in the 1920s, when arguments among women seemed more important than any common cause. The political and cultural achievements of this period were significant and the failures were equally important.

Historians have categorized the strands of the movement into radical, liberal, social, and cultural feminism, but as some note, older definitions of the period may be more descriptive. Liberal feminists, such as many members of NOW, typically argued for legal or legislative reforms within existing political systems, which they hoped would be improved with female participation. Radical feminists such as the Redstockings and The Feminists evolved critiques that focused on the evolution of male oppression, manifested in political and cultural forms. Within Radical Feminism, another political idea of radical lesbian separatism emerged, based on the notion that women could choose to form an all female-centered life. Marxists, who had historically attempted to accommodate women's rights, and feminists contributed to the construction of a new politics of Marxist-Feminism. Marxist-feminist perspectives, which had slight differences with socialist-feminism, attempted to connect women's secondary position historically with the larger questions of race and class.

Between the 1960s and the mid-1980s, these strains of feminist thought informed a variety of political initiatives and arguments. As historian and movement organizer Rosalind Baxandall observed, the women's movement remained decentralized, with few citywide organizations, and many groups with informal and shifting membership.[53] Chicana feminist groups such as Hijas de Cuauhtémoc, and Asian American associations such as Asian Sisters, organized, as did African American women's groups such as the San Francisco Third World Women's Alliance and the National Black Feminist Organization. In Boston, the Combahee River Collective sought to bring women together regardless of identity. Acting together or separately, feminists wrote, sang, taught, and demanded changes which transformed the place of women in American society.

NOW's emphasis on legal and legislative reforms resulted in an end to job advertisements that specified the gender of applicants, for example. The push for an ERA reflected the deep transformations in the women's movement, as NOW, the Women's Equity Action League, the National Women's Political Caucus, and other groups such as the United Auto Workers, the National Education Association, and the League of Women Voters joined in lobbying for the measure. Michigan Democrat Martha Griffiths introduced the ERA in House in 1971, where it passed easily, and the following year the measure won in the Senate. Signed by President Nixon, the ERA was quickly ratified by thirty states.

The success of the ERA, and the fact that it had not generated the heated conflicts between progressive women that other attempts to secure the Amendment had generated, illustrated the broad appeal of the women's movement and its changed nature. By the 1960s, women shared concerns about whether the equal protections of the Fourteenth Amendment extended fully to them, or if distinctions of gender limited women—and in turn, men—in their choices, opportunities, and obligations. Some state-funded colleges, for example, still refused to allow the tax-paying women of their state admission; clubs where lawmakers conducted informal meetings barred women and African Americans. Unlike their ancestors in the Progressive era, women in the 1970s viewed such obstacles as barriers to their rights as individuals and as women. No longer content with arguments about the need for special protections because of motherhood or femininity, women challenged protective legislation as an obstacle to equality.

A critical element of the challenge to sexual discrimination came from women theorists, scholars, and other intellectuals, who began to explore gender systematically. Women's studies as an academic discipline appeared in 1969, and through the 1970s developed as a viable, legitimate arena of scholarship. The use of gender as an analytical category of analysis won acceptance by historians, economists, sociologists, and political scientists, and increasingly sophisticated work identified issues and some solutions for gender discrimination. Academics founded journals such as *Feminist Studies* (1972) and *Signs* (1975) to further explorations and increase the legitimacy of publications.[54] An equally active community of writers contributed outside of academia to newspapers and journals such as *off our backs* (1970) and magazines such as *Ms* (1972). Collections of short writings from the movement appeared in *Sisterhood Is Powerful*, edited by Robin Morgan, and Morgana and Anzaldua's *This Bridge Called My Back*, which featured works from Chicana and Latina women.

As the women's movement grew in complexity in the 1970s, activists addressed different aspects of women's experiences. Reproductive health became the focus for some, such as the Jane Club of the Chicago Women's Liberation Union, which maintained a network of abortion providers. Other self-help collectives emphasized women's knowledge of their bodies and their reproductive choices; in 1976, the Boston Women's Health Collective published their guide in *Our Bodies, Ourselves*. Centers for victims of domestic assault, women's centers to provide information and respite, and rape hotlines also began, all viewed by activists as political responses to sexual oppression.

Within a year of the passage of the ERA, conservatives organized to contest it, and opponents to feminism created new avenues to challenge what they viewed as a dangerous agenda. Already active as a conservative Republican, in 1972 Phyllis Schlafly formed the National Coalition to Stop ERA. Schlafly toured the nation condemning the ERA for undermining the family, claiming that a change in law would force the public to endure unisex restrooms and tolerate gay marriage. Her message tapped into fears that feminists had not addressed effectively, and her ability to recruit young conservatives to her cause revealed her strategic skills. Yet Schlafly's efforts to derail the ERA were aided most by the decision in 1973 of the Supreme Court to permit legal abortions in *Roe* v. *Wade*.

The *Roe* case followed a decade of work by women activists, Planned Parenthood, and sympathetic physicians to provide legal access to abortion for all American women. By 1967, Colorado had allowed medical abortions when a mother's life was in danger, and by 1970, New York, Washington, Hawaii, and Alaska removed most restrictions on the procedure. Other states also eliminated some barriers, so that by 1973, nearly one-third of states and the District of Columbia provided some protection for women and physicians terminating pregnancies. The National Abortion Rights Action League (NARAL), founded through NOW in 1968, lobbied and sponsored marches for reproductive choice. When the Supreme Court received the case of Jane Doe, however, it remained unclear that the Court would find a sweeping protection for women. Justice Harry Blackmun's decision did not assume women had an absolute liberty to determine reproductive outcomes, but Blackmun did find for the majority that women, in consultation with their physicians, had the right of privacy in making such choices. *Roe*, in effect, legalized abortion in the first trimester, while leaving it unclear how the Court would view varied circumstances in pregnancy. The decision ignited a firestorm of controversy, fueling the growth of a conservative movement which increasingly perceived women's rights as dangerous to "the family," social order, and even national survival. The ERA suddenly became a key part of this equation.

Political activists in the women's movement did not worry at the time; the victory of abortion rights, the achievement of the ERA, and the election of new women leaders into positions of power was obviously progress. In 1972, Shirley Chisholm, the first African American woman to be elected to Congress, took her seat in the chamber, sharing responsibilities with a membership that included outspoken feminist Bella Abzug of New York. Connecticut elected Ella Grasso in 1974, the first woman to campaign for a governorship in her own right; by the end of the decade, Diane Feinstein held the gavel as Mayor of San Francisco, and Jane Byrne won the mayoral race in Chicago in 1979. The 1977 National Women's Conference in Houston, funded by Congress, drew over 20,000 women.

The Conference also opened doors for conservative women, who used state planning conventions to challenge ERA, abortion, and other feminist issues. Representatives from organizations as varied as Stop ERA and the Ku Klux Klan attended state meetings, and later the Houston Convention, to secure publicity and limit what Schlafly called the "radical, antifamily, prolesbian" agenda of women's movement organizations. By combining appeals about family life, threats of radicalism, uncontrolled sexuality, and the specter of a gay-lesbian overthrow of social order, Schlafly and other social conservatives successfully tapped in to a new political and cultural development, the expanding cultural right.[55]

During the 1960s, while women's groups, antiwar activists, Civil Rights associations and Black Panthers met and militated, conservatives regrouped after the defeat of Barry Goldwater in 1964 and the resignation of Richard Nixon in 1974. Political groups such as the Young Americans for Freedom, established in 1960; the Heritage Foundation, created in 1973; and the National Right to Life Committee, formed in 1973, challenged the availability of abortion services and the ERA with increasing fervor. An additional element appeared in 1979, the organized force of evangelical Christians, as the Moral Majority led by minister Jerry Falwell announced a new conservative politics in defense of "family values." Even at this juncture, many feminists did not fully realize the importance of such political developments. For women in the Republican Party who had championed the ERA, for example, the 1970s represented a difficult period of division, as Schlafly's influence increased within the Party. Some Republican feminists such as Mary Crisp Dent, Elly Peterson, and Mary Louise Smith worked assiduously to ensure that support for women's rights remained part of the Party's platform. By 1976, when Ronald Reagan attempted to challenge incumbent Gerald Ford for the Presidential nomination, Republican supporters for women's rights found themselves arguing that the Party should not adopt an antiwoman stance.

By 1980, Ronald Reagan's election signaled the ascendancy of a new conservative alliance. The Republican platform in 1980 abandoned the ERA and accepted a plank in support of a Constitutional amendment outlawing abortion. Some Republican Congressional Representatives had used the 1977 Houston gathering to characterize participants as "outcasts, misfits, and rejects," and "sick, anti-God, pro-lesbian, and unpatriotic."[56] Conservatives attacked the word "feminist" and the ERA in images and speeches. In 1978, when Congress voted to extend the time for the ERA to be ratified by the states, conservatives intensified arguments against it, and by 1982, when the deadline for ratification passed, activists in the women's movement understood why. Opponents of the ERA shifted the debate from women's rights to questions about gender roles for men and women, topics still replete with emotion over dependency, sexuality, and family economics. The Moral Majority, the National Right to Life Committee, James Dobson's Focus on the Family, and other conservative groups would successfully portray "feminists" as selfish, unattractive women with unshaved legs and underarms, bent on a radical agenda to dismantle the family and kill innocent babies. By the end of the 1980s, the term would find fewer young women willing to use it to identify their beliefs, and older feminists lamented what Civil Rights activist Mary Frances Berry noted as an avoidable defeat.

Ronald Reagan's presidency did mean the end of the ERA, but women could at least herald one new milestone. In 1981, the Senate confirmed Reagan's nominee, Sandra Day O'Connor, as the first female Justice on the Supreme Court. Other women also occupied important posts in the Reagan years. Jeanne Kirkpatrick served in the National Security Council and as Ambassador to the United Nations; Cabinet heads included Margaret Heckler at Health and Human Services, Ann McLaughlin at Labor, and Elizabeth Dole at Transportation. None, however, served more than two years, and all agreed with the Administration's general position on women's issues. Kirkpatrick argued for governmental support for women's advancement through appointments, but not mandates or regulations that might end "democracy and self-government."[57]

If feminists, women activists in NOW, WEAL, Chicago Women's Liberation, or Redstockings did not accomplish all that they had attempted by the

Sandra Day O'Connor became the nation's first female U.S. Supreme Court Justice in 1981 and served as an Associate Justice for twenty-four years. Courtesy of the Library of Congress.

1980s, it was clear that the women's movement had made remarkable changes in American political culture. In 1980, political scientists identified a "gender gap" in voting, as women cast their ballots for Democrats far more often than they did for Republicans. The Democratic Party in 1984 attempted to use this as an advantage against Ronald Reagan in his bid for re-election, placing Geraldine Ferraro, a Congressional Representative from New York, as the Vice Presidential nominee on the ticket with Presidential nominee Walter Mondale. Despite Ferraro's historic role, Mondale lost, but the gender gap reappeared in the election of 1988. That gender difference rested on specific views of government, with women more likely to favor environmental protection, programs for the economically disadvantaged and governmental activism, inclinations that advantaged the Democratic Party in most national elections.[58] The political gender gap remains an issue of great interest for activists and scholars alike. As the number of women in politics increases, the questions about differences among women, between women and men, and between political parties become more nuanced. For example, political scientists have argued that female Republican candidates for Senate such as Kay Bailey Hutchinson of Texas received more votes from men than women, yet Republican women running for the House of Representatives win more female than male voters' ballots. Women on the Senate Appropriations Committee have reported a significant change in raising female health issues such as breast and ovarian cancer research.

Women in the 1980s also sought and won seats to Congress and state legislatures. Aided by organizations such as the WISH List, a political fund for prochoice Republican women candidates, and Emily's List, a fundraising support for Democratic candidates, more women entered local and state races. At the end of the 1980s, women legislators made up nearly 15 percent of state representatives, but by 2005, women held approximately 22 percent of state legislative offices nationwide. Women officials continue to be a significantly smaller proportion of state legislators in the South; South Carolina, for example, has elected few women to its state assembly, while Vermont and Washington each have the largest proportion of women representatives, over a third. Women of color and those of Latin or South American descent still face barriers, however; of all women state legislators, only 18 percent claim black or Latino heritage. Even on the national level, barriers persist. Japanese American Patsy Mink of Hawaii, the first woman of color to win a seat in Congress, entered in 1965. The first woman of Puerto Rican ancestry, Nydia Velazquez, won election to the House from New York in 1993.

In 1991, the nomination of Clarence Thomas to the Supreme Court by President George Herbert Walker Bush generated an unexpected controversy over gender. As Thomas' Senate confirmation hearing appeared to be drawing to a close, Anita Hill, a law professor and prior colleague, reported that Thomas had harassed her sexually when they worked together in the Education Department and the Equal Opportunity Employment Commission. Hill's graphic televised testimony to the Senate Judiciary Committee raised new concerns over Thomas's fitness for the bench, which Thomas answered angrily. When he received the Committee's support and won confirmation by the Senate, many women believed that Hill had been sacrificed for her willingness to speak publicly about harassment.

The 1992 elections became a backlash for women voters and represented a major shift for women in office. Twenty-four women were elected to the House for the first time, raising the number of women in the House to forty-seven. In the Senate, Diane Feinstein, Barbara Boxer, Patti Murray, and Carol Mosley Braun, the nation's first African American female Senator, won their elections. Jocelyn Burdick, specially appointed to fill the remainder of her husband's term, also served. They joined Kassebaum and Barbara Mikulski of Maryland, elected in 1987. It was, as some called it, the "Year of the Woman."

The election of 1992 brought a Democratic President, Bill Clinton, to the White House, and his two terms in office brought many issues of gender to the political forefront. The Family and Medical Leave Act of 1993, long supported by female activists, provided unpaid leave for workers for the birth of a child or the illness of a family member. Clinton also appointed Madeleine Albright as Secretary of State, Janet Reno as the first female Attorney General, and Ruth Bader Ginsburg to the Supreme Court, the most vigorous record of major appointments of any president to that point. Yet Clinton's proposals for health care, led by First Lady Hillary Clinton, fared poorly in a divided Congress, and in 1996, Clinton signed the Personal Responsibility and Work Opportunity Act, which ended guarantees of state assistance for women in poverty.

By 1998, Clinton's agenda disappeared beneath the public airing of his relationship with a White House intern, Monica Lewinsky. The President's previous sexual involvements, always an issue in his political life, resurfaced as he settled a sexual harassment lawsuit brought by Paula Jones out of court. His testimony under oath, however, contained false statements. While the nation followed the investigation of Congressionally appointed Special Prosecutor Kenneth Starr, Republicans holding the majority of the House of Representatives voted to impeach President Clinton. The Senate in 1999 acquitted the President, who retained significant popularity.

Unlike the Hill-Thomas hearings, which energized women to assert their perspectives in civic life, in the 2000 election cycle, conservatives found that the sexual scandals of the past few years worked to their advantage. Democratic candidate Albert Gore confronted a self-declared

Associate Justice Ruth Bader Ginsburg received confirmation to the U.S. Supreme Court in 1993, following a distinguished career as an advocate for women's rights. AP photo/Charles Tasnadi.

born-again Christian, George Walker Bush. Another Republican, Elizabeth Dole, received little support from voters in primaries. The wooden, wonkish Gore fared badly against a confident Bush, who combined cowboy boots, past ownership of a baseball team, and an adoring wife. The Christian Right mobilized to remind voters of the importance of abortion regulations, threats to family stability, and parental rights. The election of 2000, decided by the Supreme Court, brought Bush to the White House.

Bush also continued to appoint women to significant positions in his administration. Condoleezza Rice served first as National Security

Advisor, and in Bush's second term, as Secretary of State. Christine Todd Whitman of New Jersey briefly occupied the position as head of the Environmental Protection Agency, and Margaret Spelling became Secretary of Education. Bush's Democratic opposition created the most notable first for women in politics, however, when Nancy Pelosi of California became the first female Speaker of the House of Representatives, and third in line to the Presidency, in 2007.

The elections of 2008 brought other firsts, as Democratic Senators Barack Obama of Illinois and Hillary Rodham Clinton ran for the presidency. Through the 1990s, Hillary Clinton had remained a controversial figure, defended by some as a champion of women's rights and criticized as others as a politician following in her husband's footsteps. Following Bill Clinton's two terms in office, Hillary Clinton won election as a Senator from New York in 2000 and re-election in 2006. In 2008, Clinton became the first viable female candidate for the presidency in a hotly contested campaign against Obama. Republican presidential candidate John McCain surprised voters in the summer of 2008 by choosing Alaska's Governor Sarah Palin as his vice presidential running mate. Gender again shaped the debate over whether Palin received fair treatment from the media. Despite controversies, however, Clinton and Palin proved that women could compete for the nation's highest offices.

NOTES

1. Early histories of women's suffrage often characterized winning the Nineteenth Amendment as the logical culmination of previous efforts. An emphasis on the divisions within the suffrage movement has deepened this view. See William O'Neill, *Everyone Was Brave* (Chicago: Quadrangle Books, 1971); Aileen Kraditor, *The Ideas of the Woman Suffrage Movement, 1890–1920* (New York: Columbia University Press, 1965); Ellen Carrol DuBois, *Feminism and Suffrage: The Emergence of an Independent Women's Movement in America, 1848–1869* (Ithaca, NY: Cornell University Press, 1978).

2. DeAnne Blanton and Lauren M. Cook, *They Fought Like Demons: Women Soldiers in the American Civil War* (Baton Rouge: Louisiana State University Press, 2002).

3. Linda Kerber, *No Constitutional Right to Be Ladies: Women and the Obligations of Citizenship* (New York: Hill and Wang, 1998), 81–123.

4. Sandra F. VanBurkleo, *"Belonging to the World": Women's Rights and American Constitutional Culture* (New York: Oxford University Press, 2001), 153.

5. *Minor v. Happersett* 88 U.S. 162 (1875).

6. VanBurkleo, *"Belonging to the World,"* 189.

7. "Suffrage Appeals to Lawless and Hysterical Women," *New York Times,* March 30, 1913, SM8.

8. See Anne Koedt, Ellen Levine, and Anita Rapone, eds., *Radical Feminism* (New York: Quadrangle Books, 1973); Alice Echols, *Daring to be Bad: Radical Feminism in America, 1967–1975* (Minneapolis: University of Minnesota Press, 1989).

9. Jane Addams, "Woman's Conscience and Social Amelioration," The Social Application of Religion, The Merrick Lectures for 1907–1908 (Cincinnati, OH: Jennings

and Graham, 1908), 41–60, http://tigger.uic.edu/htbin/cgiwrap/bin/urbanexp/main.
cgi?file=new/show_doc_search.ptt&doc=341; also see Jane Addams, "Hull House
(Chicago)," in *Encyclopedia of Social Reform*, ed. William D. P. Bliss (New York: Funk &
Wagnalls Company, 1908): 587–590.

10. Martin J. Sklar, *The United States as a Developing Country: Studies in U.S. History in the Progressive Era and the 1920s* (New York: Cambridge University Press, 1992); Elizabeth Sanders, *Roots of Reform: Farmers, Workers, and the American State, 1877–1917* (Chicago: University of Chicago Press, 1999).

11. Richard Wightman Fox and T. J. Jackson Lears, *The Culture of Consumption: Critical Essays in American History, 1880–1980* (New York: Pantheon Books, 1983).

12. Linda Gordon, *Heroes of Their Own Lives: The Politics and History of Family Violence: Boston, 1880–1960* (Urbana: University of Illinois Press, 2002).

13. Noralee Frankel and Nancy S. Dye, *Gender, Class, Race, and Reform in the Progressive Era* (Lexington: University Press of Kentucky, 1995); Joanne L. Goodwin, *Gender and the Politics of Welfare Reform: Mothers' Pensions in Chicago, 1911–1929* (Chicago: University of Chicago Press, 1997); Julie Novkov, *Constituting Workers, Protecting Women: Gender, Law, and Labor in the Progressive Era and New Deal Years* (Ann Arbor: University of Michigan Press, 2001); Robyn Muncy, *Creating A Female Dominion in American Reform, 1890–1935* (New York: Oxford University Press, 1991).

14. Addams, "Hull House (Chicago)."

15. Mary McDowell, "Friendly Visiting," *Proceedings of the National Conference of Charities and Corrections* (1896): 257.

16. Linda Gordon, "Black and White Visions of Welfare: Women's Welfare Activism, 1890–1945," *Journal of American History* Vol. 78, No. 2 (1991): 559–590.

17. Seth Koven and Sonya Michel, "Womanly Duties: Maternalist Politics and the Origins of Welfare States in France, Germany, Great Britain, and the United States, 1880–1920," *American Historical Review* Vol. 95, No. 4 (1990):1076–1108.

18. Meredith Tax, *The Rising of the Women: Feminist Solidarity and Class Conflict, 1880–1917* (Urbana: University of Illinois Press, 2001), 121.

19. Tax, *The Rising of the Women*, 131.

20. See Michael J. Klarman, *From Jim Crow to Civil Rights: The Supreme Court and the Struggle for Racial Equality* (New York: Oxford University Press, 2006).

21. Gerda Lerner, ed., *Black Women in White America: A Documentary History* (New York: Vintage Books, 1972), 166.

22. Beverly W. Jones, "Mary Church Terrell and the National Association of Colored Women, 1896 to 1901," *Journal of Negro History* Vol. 67, No. 1 (1982): 22.

23. Jones, "Mary Church Terrell," 24.

24. Jones, "Mary Church Terrell," 26; Evelyn Brooks Higginbotham, "African-American Women's History and the Metalanguage of Race," *Signs* Vol. 17, No. 2 (1992): 251–274.

25. Higginbotham, "African-American Women's History"; Jones, "Mary Church Terrell," 28; Anne Firor Scott, "Most Invisible of All: Black Women's Voluntary Associations," *Journal of Southern History* Vol. 56, No. 1 (1990): 3–22.

26. Jones, "Mary Church Terrell."

27. Gordon, "Black and White Visions of Welfare."

28. Paula Baker, "The Domestication of Politics: Women and American Political Society, 1780–1920," *American Historical Review* Vol. 89, No. 3 (1984): 620–647.

29. Jane Addams, *Democracy and Social Ethics* (New York: Macmillan, 1902).

30. Nancy Cott, *The Grounding of Modern Feminism* (New Haven, CT: Yale University Press, 1987), 5.

31. Joanne L. Goodwin, *Gender and the Politics of Welfare Reform: Mothers' Pensions in Chicago, 1911–1929* (Chicago: University of Chicago Press, 1997); Theda Skocpol, "The Enactment of Mothers' Pensions: Civic Mobilization and Agenda Setting or Benefits of the Ballot?: Response," *American Political Science Review* Vol. 89, No. 3 (1995): 720–730; Theda Skocpol et al., "Women's Associations and the Enactment of Mother's Pensions in the United States," *American Political Science Review* Vol. 87, No. 3 (1993): 686–701.

32. Mari Jo Buhle, *Women and American Socialism, 1870–1920* (Urbana: University of Illinois Press, 1983), 289.

33. Linda Gordon, *The Moral Property of Women: A History of Birth Control Politics in America* (Urbana: University of Illinois Press, 2007).

34. Lois Scharf, *To Work and to Wed: Female Employment, Feminism, and the Great Depression* (Westport, CT: Greenwood Press, 1980); Scharf, *Decades of Discontent: The Women's Movement, 1920–1940* (Boston: Northeastern University Press, 1987), 5.

35. Cott, *The Grounding of Modern Feminism*, 127.

36. Lorraine Gates Schuyler, *The Weight of Their Votes: Southern Women and Political Leverage in the 1920s* (Chapel Hill: University of North Carolina Press, 2006); Stanley Lemons, *The Woman Citizen: Social Feminism in the 1920s* (Urbana: University of Illinois Press, 1973); Christine A. Lunardina, *From Equal Suffrage to Equal Rights: Alice Paul and the National Woman's Party, 1910–1928* (New York: New York University Press, 1986).

37. Anne Firor Scott, "After Suffrage: Southern Women in the Twenties," *Journal of Southern History* Vol. 30, No. 3 (August 1964): 298–318; Wendy Sarvasy, "Beyond the Difference versus Equality Policy Debate: Postsuffrage Feminism, Citizenship, and the Quest for a Feminist Welfare State," *Signs* Vol. 17, No. 2 (1992): 329–362.

38. See Michael McGerr, "Political Style and Women's Power, 1830–1930," *Journal of American History* Vol. 77, No. 3 (December 1990): 864–885.

39. Sarah Jane Deutsch, "From Ballots to Breadlines, 1920–1940," in Nancy F. Cott, *No Small Courage: A History of Women in the United States* (New York: Oxford University Press, 2000), 458.

40. Scharf, *To Work and to Wed*, 330.

41. Ibid., 117.

42. Nancy Fraser and Linda Gordon, "A Genealogy of Dependency: Tracing a Keyword of the U.S. Welfare State," *Signs* Vol. 19, No. 2 (1994): 314.

43. Deutsch, "From Ballots to Breadlines," 463; see also Diane-Michele Prindeville, "Feminist Nations? A Study of Native American Women in Southwestern Tribal Politics," *Political Research Quarterly* Vol. 57, No. 1 (2004): 101–112; L. Scott Gould, "The Consent Paradigm: Tribal Sovereignty at the Millennium," *Columbia Law Review* Vol. 96, No. 4 (1996): 809–902.

44. Allan Berube, *Coming Out under Fire: The History of Gay Men and Women in World War II* (New York: Simon and Schuster, 2000).

45. In September 2008, Martin Sobel, who was convicted for treason with Ethel and Julius Rosenberg, admitted that he had spied for the Soviet Union. Sobel stated that although Ethel Rosenberg knew of her husband's activities, she did not engage in espionage. Sam Roberts, "Figure in Rosenberg Case Admits Soviet Spying," *New York Times*, September 11, 2008.

46. Susan M. Hartmann, *From Margin to Mainstream: American Women and Politics Since 1960* (New York: Knopf, 1989), 156.

47. Martha Biondi, *To Stand and Fight: The Struggle for Civil Rights in Postwar New York City* (Cambridge, MA: Harvard University Press, 2003), 166; Robert Alan Goldberg, *Enemies Within: The Culture of Conspiracy in Modern America* (New Haven, CT: Yale University Press, 2001), 24–27.

48. Hartmann, *From Margin to Mainstream*, 157.

49. Kay Mills, *This Little Light of Mine: The Life of Fannie Lou Hamer* (Lexington: University Press of Kentucky, 2007): 120–132.

50. Cynthia Griggs Fleming, "'More than a Lady': Ruby Doris Smith Robinson and Black Women's Leadership in the Student Non-Violent Coordinating Committee," in Vickie Ruiz and Ellen DuBois, eds., *Unequal Sisters: A Multicultural Reader in U.S. Women's History* (New York: Routledge, 2000): 542–553.

51. Hartmann, *From Margin to Mainstream*, 56.

52. Rosalyn Baxandall, "Re-Visioning the Women's Liberation Movement's Narrative: Early Second Wave African American Feminists," *Feminist Studies* Vol. 27, No. 1 (2001): 226.

53. The 1964 Civil Rights Act provided the key to eliminating protectionist legislation, although the extension of equal treatment would require decades of legal action.

54. See off our backs, http://www.offourbacks.org/AboutUs.htm. See also Elaine Showalter, "Women's Time, Women's Space: Writing the History of Feminist Criticism," *Tulsa Studies in Women's Literature* Vol. 3, No. 1 (1984): 29–43; Patrice McDermott, "On Cultural Authority: Women's Studies, Feminist Politics, and the Popular Press," *Signs* Vol. 20, No. 3 (1995): 668–684; Robin Morgan, *Sisterhood Is Powerful: An Anthology of Writings from the Women's Liberation Movement* (New York: Feminist Press, 2000) and *Sisterhood Is Forever: The Women's Anthology for a New Millennium* (New York: Washington Square Press, 2003).

55. Caroline Bird, *The Spirit of Houston: The First Women's Conference* (Washington, DC: Government Printing Office, 1978); Catherine E. Rymph, *Republican Women: Feminism and Conservatism from Suffrage Through the Rise of the New Right* (Chapel Hill: University of North Carolina Press, 2006).

56. Rymph, *Republican Women*, 227.

57. Rebecca Klatch, *Women of the New Right* (Philadelphia: Temple University Press, 1987), 151.

58. See Pippa Norris, *Women, Media, and Politics* (New York: Oxford University Press, 1997); Lois Duke Whitaker, *Voting the Gender Gap* (Urbana: University of Illinois Press, 2008); Kathleen Hall Jamieson, *Everything You Think You Know about Politics—and Why You're Wrong* (New York: Basic Books, 2000), 83–87.

6

⸎

Women and Law

No issue illustrates the complexities of law for women in the twentieth century better than abortion. Most Americans know that the Supreme Court "legalized" abortion in 1973 in *Roe* v. *Wade*. Both the scope and the limitations of that decision provided for continued controversy and legislation over privacy, age of consent, and the timing of the termination of a pregnancy. Legislators and advocates on both sides of "prochoice" and "prolife" battled to refine, defend, or overturn *Roe* and related laws about pregnancy. The history of abortion was not simply one of political pressure and legal suits, however. From the beginning of the twentieth century, when most states outlawed abortion, police investigated women receiving abortions, officers arrested both practitioners performing abortions and putative fathers, and prosecutors chose whether or not to pursue indictments. Hospitals and physicians complied or ignored laws, creating informal barriers or support for women "in distress." Through people working in a number of different positions, the law operated formally and informally to shape the experiences of women.

Legal scholars and historians write about "the agency" of the state in discussing the variety of ways laws can play a role in shaping society or individual lives. Higher courts interpret law, but lower courts can be seen shaping law in an equally active fashion, dismissing suits, creating case law for subsequent appeal, and interpreting existing statutes. Legislatures make laws and respond to social trends, voters, and pressure groups. Police may enforce or ignore the law, act as defenders of rights or obstacles to civil liberties, at different junctures in our national history.

Neighbors frequently act to help enforce or avoid community standards and regulations, and so become part of the fabric of any community of laws and order. What is perceived as law, in other words, remains a complicated constellation of relationships, institutions, and actors.

Given the extraordinary changes in women's roles in the twentieth century in the United States in work, family life, educational opportunities, and other areas, similar advances might be expected in law. As most legal scholars note, however, gender remains a contentious subject in American jurisprudence. The impact of gender as a force that shapes economic opportunity, for example, may have consequences beyond the obvious realms of support or job discrimination. Bankruptcy and tax law also reveal patterns that suggest that attitudes about family and women's roles have played a part in both legislation and litigation. Immigration law holds different significance for women seeking asylum from countries that practice female circumcision and for those entering the United States without the required documentation. As Supreme Court Associate Justice Ruth Bader Ginsburg has suggested, women occupy many places in American society, and laws dealing with gender may not reflect the needs of some even while responding to the experiences of others.

The most potent questions at the beginning of the century revolved around women's citizenship and the impact of gender on law. Critical debates about citizenship existed in such forms as voting rights, marriage to foreigners, the birth of children overseas, and jury duties. By 1920, the Nineteenth Amendment granted the vote, although suffrage did not clearly lead to the right to hold elective office. Congress passed laws allowing women to retain citizenship after marrying foreigners in the 1930s, and in a somewhat perverse twist, later established nationality of children born overseas to unmarried parents through the mother's nationality.[1] Women and men continued to be viewed as different types of people with unequal rights and responsibilities. Men faced a draft for military service, while women confronted unique "protections," ranging from Michigan's ban on women's work as bartenders to stipulations in state laws that men administer estates when possible. Challenges to gender discrimination began to take legal and legislative forms by the late 1960s, as a new movement for Women's Rights, and a generation of able female attorneys, came of age.

The 1970s appears in retrospect as a significant turning point for women, as new laws and interpretations provided acknowledgement of individual rights. Legislation such as the Equal Rights Amendment, the Pregnancy Disability Act, and Title IX of the Education Acts of 1972 promised to give women new opportunities. Major court decisions, from *Reed* v. *Reed*, which removed gender as a disqualification for administering an estate, and *Frontiero* v. *Richardson*, in which female military personnel won benefits for male dependents, to *Craig* v. *Boren*, which struck down laws allowing women to drink beer at younger ages than their male counterparts, seemed to indicate that the Supreme Court was moving toward a new view of gender discrimination. Any law that mandated different treatment of men and women, the Court implied, would violate the equal protection clause of the Fourteenth Amendment unless the grounds for such a law could pass the scrutiny of the courts.[2] From the 1970s until today, the Court has debated whether there are reasonable social constraints that might limit the guarantee of equal treatment of citizens. Can Congress, for example, treat unmarried parents differently if they have children born in other countries? Can a state fund separate schools for boys and girls? By 2008, the Justices had yet to apply the same strict prohibitions on gender discrimination that earlier Courts declared in effect against racial discrimination. The difference between the "heightened scrutiny" used in cases of gender, sexuality, and disability and that of "strict scrutiny" required in racial discrimination remains a contentious division among judges and justices. Ginsburg noted in her dissent to the 1998 decision in *Miller* v. *Albright* that the Court demands "'exceedingly persuasive justification,' one that does 'not rely on overbroad generalizations about the different talents, capacities, or preferences of males and females,'" to support "differential treatment of men and women."[3] Despite this clear assertion, it remains possible under current interpretations of the Fourteenth Amendment to treat men and women differently. The controversy continues to divide those who believe that the law must recognize gender differences and those who seek to remove barriers or advantages based on gender.

PROTECTIVE LEGISLATION AND GENDER DIFFERENCES

Women challenged the limitations placed on their gender throughout the nineteenth century. Although many remained relatively content, or at least quiescent, in dealing with roles that cast women as dependent and submissive, a vocal minority championed equal rights for voting and access to professions. Admission to formal legal training and formal recognition for practicing "at the bar" eluded women until 1869, when Belle (or Arabella) Babb Mansfield passed the Iowa State bar. Prior to Mansfield's achievement, women had argued cases and served as county lawyers without seeking further sanction. Mansfield's brilliance led Iowa judges to accept her application to practice law, and within a year, Iowa opened admission to the bar to all women. Ironically, Mansfield did not work as an attorney, and instead became a professor of law and history, and later a college administrator.[4]

Charlotte E. Ray, the first African American female attorney in the United States, won admission to the District of Columbia bar in 1872. The first female graduate from Howard University Law School, Ray encountered obstacles in sustaining a practice. She eventually found employment by 1879 as a teacher in New York City and abandoned her legal career. Other women also attempted to enter legal practice during the 1870s and 1880s and faced barriers from courts or legislatures. Ada Kepley, the first woman to graduate from a law school, found that her 1870 degree from Union College of Law (later Northwestern Law School) did not convince Illinois judges of her qualifications to be an attorney. Emma Barkaloo of Missouri, the first woman to attend an American law school, received admission to try cases before the Supreme Court in that state in 1870. Sara Kilgore of Michigan completed law courses at the University of Michigan in 1871 and worked with her husband.[5] Other women, such as Clara Nash of Maine, Martha Angle Dorsett of Minnesota, and Florence Cronise and Nettie Cronise Lutes of Ohio, gained admission to their states' bars in the 1870s. In 1882, Mary Hall of Connecticut and Lelia Josephine Robinson of Massachusetts won the right to practice law in their New England states. In the Utah territory, Phoebe W. Cousins began her legal career in 1872.

Myra Bradwell of Illinois faced more reluctant judges in her pursuit of a legal career. Bradwell, married to a Cook County judge, passed the Illinois bar exam in 1869, a few months after Mansfield.[6] The Illinois Supreme Court refused to approve Bradwell's application, however, citing "the disability imposed by your married condition."[7] When Bradwell objected, her application for a writ of error went to the Supreme Court. In *Bradwell* v. *Illinois*, the Supreme Court denied Bradwell's contention that she had a protected right to practice law. The 1873 case provided Justice Joseph P. Bradley with the occasion to assert that women's proper roles made them unsuitable for legal work. He claimed instead "the paramount destiny and mission of woman are to fulfill the noble and benign offices of wife and mother. This is the law of the Creator."[8] Despite this stinging rebuke to women's efforts to become attorneys, Illinois in 1872 dropped restrictions against female attorneys, and Alta M. Hulett became Illinois's first woman lawyer. Bradwell finally received admission to the bar in 1890.

Belva Lockwood, rejected by three male-only law schools before being allowed to enter the National University Law School in the District of Columbia, won the right to argue before the Supreme Court in 1879. Although the Court initially rejected Lockwood's request in 1876, the determined counselor lobbied Congress intensively, and the 1879 "Act to Relieve Certain Legal Disabilities of Women" gave the Supreme Court a mandate to recognize female attorneys. In 1880, Lockwood argued *Kaiser* v. *Stickney* before the Court.

Similar efforts to practice law in Wisconsin, North Carolina, California, and Oregon led other women to the courts and legislatures. Lavina Goodell finally won her battle for the Wisconsin bar in 1879, a year before her death. Mary Leonard's efforts in Oregon resulted in admission for women to that state's bar in 1885. Through the final years of the nineteenth century, women throughout the nation gained entrance to the legal practice. Some required a special fortitude to continue the effort. Carrie Burnham Kilgore of Pennsylvania attempted to enter legal practice in 1874. After court obstacles, she finally applied to the University of Pennsylvania Law School, which admitted her in 1881. Once she received a law degree, however, Pennsylvania authorities barred her from general practice until 1886.

The professionalization of law through the creation of the American Bar Association in 1878, and the increasing importance of law schools in determining admission to the bar, created some new opportunities for women while limiting other options. The first female lawyers came from the few universities that admitted them, such as the University of Michigan and Washington University's School of Law. The expansion of urban law schools by the end of the nineteenth century meant that "hundreds of urban women" graduated with law degrees.[9] New York University accepted female students in 1892, and two new law schools appeared to serve aspiring women lawyers, the Washington College of Law and the Portia Law School. The nation's most prestigious law schools at Harvard, Yale, Columbia, and Georgetown University continued to deny women admission, however.[10] The number of female attorneys remained small in the early years of the century; by 1920, only 3 percent of attorneys nationwide were women.[11]

Many of the women who pushed for the right to study and practice law supported the growing suffrage movement and temperance reform. Ada Kepley ran a temperance newspaper in Illinois, The Friend of the Home; Ada Bittenbinder of Nebraska became the supervisor of legal affairs for the Women's Christian Temperance Movement. Kansas attorney Mary Ellen Lease earned the nickname "Yellin' Mary Ellen" for her work for the populist People's Party in the 1890s.

The nation's first female police officers and sheriffs also appeared around the turn of the century. Chicago hired Marie Owens in 1893 but refused to allow her to wear the police uniform. Like most early female police, Owen's work focused on domestic issues, welfare concerns, and child protection. Alice Stebbins Wells, the first woman officer in the Los Angeles Police Department, petitioned the mayor and City Council for her appointment. After being sworn as an officer in 1910, Wells secured a patrol call box, a badge, and the right to make arrests. Three other women joined the department by 1912, and Wells continued to advocate female positions in national policing. The International Policewomen's

Association (later the International Association of Women Police) resulted from her efforts in 1915. By 1918, the University of California offered its first course to women in law enforcement. In many cities, however, women's entry into policing remained limited. New York City allowed women to serve as prison matrons, but restricted women's duties until 1973. Even in the face of such obstacles, New York women did advance into detective work; Police Matron Isabella Goodwin became a First Grade Detective in 1912. In the same year, Margaret Queen Adams earned an appointment as the first female deputy sheriff in the Los Angeles Sheriff's Department. Slowly, women secured the rights to wear police uniforms, to work outside of juvenile or protective services, and to carry weapons and make arrests.

During the early years of the century, many women reformers believed that knowledge of the law provided an important tool to eliminating barriers and winning access to public accommodations. As several historians note, these female activists shared an assumption that their natural rights, asserted anew by the Fourteenth Amendment to the Constitution, should secure an equal place with men.[12] Ironically, the major legal initiative to emerge beside suffrage in the early years of the twentieth century, championed by a generation of female reformers, promised to restrict women's vulnerability through equal treatment.

"Protective legislation" utilized ideas of women's special capacities as mothers and notions of superior male strength to reduce the hours and regulate the conditions of women's paid labor. Wisconsin implemented the first law of this kind in 1867 by mandating an eight-hour workday for women, although the state allowed workers to exceed the limit and offered little enforcement. Massachusetts passed a stricter set of restrictions in 1874, establishing ten-hour days for female laborers, with a maximum of fifty-eight hours of paid work during a week. The Massachusetts provision became the model for other states seeking to erect protections for female laborers. By 1896, nineteen states enacted some type of legislation limiting women's hours of work. Historian Judith Baer contended that supporters of protective legislation cited women's physical differences, women's roles as mothers, the poor conditions in many workplaces, and the absence of unionization as reasons for special laws.[13]

Protective legislation forced advocates and opponents to engage a variety of legal questions, from the rights of individuals to contract their labor to the meaning of equal protection under the Fourteenth Amendment. Laws limiting women's work presumed a set of relationships among women and families, workers and the state, and employers and those who labored for them. The Supreme Court emphasized the free rights of contract in what some historians term the "Lochner era," after the pivotal decision in *Lochner* v. *New York*. In that 1905 case, the Court held that the due process protections of the Fourteenth Amendment ensured individual workers the ability to negotiate separately with employers over work hours. The decision toughened employers' resistance to state efforts to regulate working conditions and hours. In 1908, the Justices found an exception in *Muller* v. *Oregon*, which upheld Oregon's restrictions on women's work hours. The Court declared, "the physical well-being of woman becomes an object of public interest and care in order to preserve the strength and vigor of the race." Restrictive protections served to insure women's ability to be or become mothers, the Court concluded unanimously. Simply, the Court determined that states could limit women's work because of their "natural" reproductive roles. In 1917, the Court reached a similar finding in *Bunting* v. *Oregon*, ruling on a ten-hour working day.

The *Muller* decision did not ensure the constitutionality of other protective laws, however. Efforts to assure minimum wages for female workers provoked particular dissension from employers. Between 1912 and 1915, twelve states enacted provisions for women's pay, invariably basing the minimum on the assumption that few if any women supported dependents. Organized labor, both through unions and the increasingly powerful American Federation of Labor, argued vehemently against legally mandated wages for men on the basis that collective bargaining would secure higher pay. Minimum wages, they contended, could quickly become the maximum employers would offer. In 1923, the Supreme Court struck down a District of Columbia minimum wage provision in *Adkins* v. *Children's Hospital*, ruling that such laws infringed upon freedom of contract. The regulation of hours, the Court determined, differed from a negotiation for wages because pay did not reflect a public interest in protecting specific workers. The Court continued to use the *Lochner* standard of due process protections to strike down attempts to win minimum wage laws until the New Deal, while upholding restrictions on hours.[14]

Protective legislation stirred strong dissention between women's organizations in the 1920s, as the National Women's Party led by Alice Paul challenged the idea that law should accommodate gender differences. Paul proposed an amendment to the Constitution that would assert equal rights for men and women, and she and her followers argued that laws sustaining gender differences harmed women. Many female reformers active in Progressive era causes from women's suffrage to social settlements disagreed vehemently and contended that protective legislation provided the only safeguards available to working women. Throughout the decade, women's organizations battled over the benefits and disadvantages of protective legislation. The disputes served to limit feminist politics during this period and meant hard choices for reformers during the 1930s. In the wake of the Great Depression, female activists still debated the merits of labor laws that applied equally to men and women.

Julia Lathrop, Jane Addams, and Mary McDowell worked to extend the ideas of settlement house work and women's suffrage. In 1913 they lobbied Congress for a federal suffrage amendment. Courtesy of the Library of Congress.

Ultimately, most backed the Wagner Act in 1935 and the creation of a National Labor Relations Board. In 1937, the Supreme Court's decision in *West Coast Hotel* v. *Parrish* finally overturned the barriers of Lochner, as the Court asserted the constitutionality of legal pay minimums. The next year, despite persistent discussion, women reformers supported the passage of the Fair Labor Standards Act, which required minimum wages for men and women.

As historians note, however, the Fair Labor Standards Act did not eliminate protective legislation or provide relief to the majority of female workers. Written to cover only certain categories of work, the law applied to only 20 percent of the nation's fifty-five million workers.[15] Of those, less than 14 percent of female laborers worked in occupations included in its provisions. Some women's organizations, such as the National Consumers' League, still fought vigorously for protective legislation. Up to the 1960s and passage of the Civil Rights Act of 1964, adherents of special protection for women's work remained adamant about the need for separate laws covering female workers.

Law in the late nineteenth and early twentieth century offered equally ambiguous solutions to women's property rights, citizenship, and child custody. Legal scholar James Schouler examined the laws for family matters, or domestic relations, in 1870 and concluded that "confusion and uncertainty" prevailed.[16] Some states limited the constraints of *coverture*, the common law assumption that a husband administered his wife's property as family head. The Married Women's Property acts which granted married women the rights to own property in their own names, to sue or be sued, and to administer estates, eventually erased centuries of legal restrictions, although such changes did little to change patterns of family earning or male control.[17]

A similar problem of ambiguity confronted American women who married foreigners. In the late nineteenth century, courts held that American brides lost their citizenship when they married men from other countries. A well-connected few, such as President Ulysses S. Grant's daughter, managed to have their citizenship restored by Congress. In 1907, the Expatriation Act closed even that door, asserting that a woman's citizenship conformed to her husband's. The Alien Property Custody Act, enacted in 1917, allowed the government to seize the holdings of Germans and other "enemies" during wartime, a law that equally penalized American wives of certain foreigners. The Cable Act of 1922 attempted to end such discrimination by allowing women to retain United States citizenship after marriage to men eligible for American naturalization. The provisions excluded Japanese and Chinese applicants, although in 1931, American women married to Japanese men received the right to retain their citizenship. Most restrictions against Asians persisted after World War II. For example, the War Brides Act of World War II banned applications from women from the "Asian Barred Zone." The Soldier Brides Act of 1947 amended the law to allow Japanese wives of American servicemen to enter the country.[18]

A similar resistance to granting women unimpeded rights appeared in laws conferring citizenship on children. Throughout the twentieth century, statutes granting American citizenship to children born abroad to American parents, or to children born in the United States to foreign-born parents, established different criteria for mothers and fathers. American mothers could not claim citizenship for their children born overseas at all until 1934; by 1989, federal courts finally allowed such offspring to become citizens. Unmarried parents continue to face different tests for conveying American citizenship, however, with fathers required to establish paternity and residency. Mothers of children born out of wedlock outside the United States do not share that burden, as the Supreme Court held in *Tuan Anh Nguyen* v. *INS* in 2001.

Immigration statutes and practices throughout the twentieth century have favored particular forms of family relationships and created obstacles for those who did not fit a preferred ideal. At the century's beginning, immigration officers at Ellis Island exercised a unique policing authority when foreigners entered and could label individuals guilty of "moral turpitude" or assess mental status. Female arrivals could not leave Ellis Island without a male relative or guardian, due to the perception that unaccompanied women would become dependent or victims—or purveyors—of vice. A 1932 study of immigration practices concluded that inspectors used "mental pigeonholes" to characterize arrivals by desirable or undesirable characteristics. A similar 1988 study documented the significance of stereotypes in assessing immigrants. The author found one inspector willing to speak openly about how he perceived the women of some nationalities had a propensity to lie, others to alter documents, and still others to smuggle food.[19] These extra-legal procedures shape women's experiences of law and order in ways that historically have differed from those of men. Perhaps the most compelling difference remains the battle to win asylum by women and girls who refuse to undergo genital mutilation, a traditional practice among some cultures. Despite continued advocacy in the United States by a variety of organizations, women who have received or fear genital mutilation are not routinely granted the right to stay. In 1994, Toganese citizen Fauziya Kasinga requested protection and asylum and was held in detention for two years pending the successful resolution of her petition. Yet as late as 2007, the Immigration Appeals Board of the Department of Justice ordered a Malian woman to return to her country, disregarding claims that she would be forced into an unwanted traditional marriage. INS officials continue to insist that because female genital mutilation occurs only once, women cannot reasonably fear repeated violence, a position that has been challenged by the Second Circuit U.S. Court of Appeals.[20]

Throughout most of the century, women repeatedly discovered that gender differences played a substantial part in other laws as well. Winning the vote in 1920, for example, did not extend the franchise to all American women. Native American women ultimately received the ballot in 1924, and Puerto Rican women in 1929. Full universal suffrage arrived for Puerto Rican women in 1952, after a literacy requirement was eliminated. Jury service, which some believed might follow quickly after the vote, also required additional effort. In 1879, the Supreme Court upheld the exclusion of women from juries; *Strauder* v. *West Virginia* determined in part that a state "may confine the selection to males."[21] Other courts also repeated the belief that prohibiting women from jury service spared female citizens from a duty that might offend their morality or delicate sensitivities. A few states allowed women to serve on juries; Utah, Washington, Kansas, Michigan, New Jersey, and California mandated the obligation soon after female residents gained the vote. Oregon went a step further, and required at least one female juror in cases involving children. In Illinois, New York, and Massachusetts, lengthy legislative battles preceded legislation allowing women to be impaneled.

During the war years, the issue of excluding women became a central part of cases of Donald and Edna Ballard, a son and mother accused of mail fraud. The Ballards insisted that an all-male jury deprived Edna of a fair hearing. The Supreme Court overturned the Ballard's conviction, with Justice William O. Douglas asserting in his decision that "the sexes are not fungible." Douglas wrote that "a flavor, a distinct quality, is lost if either sex is excluded."[22] When Gwendolyn Hoyt stood trial for the murder of her husband in Florida in 1957, however, the potential jury pool consisted of 3,000 men and only 35 women. An all-male jury convicted Hoyt, and her attorneys appealed. The Supreme Court upheld her conviction in 1961, refusing the notion that gender might create special categories of legal consideration. If some women were able to volunteer for jury duty, the majority concluded, their absence from any particular jury was not evidence of discrimination. In this case, the Court avoided the opportunity to recognize the unique obstacles posed by gender in the law, even as the Justices were applying that type of construction to race.[23]

The final remedy to the inequities of *Hoyt* arrived after the Civil Rights Act of 1964 enforced equal protection within the law. In *Reed v. Reed*, American Civil Liberties Union attorney Ruth Bader Ginsburg convinced the Court that Idaho laws that preferred men as administrators of estates violated the Constitution's prohibition against discrimination. That opening allowed for other protections from gender discrimination, and in 1975, the Court agreed with Billy Taylor's claim that the absence of women on the jury of his kidnapping trial was unfair. *Taylor v. Louisiana* overturned Hoyt, and finally clarified the right of women to perform jury duties.

Federal and state tax policies followed a similar trajectory. Throughout the nineteenth century, activist women protested "taxation without representation," citing the unfairness of taxing citizens for property or schools without granting the vote. The adoption of federal income taxes in 1913 created new problems. Before 1948, couples in community property states (California, Louisiana, and New Mexico) were able to divide their income in order to pay lower taxes. In other states, marriage still meant two individual returns and a higher tax rate for the family income. The Congressional decision in 1948 to offer a joint return for married couples offered some relief, yet this support for marriage continued the disadvantages of single mothers and other heads of household. A revision in 1969 aimed to end what some had termed a "marriage penalty," yet single parents received little assistance from tax codes that reinforced a family ideal.[24]

During these years, women gained increasing access to the legal profession. Florence Allen became the first woman to be a state Supreme Court justice, earning a place on the Ohio bench in 1922. By 1928, Genevieve Rose Cline received an appointment to the U.S. Customs Court as the first female federal judge. Franklin D. Roosevelt appointed Allen to the Sixth Circuit Court of Appeals in 1934, making her the first woman on a federal appellate court. Burnita Shelton Matthews became the first district court judge in 1949. Elite law schools slowly admitted women. Yale inadvertently failed to specifically bar women applicants, and in 1886, Alice Rufie Jordan received recognition for completing all required courses. Yale moved promptly after the "Jordan incident" to reserve admissions for males only until 1918. In 1929, Margaret Spahr became the first female graduate of Columbia Law School; Harvard finally accepted women in 1950. African American women faced equally daunting challenges in getting a legal education. As late as 1940, fewer than sixty African American women practiced law in the United States.

For those women determined enough to become attorneys, barriers remained. Ruth Bader Ginsburg transferred from Harvard Law to Columbia after her marriage and worked on the law reviews of both. Even though Ginsburg graduated at the top of her law class, she received no offers from law firms. Sandra Day O'Connor recalled a similar experience after her graduation from Stanford Law School. Despite finishing in two years, working on the law review, receiving the honor of the Order of the Coif, and graduating third in her class, O'Connor resorted to working as a governmental attorney when she failed to receive any invitations to join a legal firm. A 1957 study of New York City law firms discovered that of 1,755 women attorneys listed in legal directories, only eighteen worked for large firms.[25]

The most substantial changes for women in law, as practitioners and as citizens, emerged as part of the Women's Rights movement in the 1960s and 1970s. The first course on women and law offered at a law school appeared at New York University's School of Law in 1969. In 1971, women activists created the Women's Legal Defense Fund to litigate and monitor laws on women's issues. In the next year, the Women's Rights Project of the Center for Law and Social Policy was formed, which became the National Women's Law Center in 1981. The appointment of a woman to the Supreme Court remained the most remarkable achievement, however. In 1981, President Ronald Reagan nominated O'Connor, by then a judge on the Arizona Court of Appeals, to the bench. Ginsburg became the second female Justice in 1993. As notable, in the same year, Congress confirmed the first female Attorney General of the United States, Janet Reno. By 1995, even the most august bodies of American law seemed transformed, when the American Bar Association named its first female president, Roberta Cooper Ramo.

Other legal developments prior to 1964 reinforced gender differences in the law. In the 1948 case of *Goesaert* v. *Cleary*, the Supreme Court

Women Strike for Peace picketed the United Nations in 1962 during the Cuban Missile Crisis. AP photo.

upheld a Michigan law limiting bartending jobs to men, unless a woman was "the wife or daughter of the male owner." The Court in 1927's *Buck* v. *Bell* allowed thirty states to retain laws similar to a Virginia statute, which lead to eighteen-year-old Carrie Buck's forced sterilization. By 1942, the Justices limited the ability of states to sterilize prisoners or individuals convicted of "habitual" crimes of moral turpitude in *Skinner* v. *Oklahoma*. The decision did not overturn the earlier Buck decision, however; by the 1970s, forced sterilization gradually ended as a matter of practice.[26]

The Court ruled on other aspects of sexuality, slowly setting the stage for major discussions about privacy and reproduction. Margaret Sanger challenged the so-called "Comstock law" bans on birth control information in 1918, and as a result the New York Court of Appeals determined that physicians could dispense contraceptive material. Not until the colorfully named *United States* v. *One Package of Japanese Pessaries* in 1936 would the Supreme Court invalidate laws banning the importation of contraception for medical use. By the 1960s, in *Griswold* v. *Connecticut*, the Court under Chief Justice Earl Warren overturned a Connecticut law that prohibited doctors from prescribing contraception or giving contraceptive information. The decision, written by Justice William O. Douglas, found broad protections for privacy in the First, Fourth, and Fifth Amendments of the Constitution. The marital relationship should not be subjected to an invasion of "protected freedoms," Douglas wrote. This decision became a somewhat unexpected key to the controversies that followed.[27]

In 1971, Justice William Brennan wrote the decision in *Eisenstadt* v. *Baird*, which extended the protection for contraceptive use to single individuals. In summing up the case, Brennan indicated that "the decision whether to bear or beget a child" remained a private and individual matter. In 1973, the Court responded to increasing pressure to consider the issue of abortion; by that time, over fifty organizations, religious associations, and medical groups publicly supported more liberal abortion statutes.

In the decision of *Roe* v. *Wade*, and the accompanying case of *Doe* v. *Bolton*, the Court struck down all states laws prohibiting women's access to medically safe abortion services. Justice Harry Blackmun wrote for the majority that state laws prohibiting medical abortion services "without regard to the stage of her pregnancy and other interests involved violate the Due Process Clause of the Fourteenth Amendment, which protects against state action the right to privacy, including a woman's qualified right to terminate her pregnancy." Blackmun tempered the decision, however, stating that "though the State cannot override that right, it has legitimate interests in protecting both the pregnant woman's health and the potentiality of human life, each of which interests grows and reaches a "compelling" point at various stages of the woman's approach to term."[28] Blackmun constructed the protection of a woman's privacy in terminating a pregnancy, and the state's interest in regulating access to abortion, on the basis of a three-trimester model. In the first trimester, a woman's right to determine whether to end a pregnancy "must be left to the medical judgment of the pregnant woman's attending physician," the Roe decision held. The second trimester might be subject to regulation related to maternal health. Blackmun reached this position in a compromise with Justices Thurgood Marshall and William Brennan, who worried during discussions about the practicality of a twelve-week limit on poor women. Blackmun left the third trimester, the seventh, eight, and ninth months of pregnancy, to greater state intervention. The decision provided some guidelines, mandating that "the State, in promoting its interest in the potentiality of human life, may, if it chooses, regulate, and even proscribe, abortion except where necessary, in appropriate medical judgment, for the preservation of the life or health of the mother."[29]

Roe ignited a firestorm of protest and a continuing legal assault on its protections. It has been suggested that the decision sparked over thirty years of debate in law and policy. Opponents began to push for state restrictions and test the limits of *Roe*. In 1976, following Missouri's efforts to restrict abortion, the Court ruled that mandating spousal consent and broad parental approval rights violated *Roe*. The Court continued to refine available reproductive rights, however; in 1977, for example, the Court upheld refusals by Pennsylvania and Connecticut to allow Medicaid funding for abortions. The Justices also ruled that public hospitals did not have to perform nontherapeutic abortions.[30] Reproductive rights became increasingly politicized in the wake of such decisions. By 1980, the Republican Party included a plank in its party platform supporting the end to Roe, either through a transformed and prolife Supreme Court that would ideally overturn the decision, or a Constitutional amendment to abolish abortion.

The addition of the first female justice to the Court did not have a dramatic impact on reproductive health cases. In 1983's *City of Akron* v. *Akron Reproductive Health*, the Court determined that a twenty-four-hour waiting period for abortion services created an "unduly burdensome" barrier. Further efforts to constrain abortion services in Pennsylvania included "printed materials to include a statement that there are agencies willing to help the mother carry her child to term and to assist her after the child is born and a description of the probable anatomical and physiological characteristics of an unborn child at 'two-week gestational increments'." In *Thornburgh* v. *American College of Obstetricians and Gynecologists*, the Court decided that the provisions of the law interfered with the private decisions between a woman and her physician. Yet in 1989, the Court returned to the issue of state limits in *Webster* v. *Reproductive Health Services*. Moving toward a two-phased construction of pregnancy into periods of before and after fetal viability, the Justices ignored a preamble to the Missouri law that stated that life begins at conception. That premise did not influence or affect the statutory provisions or limits, the Justices held. They allowed the restrictions imposed by Missouri, which blocked the use of state monies or employees in abortion services. The direction of the Court continued in 1992, in *Planned Parenthood* v. *Casey*. This decision fully articulated the concept of viability as a critical marker in policy, and allowed for a twenty-four-hour waiting period and parental notification. At the same time, however, a new five Justice majority emerged as Justice David Souter joined O'Connor, Anthony Kennedy, John Paul Stevens, and Blackmun. The Justices used the decision to state that they did not foresee overturning the essential privacy provisions of *Roe*, and urged, "the contending sides of a national controversy ... end their national division by accepting a common mandate rooted in the Constitution." Yet a new challenge to *Roe* emerged in 2000, when a Nebraska law prohibiting abortion in the third trimester came before the Court in *Stenberg* v. *Carhart*. The Court found that Nebraska's law placed obstacles on the ability of physicians to perform procedures and overturned the statute. A second attempt to restrict late abortions arrived at the Court in 2007 as *Gonzales* v.

Carhart. In this case, a majority of Justices upheld a federal law limiting third trimester abortions. In her dissent, Justice Ginsburg argued that the right to terminate a pregnancy constituted an issue of equal citizenship for women.[31]

The *Roe* case, and its opponents' determination to overturn it, shaped state and national politics throughout the final years of the twentieth century. Nationally, the Republican Party consistently placed the elimination of legal abortion in its platforms, and support for a prolife position appeared to be a key consideration for Republican candidates. At the same time, however, prochoice Republican leaders such as Hawaii's Governor Linda Lingle, New Jersey's Governor Christie Whitman, and Connecticut's Governor Jodi Rehl, and Senators Olympia Snowe and Susan Collins, maintained a visible alternative for voters. The question of abortion rights came to the fore in the 2008 vice presidential nomination of Alaska's Governor Sarah Palin by the Republican Party. Palin's ascension to the ticket, despite her recent election to a governorship, stemmed from the recognition by party advisors that other candidates with prochoice records would not fit the party ticket or the agenda of most delegates. By contrast, the Democratic party found that prochoice voters allied themselves more readily with the Democratic ticket of Barack Obama and Joseph Biden.

While the access to abortion services continued to generate dissension, other changes in laws governing sexuality and reproduction offered greater freedoms and protection, reflecting shifting social ideas. In 1967, the Court's decision in *Loving* v. *Virginia* ended state laws that barred marriage between individuals of different races. At the same time, women's organizations pushed for new laws and procedures in rape prosecutions. Massachusetts moved in 1968 to eliminate the need for women to provide evidence of their resistance to an attack; increasingly, states also began to incorporate rape shield laws, which put a woman's sexual history out of bounds in prosecution. By the late 1970s, states also allowed prosecutions against marital partners for rape. In the same period, women's organizations began to open rape crisis centers. Such concerted actions had a significant impact on the public perceptions of rape and women's abilities to find redress after an assault. In 1984, the Victims of Crimes Act allowed for federal funding for sexual assault hotlines. Women's efforts on behalf of women in violent relationships also lead to new supports; in 1974, the first shelter for battered women opened in St. Paul, Minnesota. Domestic violence programs received federal support in the 1984 Crimes Act. The Sexual Abuse Act of 1986 brought federal law into line with many of the changes which had taken place in revised state laws. By 1994, the Violence Against Women Act, repeatedly brought to Congress by Delaware Senator Joseph Biden, established new guidelines for the federal prosecution of rape, and funding for programs to aid victims of rape or domestic violence.[32]

The path to equality at work began legally with the Equal Pay Act of 1963, which mandated equal wages for men and women doing the same jobs. As many scholars noted, however, segregation by gender in the labor force historically has meant that the majority of jobs is done primarily by pools of male or female workers. As a result, equal pay demands involve a relatively small minority of workers. As the Women's Movement grew, advocates of economic equality began to draw attention to other issues of pay equity, such as comparable wages for jobs with equivalent challenges and requirements. The 1964 Civil Rights Act provided an important legal foundation for job protection; Title VII in the act prohibited discrimination on the basis of sex in hiring, promotion, and work conditions. Protective legislation, the favored strategy of earlier female activists for sustaining rights for working women, became obsolete. The act also created the Equal Employment Opportunity Commission (EEOC), with the mandate to ensure the effective administration of the new law.

The early EEOC lacked enforcement or litigation powers, but its staff turned immediately to accepting complaints and investigating work conditions. In 1966, the EEOC started requiring companies with more than one hundred workers to file employment (EEOC-1) reports. Using this information, the Commission held public hearings to document patterns of discrimination. A number of job practices that had traditionally separated work into male or female spheres fell under EEOC scrutiny. By 1966, newspapers no longer continued the practice of running job ads as "help wanted male" or "help wanted female." By 1968, the EEOC worked to eliminate state protective laws that had provided special provisions for women workers.

The case of *Phillips* v. *Martin Marietta Corporation* in 1971 sustained the ruling that companies could not refuse to hire women with school-aged children. The Court also made clear that exceptions to the Civil Rights Act—bona fide occupation qualifications—must be narrowly construed. "BFOQ" considerations continued to be a major element in framing gender differences in hiring and employment. In *Weeks* v. *Southern Bell*, the Fifth Circuit Court ruled that women could not be barred from jobs by physical requirements for lifting heavy objects.[33]

By 1972, Title IX of the Education Act erected protections against gender discrimination in education (including school athletics), and Congress provided the EEOC with enforcement and litigation authority. In addition, the equal protection against job discrimination was legislatively extended to governmental employees. *Frontiero* v. *Richardson* confronted the Court with a clear issue of sexual discrimination. Sharon Frontiero, as a lieutenant in the Air Force, had applied for dependent benefits for her husband Joseph. Although female dependents routinely received housing and medical service, the Air Force insisted that the Frontieros prove that Joseph received at least half of his support from his wife. Arguments

Fannie Lou Hamer worked to organize the Mississippi Freedom Summer for the Student Nonviolent Coordinating Committee and fought in 1964 for recognition of civil rights workers within the Democratic Party. Courtesy of the Library of Congress.

against the discrimination were presented to the Court by the Southern Poverty Law Center and attorney Joseph Levin, who was joined in an amicus curiae role by American Civil Liberties Union lawyer Ruth Bader Ginsburg. The decision, written by Justice William Brennan, constructed a new standard for appellants; following the decision in *Reed* v. *Reed,* the Court said that "we can only conclude that classifications based upon sex, like classifications based upon race, alienage, or national origin, are inherently suspect, and must therefore be subjected to strict judicial scrutiny."[34] The Court did not follow Brennan's recommendation, however. In *Craig* v. *Boren,* the Justices instead established criteria of "intermediate scrutiny," allowing for some instances of gender difference.

The case of *McDonnell Douglas* v. *Green* in 1973 created additional qualifications for proving sexual discrimination. In this decision, the Court laid out the steps for proving or disproving a charge of bias. In making a complaint, an individual had to prove membership in a "protected group" under Title VII, and that an application had been made for employment. The individual also had to prove qualifications for the position, and demonstrate that the employer rejected a legitimate application and accepted ones from other people. At the next stage, the plaintiff had to establish proof of discrimination. The employer, as defendant, might respond by showing how the circumstances in question were not caused by bias, but resulted from legitimate expectations. Finally, a plaintiff had to demonstrate either that the explanation by the employer was insufficient, in error, or otherwise at fault. These procedures established greater legal hurdles for women to prove employer bias.[35]

It has been contended that the Court's use of the same standards it applied in case of racial discrimination represented a significant legal turning point. By assuming the equivalency of race and gender, the Court presumed that sex discrimination arose "out of traditional, old-fashioned or outmoded habits of thinking."[36] This construction did not provide for the possibility that sexual discrimination could occur in ways that did not affect all women. In the cases following the Craig decision, the Court did reach equally controversial conclusions. In *Gedulig* v. *Aiello*, the Justices determined that a California insurance program that did not cover pregnancy did not discriminate against women, as pregnancy itself was not a sex-based classification. This and another pregnancy-related case, *General Electric* v. *Gilbert*, led Congress to pass the Pregnancy Disability Act of 1978, mandating legal protection for pregnant women at work and with insurance programs.[37]

Overall, the early 1970s nonetheless marked a period of sustained legal efforts to create greater gender equity. Congress moved to eliminate sexual discrimination in access to credit in 1974. The equal application of public benefits in *Weinberger* v. *Weisenfeld* in 1975 ensured that widowers might be entitled to a wife's Social Security survivor benefits. Two years later, *Califano* v. *Goldfarb* voided gender distinctions in Social Security Income (SSI) benefits. The EEOC centered its investigations in this period on four large corporations, filing "commissioner charges" against General Electric, General Motors, Ford Motor Company, and Sears Roebuck. The Commission reached settlements with a number of companies for discriminatory practices; General Electric paid $29.8 million in back pay to its employees in 1978. Steel companies and steelworker unions agreed to a $31 million settlement for female employees, while the Duquesne Lighting Company offered $1.7 million for its workers. Other settlements with Ford Motor Company, General Motors, Westinghouse

Electric, and Minnesota Mining allowed for improvements in work practices and compensation for past discrimination. In its case against Sears
Roebuck, however, the EEOC did not prevail. Instead, after nearly ten
years of litigation, the Seventh Circuit Court of Appeals ruled that the
EEOC could not prove that Sears intentionally hired men for commission
sales of large appliances. The case generated significant discussion among
historians, as two leading scholars testified on both sides of the case. Rosalind Rosenberg offered historical evidence for Sears that suggested
women did not apply for the types of jobs under scrutiny. Alice Kessler-
Harris offered a substantially different interpretation for the EEOC, as she
cited patterns of more subtle discrimination. Ironically, perhaps, the Seventh Circuit Court of Appeals later found that the EEOC proved a case
against Sears for failing to accommodate a worker's disability.[38]

The issue of sexual harassment emerged as a new focus of legal activity
in the 1980s. The EEOC generated guidelines for defining harassment in
1980, specifying that both a "quid pro quo," or work in exchange for sexual favors, and the presence of a hostile work environment, constituted
distinct forms of harassment. The Supreme Court upheld these rules in
Meritor Savings Bank v. *Vinson* in 1986. Subsequent decisions established
that supervisors were legally responsible for the harassing behavior of
employees, and the ability of plaintiffs to sue for damages. Two later cases
provided an extension of protection to gays and lesbians and allowed for
workers to file a class action suit against an employer for failing to redress
complaints of a hostile environment.[39]

Through the decade, the Supreme Court addressed the parameters of
gender rights in a series of decisions with mixed results for women. In
Wengler v. *Druggists Mutual Insurance Company*, the Justices declared
that gender discrimination must be "justified" by "important governmental objectives"; in this case, a widower was entitled to his wife's death benefits. A similar ruling for a male plaintiff in *Mississippi University for
Women* v. *Hogan* found the state-supported university could not reject
male applicants. The *County of Washington* v. *Gunther* in 1981 established the idea of "pay equity," when the Court determined that plaintiffs
could make an argument on the basis of comparable rather than identical
jobs. In 1984, the Court determined that the U.S. Jaycees could not refuse
female members due to the public nature of the organization. (In 2000,
however, the Court determined that the Boy Scouts of America could use
their rights of freedom of association to bar the membership of gay men.)
In *Rostker* v. *Goldberg*, the Justices rejected arguments that the military
draft should apply to women as well as men, refusing an invitation to
overturn the Congressional mandate for an all-male conscription.[40]

Two major decisions in the 1990s extended gender protections. In *International Union, UAW* v. *Johnson Controls*, the Court found that a company

that limited work to women without the ability to bear children violated their rights. As significant, the Justices raised the issue of protection for male workers. By 1996, the Justices ruled that the state-supported Virginia Military Institute had to admit female students. The Court also allowed students to bring sexual harassment cases against school districts that did not respond to complaints in *Davis* v. *Monroe County Board of Education*.[41]

These decisions came in the wake of the contested 1991 appointment of a new Justice, Clarence Thomas, to the Supreme Court Bench. When the nation's first African American Justice, Thurgood Marshall, retired from the Court, advocates for civil rights worried that President George H. W. Bush would use the opportunity to name a conservative. Thomas' nomination indeed dismayed many advocates of civil and women's rights, who were troubled by Thomas's history as director of the EEOC in the 1980s. The confirmation hearings focused on allegations from several female employees at EEOC and from Thomas' former position at the Department of Education. The testimony of law professor Anita Hill before the Senate Judiciary Committee led Thomas to call the proceedings a "high tech lynching." Thomas's eventual confirmation led to a political backlash in the 1992 elections and resulted in victories for a significant number of female candidates. Thomas has voted with the conservative bloc on the Court, most frequently siding with Justice Antonin Scalia.[42]

In the 1990s, legal cases involving Title IX of Educational Amendments of 1972 finally arrived at the Court. When originally drafted, Title IX prohibited discrimination by sex in public educational programs. In 1979, the Office of Health, Education, and Welfare under President Jimmy Carter added a three-part test for implementation, requiring "full and effective" accommodation of an underrepresented sex in athletics. In other words, in order to receive federal funding, schools had to provide opportunities for males and females to ensure more equivalent programs. The rules generated heated debate over the nature and practicality of equal opportunities. Would women be wrestlers, for example, or young men gymnasts? In 2002, a Committee on Opportunity in Athletics held public hearings to consider the viability and consequences of Title IX. By 2005, the Committee reported a clarification, which attempted to give new weight to school efforts to achieve equity in athletic programs. Even with such an open process, however, several cases from Title IX came before the Supreme Court. In *Franklin* v. *Gwinnett County Public Schools* in 1992, the Justices determined that schools not complying with Title IX could be sued for both punitive and compensatory damages. Studies by the Women's Sports Foundation credits Title IX with a dramatic increase in women in athletics. In 1971, fewer than 300,000 women and girls participated in school sports; by 1997, almost three million did so.[43]

Another contested area of law in the 1990s came from growing demands by gay and lesbian organizations for the right to marry and assume legal domestic and parental roles. In 1993, the Hawaii Supreme Court determined that same-sex marriage would be constitutional in that state unless specifically banned. In response, the Hawaii legislature prohibited gay and lesbian marriage by statute. In Alaska, the state legislature passed a marriage bill requiring that parties to marriage must be one male and one female. Similar legislation came before Congress in 1996, as the Protection of Marriage Act made heterosexual marriage the federal standard. The act also allowed states to ignore same-sex marriages conducted in other states and to deny marriage benefits to those who had been married elsewhere. States began to pass similar laws. Vermont and Connecticut moved in a different direction, and each legalized civil unions for gays and lesbians. While not legally marriage, the civil union provided partners with the same benefits and responsibilities of marital partners. The Massachusetts Supreme Court finally recognized same-sex unions in 2003, determining that any barrier would be unconstitutional in that state. In 2004, Massachusetts became the first state to recognize same-sex marriage, but legislators moved rapidly to ban such marriages by nonresidents. In 2006, New Jersey also recognized civil unions. In 2008, California allowed for same-sex marriage and allowed those from other states to conduct marriage ceremonies in the state.

By the end of the twentieth century, the Supreme Court appeared poised in decisions such as *United States* v. *Virginia* to move gender discrimination to a level of strict scrutiny, which might eliminate many arguments for the perpetuation of gender differences in law. As the new century progressed, however, the Court increasingly assumed a more conservative composition under new Chief Justice John Roberts. With the retirement of Justice Sandra Day O'Connor, and the appointment of Samuel Alito as her successor, court watchers became more concerned about retaining the advances of the previous decades. New challenges, such as laws on same-sex marriage and attempts to end *Roe* v. *Wade*, occupied the legal agenda. Two cases raised special concerns for women activists. In 2007, the Court ruled that wage discrimination must be reported within 180 days of the first instance of the discrepancy. In this case, Lily Ledbetter discovered that she had been paid substantially less than male supervisors at a Goodyear Tire plant in Alabama for nineteen years. A jury awarded Ledbetter $3.5 million in back pay and damages, and Goodyear appealed. The Court determined that Title VII of the Civil Rights Act mandated the time limit, but Justice Ginsburg argued in her dissent that such a conclusion ignored the incremental nature of discrimination in salaries. As a practical matter, the decision in *Ledbetter* v. *Goodyear Tire* limits the ability of workers to bring such cases to court. In another controversial decision, *Jespersens* v. *Harrah's Operating Company*, the Ninth Circuit Court of Appeals found that makeup requirements for female employees were not discriminatory, and that different standards of grooming for men and women did not impose a burden on women.[44]

Laws covering marriage, divorce, child custody, and support also concerned many women by the end of the twentieth century. Throughout the century, attitudes toward divorce grew increasingly lenient. Historians have found that women increasingly sued for divorce, for example, evidence of a growing belief in the importance of marital happiness. Some states retained strict grounds for divorce; in New York, adultery remained one of the few possibilities for securing a legal end to marriage. As a result, husbands and wives sometimes faked an "affair" with a willing (or paid) "correspondent," a practice lampooned in film and fiction. Other states such as Indiana and Nevada offered more generous methods of securing divorce, with short residency requirements for those filing. In New Mexico, marital "incompatibility" appeared in 1933 as a ground for dissolution; California moved to "no-fault" divorce in 1970. By the end of the century, most states had adopted similar statutes, allowing couples to end marriage without excessive costs or litigation. As legal scholars have noted, the idea of marital choice informed many of these changes, as legislatures took an increasingly liberal approach to marriage and cohabitation. At the same time, however, the older form of "common law marriage," in which partners could constitute a union without a marriage ceremony if they continued to reside together for seven or more years, disappeared from most state law. Only nine states retained common law provisions by the end of the century. Cohabitation between unmarried partners became more commonplace, and the demand for legal rights for domestic partners resulted in an increasing numbers of employers offering benefits to nonmarital partners. In 1995, Vermont offered partnership benefits to state employees, and in 1997, Hawaii extended domestic partner benefits to all same-sex couples. In 1981, the California case of *Marvin* v. *Marvin* established the award of "palimony," or support to a non-marital partner at the termination of a long-term relationship.[45]

It has been suggested that a presumption of choice has become an increasingly significant part of the American notions of family and gender in the twentieth century. As individuals choose when and whom to marry, whether to have children, and how to organize family relationships, they expect law to validate their preferences. The ability to choose, however, remains a point of political contention, as Americans continue to use law to frame such essential issues as work, childbearing, and marriage.[46]

The progress of women in the legal profession remains equally uncertain. Although women now constitute almost half of law school students, other statistics reveal key differences between male and female attorneys. The American Bar Association reported in 2006 that women earned 70.5

percent of what males received, for example. Only 15 percent of Fortune 500 companies had women as general counsel; slightly less than one-fourth of District Court Judges were women. Private law firms offer a similar picture, with women accounting for 44 percent of associates but only 18 percent of partners. Even the Supreme Court mirrors the difficulties women face. As clerkships with the Court remain a major stepping stone to a significant legal career, women are less likely to work for the Court. Between 2000 and 2008, Justices Stephen Breyer, Ruth Bader Ginsburg, and Sandra Day O'Connor had a roughly equal number of male and female clerks. In comparison, only 7 percent of Justice Antonin Scalia's clerks were women. Female attorneys made up only 11 percent of Justice Anthony Kennedy's clerks in the same period.[47]

NOTES

1. Linda Kerber, *No Constitutional Right to Be Ladies: Women and the Obligations of Citizenship* (New York: Hill and Wang, 1998); see also Michael Grossberg, *Governing the Hearth: Law and Family in Nineteenth-Century America* (Chapel Hill: University of North Carolina Press, 1985).

2. Cass Sunstein, *Designing Democracy: What Constitutions Do* (New York: Oxford University Press, 2001), 176.

3. *Miller* v. *Albright* 523 US 420 (1998).

4. Karen Berger Morello, *The Invisible Bar: The Woman Lawyer in America, 1638 to the Present* (Boston: Beacon Press, 1986); see also Women's Legal History Project at Stanford University, http://womenslegalhistory.stanford.edu/papers/sleeth.pdf.

5. "First Women's Law School Opens This Fall; Professor Joseph Henry Beale of Harvard Law School, Head of New Institution, Tells What He and His Colleagues Hope to Accomplish," *New York Times*, October 3, 1915.

6. The first bar examinations were administered by judges and did not always require a written test.

7. Morello, *Invisible Bar*, 16.

8. *Bradwell* v *Illinois* 83 US 130 (1872).

9. Morello, *Invisible Bar*, 67.

10. The "elite" law schools include Yale, Columbia, Harvard, Stanford, and the University of Pennsylvania, among others. This designation does not imply that other law schools had inferior students or faculty but indicates the degree of prestige traditionally accorded to graduates.

11. Nancy Woloch, *Women and the American Experience* (New York: McGraw Hill, 2006), 284.

12. Issues of Fourteenth Amendment rights and women's equality are covered through a variety of perspectives by Kerber; Marylynn Salmon, *Women and the Law of Property in Early America* (Chapel Hill: University of North Carolina Press, 1986); Nancy Isenberg, *Sex and Citizenship in Antebellum America* (Chapel Hill: University of North Carolina Press, 1998); Evan Gerstmann, *The Constitutional Underclass: Gays, Lesbians, and the Failure of Class-Based Equal Protection* (Chicago: University of Chicago Press, 1999); Garrett Epps, *Democracy Reborn: The Fourteenth Amendment and the Fight for Equal Rights in Post-Civil War America* (New York: Henry

Holt, 2006); Martha Minow, *Making All the Difference: Inclusion, Exclusion, and American Law* (Ithaca, NY: Cornell University Press, 1990).

13. Judith Baer, *The Chains of Protection: The Judicial Response to Women's Labor Legislation* (Westport, CT: Greenwood Press, 1978), 23.

14. Michael J. Phillips, *The Lochner Court, Myth and Reality: Substantive Due Process from the 1890s to the 1930s* (Westport, CT: Praeger, 2001).

15. Alice Kessler-Harris, *In Pursuit of Equity: Women, Men, and the Quest for Economic Citizenship in Twentieth-Century America* (New York: Oxford University Press, 2001), 105.

16. Kerber, *No Constitutional Right to Be Ladies*, 39.

17. Salmon, *Women and the Law of Property*; Nancy F. Cott, *Public Vows: A History of Marriage and the Nation* (Cambridge, MA: Harvard University Press, 2000).

18. For a fuller discussion of the meanings of gender and citizenship, see Peter W. Bardaglio, *Reconstructing the Household: Families, Sex, and the Law in the Nineteenth-Century South* (Chapel Hill: University of North Carolina Press, 1998); Hendrik Hartog, *Man and Wife in America: A History* (Cambridge, MA: Harvard University Press, 2000); Kerber, *No Constitutional Right to Be Ladies*.

19. Janet A. Gilboy, "Implications of 'Third-Party' Involvement in Enforcement," *Law and Society Review* Vol. 31 (1997): 505–530.

20. "International Trafficking in Persons, Especially Women and Children," *American Journal of International Law* Vol. 95 (2001): 407–410; Patricia R. Pessar and Sarah J. Mahler, "Transnational Migration: Bringing Gender In," *International Migration Review* Vol. 37 (2003): 812–846.

21. Kerber, *No Constitutional Right to Be Ladies*, 133.

22. Ibid., 177–217.

23. Ibid.

24. Ibid., 122; See also Carolyn C. Jones, "Split Income and Separate Spheres: Tax Law and Gender Roles in the 1940s," *Law and History Review* Vol. 6, No. 2 (1988): 259–310.

25. Morello, *Invisible Bar*, 205.

26. *Buck v. Bell* 240 U.S. 200 (1927); *Goesaert v. Cleary* 335 U.S. 464 (1948); *Skinner v. State of Oklahoma ex rel Williamson* 316 U.S. 535 (1942).

27. *United States v. One Package of Japanese Pessaries*, 86 F.2d 737 (2nd Cir. 1936); *Griswold v. Connecticut*, 381 U.S. 479 (1965).

28. *Roe v. Wade*, 410 U.S. 113 (1973); *Doe v. Bolton*, 410 U.S.179 (1973).

29. *Roe v. Wade*.

30. See *Poe v. Ullman*, 367 U.S. 497 (1961); *Eisenstadt v. Baird*, 405 U.S. 438 (1972).

31. *Stenberg, Attorney General of Nebraska, et al. v. Carhart*, 530 U.S. 914 (2000); *Gonzales v. Carhart* 550 U.S. ___ (2007).

32. *Loving v. Virginia*, 388 U.S. 1 (1967).

33. *Weeks v. Southern Bell*, 408 F.2d 228 (5th Cir.).

34. *Frontiero v. Richardson*, 411 U.S. 677 (1973); *Reed v. Reed*, 404 U.S. 71 (1971).

35. *McDonnell Douglas v. Green*, 411 U.S. 792 (1973).

36. Reva Siegel, "The Modernization of Marital States," *Georgetown Law Journal* Vol. 82 (1994): 2127–2211.

37. *Geduldig v. Aiello*, 417 U.S. 484 (1974);*General Electric Co. v. Gilbert*, 429 U.S. 125 (1976).

38. *EEOC & Keane v. Sears Roebuck & Co.*, 233 F.3d 432—7th Cir. 2000; Ruth Milkman, "Women's History and the Sears Case," *Feminist Studies* Vol. 12, No. 2 (1986): 375–400.

39. *Meritor Savings Bank* v. *Vinson*, 477 U.S. 57 (1986); *Thibodeau* v. *Design Group One Architects, LLC*, 802 A.2d 731 (Conn. 2002); *Jenson* v. *Eveleth Taconite Co.*, 139 F.R.D. 657, 667 (D. Minn. 1991).

40. *Wengler* v. *Druggists Mutual Ins. Co.*, 446 U.S. 142 (1980); *County of Washington* v. *Gunther*, 452 U.S. 161 (1981); *Rostker* v. *Goldberg*, 453 U.S. 57 (1981); *Mississippi University for Women* v. *Hogan*, 458 U.S. 718 (1982), *Boy Scouts of America* v. *Dale*, 530 U.S. 640 (2000).

41. *Automobile Workers* v. *Johnson Controls, Inc.*, 499 U.S. 187 (1991); *Davis* v. *Monroe County Board of Education*, 526 U.S. 629 (1999).

42. See Jane Mayer and Jill Abramson, *Strange Justice: The Selling of Clarence Thomas* (New York: Houhgton Mifflin, 1994); Clarence Thomas, *My Grandfather's Son: A Memoir* (New York: HarperCollins Publishers, 2007).

43. Title IX of the Education Amendments of 1972; *Franklin* v. *Gwinnett Cty. Public Schools*, 911 F.2d 617 (CA11 1990); Women's Sports Foundation, "Understanding Title IX and Athletics 101," http://www.womenssportsfoundation.org/Issues-And-Research/Title-IX.aspx.

44. *Ledbetter* v. *Goodyear Tire & Rubber Co.*, 550 U.S. ___ (2007); *Jespersen* v. *Harrah's Operating Co.*, No. 03–15045 (9th Cir. Apr. 14, 2006).

45. Glenda Riley, *Divorce: An American Tradition* (New York: Oxford University Press, 1991); Robert L. Griswold, *Family and Divorce in California, 1850–1890: Victorian Illusions and Everyday Realities* (Albany, NY: SUNY Press, 1982); Elaine Tyler May, *Great Expectations: Marriage and Divorce in Post-Victorian America* (Chicago: University of Chicago Press, 1980).

46. Lawrence M. Friedman, *Private Lives: Families, Individuals, and the Law* (Cambridge, MA: Harvard University Press, 2004).

47. American Bar Association, Commission on Women in the Profession, http://www.abanet.org/women.

7

———∽∾∾∾———

Women and Religion

The 3,000-seat Angelus Temple in Los Angeles offered a spectacular show to those who entered its doors. Opened in 1923 to house the Four-square Church of preacher Aimee Semple McPherson, the Temple attracted the faithful and the curious to hear a positive message about salvation and Christ's second coming. Lavish shows focused on patriotism, religious stories, and the promise of healing always ended with McPherson's clear, vivid parables and sermons. Together with her mother, Minnie Kennedy, McPherson managed a growing enterprise earning thousands of dollars a week, including the first religious radio station, KFSG, as one of America's most prominent evangelists.

McPherson occupies a fascinating niche in the history of women and religion in America's twentieth century. Her celebrity foreshadowed the later efforts of fundamentalists such as Tammy Faye Baker and Beverly LaHaye, who successfully mobilized women through new organizations and the media. McPherson championed social work among the poor and equal access for African Americans, at one point facing down an audience filled with Ku Klux Klan members. McPherson asserted a woman's right to preach and lead a religious organization, a claim rooted in the nineteenth century and yet still controversial in the new century. Like many women, however, McPherson also found herself defined by sexuality and challenged by the difficulties of balancing personal life and public achievements.

McPherson, born in Canada, married a young evangelical minister, Robert Semple, in 1908, and the couple became missionaries to China, where Robert died in 1910. McPherson returned to the United States with an infant daughter, began work for the Salvation Army, and remarried. When she and her new husband, Harold McPherson, had a new baby, Aimee McPherson struggled with depression and dissatisfaction. She left home to begin a career as an itinerant preacher, joined by her mother in 1918. As she traveled the nation, McPherson attracted larger and larger audiences, and by the time she settled in Los Angeles, she had perfected an appeal as a Pentecostal. She shared the beliefs in the power of God's Holy Spirit to create miracles, from the practice of followers spontaneously speaking in unknown languages (glossolalia) to faith healing. As the Foursquare Church began in Los Angeles, McPherson routinely drew thousands to the Angelus Temple.

Scandal followed in the wake of her growing influence, however. As McPherson condemned the teaching of Darwin and evolution, she attracted political and religious enemies. She faced accusations of having an affair with her married radio engineer, Kenneth Ormiston. Then, on May 18, 1926, something more spectacular occurred: Aimee Semple McPherson disappeared after a swim on Venice Beach. For weeks, her supporters stood at the beach mourning her loss and hoping for a miraculous return. On June 23rd McPherson walked into the town of Agua Prieta, Mexico, claiming that she had been kidnapped by "Steve," "Mexicali Rose," and "Jake." The Los Angeles police did not believe her, noting that her shoes and clothes showed no evidence of the dusty desert or her supposed escape. A grand jury convened to investigate turned into a trial of McPherson's honesty.

For her devotees, McPherson's claims seemed valid, and for them, her appeal remained solid. For others in Los Angeles, the possible affair and strange tale of abduction made McPherson questionable, if not vulgar. Although she continued to minister until her death in 1944, her fame remained diminished in an increasingly insecure life. Sexual innuendo and rumor had upset McPherson's career as one of the nation's leading ministers.[1]

Aimee Semple McPherson's story illustrates both the potential and the pitfalls for women who sought new avenues of religious expression in the twentieth century. Throughout the past hundred years, Americans assumed that women's moral instincts and innate piety endowed them with a natural proclivity to religious life. Women's opportunities for leadership remained circumscribed, however, as many denominations prohibited women from becoming priests, ministers, or rabbis. Despite such limitations, women pioneered new roles in the churches that allowed them to be ordained, and in a vast array of organizations focused on spiritual commitment. Women transformed notions of Christianity as well, infusing a more wrathful Protestantism with images of a friendly, compassionate Jesus. Hymns such as "Jesus Loves Me" by Anna B. Warner or

Evangelist Aimee Semple McPherson continued to intrigue reporters in 1928, two years after her mysterious disappearance from Venice Beach, California. AP photo.

"I Need Thee Every Hour" by Annie Sherwood Hawks celebrated a new closeness with a loving God.[2] In the ideals of domesticity, maternal love merged with concepts of devotion, making women the religious authority of the family in place of the increasingly outward-orientated father and husband.

By the end of the nineteenth century, women had responded to these changes in a variety of ways. Some used their religious authority to legitimate activities outside of the home that might otherwise seem inappropriate. Missionary work, a part of evangelical tradition since the beginning of the nineteenth century, attracted growing numbers of women. By 1900, nearly 5,000 Christian women, nearly 60 percent of all volunteers, worked as missionaries in seemingly exotic locations such as China, Burma, and Japan; thirty-three denominations established missions between 1861 and 1894. Mission boards counseled women to remain submissive to their missionary husbands, but single women found a new freedom from "angry debate" over feminine ideals.[3]

Women also served on or created new organizations within their denominations. In the Presbyterian Church, for example, the San Francisco-based Women's Occidental Board of Foreign Missions created "rescue" programs for Chinese women forced into prostitution; others focused on "home missions" to educate children or provide aid to the poor.[4] For Jewish women, participation in the Philadelphia Hebrew Relief Association for Sick and Wounded Soldiers, or the Ladies' Sewing Society of the United Hebrew Relief Association, allowed for philanthropy and activism.[5] Women used their religious affiliations to begin Sunday schools, assistance for the needy, and homes for orphans or "fallen" women. In Galveston, Texas, for instance, women played a central role in organizing Sunday schools, believing that religious education countered the corrosive effects of secular life. They also worked to create programs for young adults and children; the "Sunbeam" society of Galveston's First Baptist Church worked with children as young as five to ensure Christian education.[6]

Religion also became a key motivation for organizations with no denominational identity. The Charity Organization Societies, begun after the Civil War, maintained a largely Protestant orientation in appeal and clientele, but individual societies offered aid to Jewish and Catholic applicants. For women, the role of "friendly visitor" presented opportunities to travel within their communities without chaperones and to voice concerns about "unladylike" subjects, such as criminal behaviors or alcoholism. The Women's Christian Temperance Association (WCTU), founded in Chicago in 1873, emerged as the most vigorous organization of reforming women. When Frances Willard became president in 1879, she adopted the motto of "Do Everything," urging a growing membership to oppose saloons and take on charitable work. She linked the spiritual purity of the home with women's activism, and continued a religious appeal for women to "bless and brighten every place." For many women, the WCTU served as an opportunity for activism in keeping with a domestic role, and by 1911, the organization claimed almost half a million members.[7]

By the turn of the century, other women's associations developed with only vague religious claims, such as the General Federation of Women's Clubs. Social settlements, which drew a new generation of young, college-educated women into reform, straddled a more nuanced line between religion and secular life. Most rejected denominational affiliations, religious services, and proselytizing. The settlements practiced "not institutional religion, ... not denominational religion," Dean George Hoges told a gathering of charity workers. Nevertheless, "there is love in it for God and man," he declared.[8] Jane Addams assured wealthy contributors that Chicago's Hull House would adhere to a sense of religious fellowship, and routinely linked Christian ideals with settlement values. Repeatedly, settlement advocates connected largely Protestant religious principles with social reform while insisting that they welcomed Catholics, Jews, and Protestants. The settlement concept tied the teachings of Social Gospel, which had promoted religious work and social reform, with the desire of women for more public roles. The settlement houses that flourished before the 1920s in large and small cities allowed female activists to blend piety and philanthropy into a professionalizing social work.

The majority of settlements served diverse communities but typically offered most of their services to immigrants. Some, such as the White Rose Mission in New York, focused on aiding local African American residents. Because the organized settlements rejected denominational connections, however, the National Federation of Settlements, formed in 1911, excluded the Mission from membership. Many settlements with religious ties offered programs for African American, and most were formed by groups of religious black women affiliated with churches. It has been suggested that policies of the National Federation led to "self-defeating and discriminatory policies," which unfairly discriminated against race and religion.[9] At the least, such limitations did reflect an unwillingness on the part of white reformers to consider the role of churches in African American life.

Since the Civil War, churches had provided the framework for social services, education, and activism in the African American communities of the South. Blacks preferred African American congregations; the National Baptist Convention, formed in 1894, grew to be the largest denomination by 1900, with over two million members. The African Methodist Episcopal Church had about half a million members, and fundamentalist faiths continued to expand in the early twentieth century. The "Holiness" movement developed as well, infusing one part of African American religion with a distinctive, joyous style of singing and praise. Overwhelmingly, men headed churches as ministers, bishops, deacons, remaining responsible for issues of theology and administration. Women provided the social core of these Southern churches, however, organizing community events, operating schools, and assisting the poor. Black leader W. E. B. DuBois noted in 1899 that community life centered in churches, from weddings to club meetings; in the South, as segregation limited the public spaces, churches remained accessible and open to all.[10]

The Sunday collections often went to the poor, and churches actively supported schools, colleges, orphanages, and homes for the aged. Some churches managed day nurseries, courses in cooking and sewing, and recreation. Women's pivotal role in ensuring that such work was done effectively allowed for more public roles and new avenues for activism. In 1906, women's participation in the National Baptist Convention reached record levels, with two-thirds of the memberships. Within the Convention, women formed a Women's Convention in 1900 that would eventually claim more than a million female participants. The Convention allowed women to advance as women and provided an opportunity to consider how race and gender structured their experiences.[11]

Religion served as an entrance into political and club work as well. The National Association of Colored Women had nearly one hundred thousand members in 1920, many who came into the organization from church associations. Women such as Nannie Helen Burroughs and Francis Ellen Watkins Harper used their connections with their churches to argue for African American rights in the face of disenfranchisement and Jim Crow laws. The relationships among advantaged women and those experiencing hardship did not remain untroubled, however; at times, African American women of the middle class worried that poor women created their own problems, and some described their clients as backward or uneducated.[12] Such attitudes complicated the politics of service and religion, even as women's organizations struggled to improve conditions. At the same time, social activism couched in religion allowed African American women to more safely confront the deepening racism of the Jim Crow South, as resistant whites remained less likely to challenge Christian associations.[13]

Women's religious associations also played a significant role in immigrant communities, providing needed social services, a sense of connection, and reinforcement of valued traditions. For Jewish immigrants, for example, Hadassah, the Women's Zionist Organization of America, focused on assistance to Palestine and education of American Jewish families. Formed in 1912 by Henrietta Szold, Hadassah rapidly adopted programs to assist in the establishment of a Jewish homeland, providing a visiting nurse service and other forms of relief. By 1933, the Youth Aliyah (Jugendaliyah, Aliyat Hano'arn) funded by Hadassah allowed over 100,000 German Jewish children to establish homes in Palestine.[14]

Within the American Jewish community, religious possibilities also multiplied; Reform Judaism, begun in Europe and established in the United States by Rabbi Isaac Meyer Wise in the 1870s, offered a vehicle for adapting to modern American life. Criticized by more Orthodox Jews who insisted on upholding all 613 laws of the Torah, the use of Hebrew, and strict gender roles, Reform Jews found themselves at odds with many immigrant arrivals. A third type of Judaism emerged from the discontent some felt with both perspectives, attempting a moderate path. Conservative Jews objected to the rejection of kosher laws, and by the early twentieth century had established their own theological center, the Jewish Theological Seminary in New York City. Each division within the Jewish community worked vigorously to provide religious guidance and social services to the growing number of new Jewish arrivals. By 1924, when immigration to the United States slowed because of new legal restrictions, approximately three million of Europe's twelve million Jews had emigrated to America.[15]

Women's organizations also emphasized issues of identity and sisterhood. The National Council of Jewish Women, formed in 1893, stressed
the challenges of anti-Semitism and the need to confront religious "perse-
cution." Women in the Reform community established a National Federation of Temple Sisterhoods in 1913, linking fifty-two local associations in
charity work and mutual support. The Women's League of the United
Synagogues of America, formed in 1918, also allowed women to do relief
work, provide aid to Jewish libraries or community associations, and develop religious identity.[16]

Women's work in the home also ensured the continuity of religious traditions and culture. For Jewish immigrant women, maintaining their faith in a
predominantly Christian nation required a distinct set of household labors.
To celebrate the Sabbath, women cleaned their homes, prepared meals
according to kosher standards (kashruth), and arranged family life so that
the Sabbath would be a day of no work and religious observance. Orthodox
women also maintained the tradition of the mikvah, a ritual cleansing after
menstruation, and adhered to the niddah, religious law prohibiting inter-
course during menstruation. Reverence for study of the Torah meant that
devout men sometimes remained outside of the labor force while women
worked, although such practices fell under increasing criticism.[17] Though
the first decades of the twentieth century, Jewish identity remained strong
even as new generations began to transform practices. By the 1920s, only 10
percent of Jews kept kosher households, for example.

For other immigrant women, religion also shaped life in America. For Italians, Poles, and Hungarians, efforts to continue traditional celebrations,
foods, and beliefs structured associations, work life, and childrearing. Among
Mexican Americans, such beliefs as reverence for Our Lady of Guadalupe
allowed for a combination of Native and Catholic heritages, and perpetuated
a distinct culture, upheld by women, in Latino communities. Asian women,
too, helped new arrivals at the turn of the century. Federal restrictions dramatically limited the number of women from China who could enter the
United States; most who did came in a distinctly subordinate position to
husbands and fathers, a position mandated by Confucian tradition. Some
Chinese immigrants arrived as Christian converts, influenced by American
missionaries. Among Koreans, the majority of those immigrating to the
United States were Christian, although fewer than twenty percent of citizens
described themselves that way in Korea. The Japanese women who entered
the United States came as family members, and prior to leaving Japan had to
go before review boards to ensure their ability to maintain Japanese honor.
Such strictures did not prevent the development of "picture brides," women
who came to America after arranged marriages with men who had already
immigrated. Much like other immigrants, Japanese women sustained their
religion and customs. Both Buddhist temples and Japanese-language classes

for children provided continuity with Japan, and on celebration days, women wore traditional dress.[18]

Native Americans faced perhaps the most stringent limitations on practicing their religions. The establishment of "Indian schools" separated children from their families and their traditions in the late nineteenth century; reservations and federal law restricted traditional practices that provided the foundations of Native American spiritual life. Even with the protections of citizenship guaranteed in 1924, many Indians faced state or local laws that inhibited religious celebration. The preservation of customs and religious rituals often fell to informal or extra-legal conservation. The Indian Reorganization Act of 1934 ended restrictions on Native practices, and by 1940, six Native American linguistic groups still persisted in North America. Most Native American groups openly resumed the performance of traditional rituals, although women typically occupied secondary roles. In groups with matrilineal focus, female decision-making and leadership remained part of the fabric of Native life. For most groups, women retained central roles in organizing community events, making foods and maintaining the domestic traditions essential to religious and cultural continuity. In 1978, Congress moved to provide some assistance to the growing movement by Native groups to restore religious rights, passing the American Indian Religious Freedom Act. In 1994, the preservation of Indian rights was supplemented by the Native American Cultural Protection and Free Exercise of Religious Act.[19]

Another religious minority that emerged in the nineteenth century with controversial practices became a major denomination in the twentieth century. The Church of Jesus Christ of Latter-Day Saints, or Mormonism, began in the 1830s in upstate New York. Founder Joseph Smith declared that the angle Moroni had revealed the Book of Mormon written on gold plates. When Smith and his followers translated the plates, they constructed a unique Christian religion that encouraged capitalist virtues and male-dominated family life. As the Mormons moved from New York westward to Illinois, however, other Americans objected to the faith's growing popularity and to its quiet practice of multiple marriage, or polygamy. In 1844, after settling in Nauvoo, Illinois, Smith revealed a plan in which he would become king in the United States. Distraught neighborhoods killed Smith and his brother Hyrum, forcing his successor, Brigham Young, to lead the Illinois Mormons to a new settlement in the Utah territory. The religious continued to practice polygamy as the community expanded, but in 1882 Congress made multiple marriage illegal. In order to gain admission to the United States as a territory and later as a state, the Church abandoned the practice in 1890, although small communities of Mormons continued to organize around it throughout the twentieth century.

The status of women within the Church continues to provoke controversy among scholars. Mormon women cannot serve in the highest levels of their denomination and remain excluded from its most sacred spaces. Following the early teachings of Joseph Smith, devout Mormons believe that while men and women may have "equality," God destines each for different roles. Viewing the family as the "most sacred" social institution, contemporary Mormon leaders such as Gordon B. Hinckley declare "fathers are to preside over their families in love and righteousness and are responsible to provide the necessities of life and protection for their families. Mothers are primarily responsible for the nurture of their children. In these sacred responsibilities, fathers and mothers are obligated to help one another as equal partners."[20] Women exercise leadership through the Relief Society, founded in 1842, providing assistance to Mormon families and religious education. Analysts of religion debate whether women exercise full autonomy or gain deeper satisfaction through gender-segregated activities, with some suggestions that the sisterhood of wives might provide support in a largely female setting.[21] In contrast to such arguments, Mormon Sonia Johnson formed Mormons for the Equal Rights Amendment in 1976, and continued open criticism of Latter Day Saints (LDS). In 1979, the Church excommunicated Johnson. Since the 1980s, feminist disagreement from within the LDS has been seen to be limited as church leaders emphasize the importance of women's contributions.[22]

Some mainstream Protestant churches refuse to recognize the Church of Jesus Christ of Latter-day Saints as a Christian denomination, despite shared beliefs in the importance of Christ as a divine presence. The Lutheran Church–Missouri Synod explicitly declared Mormonism outside of the basic tenets of Christianity, for example, and other Christians sometimes contend that LDS believers do not share essential beliefs about sin, God, salvation, and resurrection. Nevertheless, LDS has grown dramatically in the twentieth century, claiming over twelve million members worldwide by 2005.[23]

By the 1920s, a new religious force began to shape the national dialogue on faith. Christian groups sharing a belief in biblical inerrancy expanded their congregations, took denominational forms, and begin to have a significant cultural and political impact. Many described themselves as "fundamentalist," following the guidelines of *The Fundamentals*, published in twelve volumes between 1910 and 1915 by Milton and Lyman Steward. Ministers and clergy with the same concerns about the changes in Christian theology shared ideas put forward by theologians such as J. Gresham Machen and A. A. Hodge, professors at the Princeton Theological Seminary. Some of those involved had belonged to the Niagara Bible Conference, an annual meeting held from 1876 to 1897 by Protestant pastors and leaders who adhered to common beliefs about salvation, divine will, and Christ's return to earth. It has been suggested that this type of fundamentalism drew on nineteenth century religious traditions of revivalists and premillennialists, who believed Christ would return to earth before the end of worldly society.[24]

By the 1920s, a portion of the religious community merged their ideas with other anxieties in a rapidly changing nation. Those defining themselves as "fundamentalists" worried about the corrosive impact of Darwinian science and the possible erosion of religious beliefs in mystical or supernatural events. Many advocated a return to modesty in women and a more demure public sexuality, as movies, public amusement parks, and music suggested more risqué behaviors. World War I also prompted a fervent patriotism that tied Christianity to nationalism in new ways and premillennialism with military conflict.[25] Fundamentalism also became a potent response to urbanization, as Americans moved from rural areas into towns and cities. Despite a popular identification with uneducated farmers and unsophisticated sharecroppers, fundamentalist churches maintained an important presence in the cities. The World's Christian Fundamentalist Association gathered in Philadelphia in 1919, for example, to create an organizational structure. The Association linked bible colleges, small churches, ministers, and new religious organizations, holding annual meetings in Chicago, Denver, and Los Angeles. Other fundamentalist groups, such as the Fundamentalist Fellowship of Baptists, emerged from dissent over the supposedly liberal direction of mainstream denominations. Even with this movement toward some centralization, however, fundamentalists remained resistant to developing a strong federation or a single organization to oversee congregations. American fundamentalism in the 1920s remained a "disorderly conglomeration of often competing constituencies", separated by suspicion and doctrinal nuances.[26]

For all of the disunity among congregations, fundamentalist clergy with few exceptions agreed upon a core of ideas about women, family, and sexuality. While preachers thundered from the pulpit or railed in the revival tent, women in mainstream denominations tended to dismiss their admonitions as marginal declarations out of touch with social changes. In doing so, many female observers ignored the ways in which fundamentalism reshaped debates over women's roles and the possibility of shifting attitudes which would limit women's access in religious life. Fundamentalism contained a vehement challenge to new roles for women and new promises of virility for men.

The dominance of women in mainstream congregations of the late nineteenth century shifted by the 1920s, as men worked to limit women's access to religious committees and assert masculine authority. Even those denominations such as the Presbyterians, which considered allowing women to vote on congregational matters, retreated from a full assertion of women's religious equality. For fundamentalists, the movement to reassert male control of church matters came as statements of the importance of religion in public affairs. Ministers promoted an image of a robust Christ, replacing the feminized stereotype of the nineteenth century. Jesus was a businessman, Bruce Barton explained; the Baptist *Bible Champion* boldly declared that Christ was "the most manly of men."[27] The virile Christ could only have men as his true representatives, and only men legitimately controlled both the family and the state.

Women heard that the injunctions of Saint Paul in the New Testament ensured their docility and subordination. Women's ministry upended the true nature of the Church; biblical infallibility underlined the importance of adhering to the unambiguous injunctions. When Paul wrote that women should "keep silent" in churches, many fundamentalists believed, he relayed God's wisdom on female submission.[28] Women's place remained the home, where they fulfilled the "divinest function of life" as mothers.[29] This declaration obviously challenged women's entrance into professions, the voting booth, and political life, and heralded a new passivity that defined women solely in relationship to Christ and husband. Yet ministers also shifted the religious image of women, from the naturally pious ideal of the nineteenth century to the innately wicked, sexualized temptress and betrayer. Mary and Martha gave way as symbols in fundamentalist literature to Jezebel, Bathsheba, and Lot's wife.[30] The World's Christian Fundamental Association proclaimed the dangers of the "maelstrom of modern infidelity."[31]

Fundamentalists famously attacked ideas in the 1920s that appeared to threaten moral order. Not only did ministers inveigh against sexual license, they declared the immorality of dancing, many forms of modern music, and motion pictures. Most threatening of all, however, was the scientific concept of evolution; Darwin's theories demeaned God and belittled the biblical story of human existence.[32] Challenges to the teaching of evolution represented one effort to undermine a science that denied the supernatural and the literal Bible. In Dayton, Tennessee, the trial of teacher John Scopes for teaching evolution generated worldwide publicity and fundamentalist fervor. Although Scopes was convicted of violating a Tennessee law, the ridicule attached to the fundamentalist position on such biblical stories as Jonah and the Whale meant that in the years between 1925 and the 1970s, "fundamentalists rarely ventured outside of the evangelical subculture."[33]

Within the African American community, fundamentalism and a growing Pentecostal movement attracted parishioners. Unlike the fundamentalism spreading among white Christians, the religious sentiment in African American churches included a more vocal and active role for women. Belief in the spiritual power of the "Holy Ghost" and emotional expressions of religious inspiration spread among those drawn to Pentecostalism. The "Sanctified Church," as participants called it, connected the Holiness and Pentecostal faiths, and provided African American women a continued prominence in teaching and contributing to their faith.[34]

For Catholics, the 1920s represented an important period of growth following the arrival of millions of Catholic immigrants to the United States.

As early as 1850, the Roman Catholic Church had the largest membership of any denomination in America, and by 1884, the Third Plenary Council of American Bishops concluded that each parish must open a Catholic school and provide services. Within the church, women faced clear choices: a life as a wife, mother, and devout lay worker, or as a "sister" in a religious order. The majority chose to follow the path of domesticity, yet adhering to religious precepts was not always easy or simple.

For many immigrant families from Southern or Eastern Europe, the church offered assistance to alleviate poverty, education in a parochial setting, and a focus for community life. For the very poor, Catholic social services provided orphanages (including the possibility of temporary shelter for children), homes for the aged, rudimentary health care, guidance for unmarried women new to cities, and help finding work. Some Catholic societies focused on service to a specific area or type of client; Boston's League of Catholic Women devoted energies to Italian immigrants. Irish Catholic women in another part of Boston established the Guild of Our Lady for enrichment, theater, and meetings.[35] Polish women also saw the local Catholic church as one critical center of local life, sustaining Polish language and customs in such exotic locales as New York and Chicago. By 1916, over 1,200 Catholic parishes in the United States ministered exclusively in languages other than English.[36] This type of "ghetto Catholicism," as one scholar termed it, allowed immigrants to assimilate into American institutions and culture at their own pace and with their own identities. The Catholic parish also provided a space for building political associations and economic connections. At the same time, however, it isolated many and contributed to continued suspicion among Protestants about Catholic "difference" and inferiority.[37]

Catholic leaders provided idealized roles for women who chose marriage and family over religious life. The Archbishop of Baltimore, Cardinal James Gibbons, reminded women in 1919 that even with the vote, women should "maintain their true dignity" based on the "power of gentleness." Women learned from the Boston League of Catholic Women that "under the authority of her husband," a woman "rules the Christian home" where she fulfilled her highest duty to God and country.[38] Priests delivered clear injunctions about personal purity, and the Virgin Mary remained a powerful model of idealized womanhood. Young Catholic women also learned the importance of marriage to another Catholic, and the preservation of Catholic tradition, as well as guidance of God's role in shaping family size. Even as more and more American women employed mechanical means for birth control such as the diaphragm, Catholic women were told by the Church hierarchy that limiting births stood in violation of divine will; sex in marriage should be reserved for procreation, not pleasure. Divorce, too, threatened the Catholic family; couples understood that the Catholic marriage would not be easily dissolved. Church officials urged Catholic men to choose carefully when picking a wife. The Notre Dame *Religious Bulletin* warned men, "Don't wait until after marriage to domesticate her. If she doesn't know how to run a home, you won't have a home."[39]

The Second Vatican Council held by Pope Jon XXIII in 1962 (and ended in 1965 under Pope Paul VI) loosened some of the restrictions the church placed on women. While the Pope did not abandon the belief that women's highest calling remained motherhood and marriage, he did concede that some women needed to work outside their homes. Other factors eroded the relationship between Catholic women and the Roman church, however. As more Catholic families became upwardly mobile, for example, more choices about schools, neighborhoods, and culture pulled some families away from Catholic networks. World War II and the G.I. Bill meant other opportunities, and anti-Catholic stigma, which in 1928 contributed to the defeat of presidential candidate Alfred E. Smith, declined in the United States. As important, the growing movements for civil rights and women's rights in the 1960s would implicitly challenge hierarchical authority.

Catholic women choosing a religious life could join one of over two hundred orders in the United States. Service might include work in a parochial school, which numbered nearly 4,000 at the turn of the century, or Catholic hospitals or academies. The religious orders varied in structure, history, and obligations, but all shared vows of obedience, poverty, and chastity. The Sisters of Mercy, predominantly Irish, began in the United States in 1843, and established themselves in Pittsburgh, New York, and San Francisco within two years. The Ursuline sisters, with a tradition stretching back to sixteenth-century Italy, also arrived in the mid-nineteenth century; the Little Sisters of the Poor, from France, brought their focus on work with the aged to New Orleans and New York after the Civil War. An order of women of African descent, the Oblate Sisters of Providence, developed in Baltimore, Maryland, in 1829, followed by the African-American Sisters of the Holy Family in 1842. These and the many other communities of women religious provided nursing, aid, and teaching for both Catholic institutions and the needy. To a significant extent, they served as one of the first large welfare networks in the United States. That role shifted after the reforms of the Progressive era, as secular women and local governments began to assume the tasks previously performed by sisters. Nor did Progressive female reformers appear to recognize how similar their social settlements were to the communities of women living in religious communities.[40] Despite canon law changes that limited the autonomy enjoyed by most women's orders, the number of women who dedicated their lives in Catholic religious communities increased up to the 1960s.

Catholic nuns provided many services for the church throughout the century. Two nuns clamming on Long Island in 1957 kept their habits on while they worked. Courtesy of the Library of Congress.

The social shifts that changed women's lives in the 1920s, from winning the vote to the development of a new type of companionate marriage, also brought changes in religious life. Progressive reform led to the development of social work, for example, which increasingly moved charitable work away from volunteers. One historian noted that the "severing of Protestant Christianity from liberal social reform" also reinforced connections between conservative religion and opposition to progressive legislation. The Catholic Church campaigned for the defeat of a child labor amendment and condemned contraception and public expressions of sexuality in movies or magazines. Some fundamentalists rejected racial equality, championed nativist initiatives, and embraced a strong anti-Semitism. To a significant extent, America seemed more secular and more materialistic in this period as well, a concern that led Robert and Helen Merrill Lynd to assess the state of religion in "Middletown" at mid-century.[41]

The crisis of the Great Depression brought other religious concerns to the forefront of American life. The absence of governmental welfare structures or reliable relief meant that families in desperate economic need turned to churches and charities for assistance. By 1932, the resources of most were stretched past the breaking point. The best efforts of localities, religious organizations, and states proved to be inadequate for meeting the challenge of such widespread need. As he took office in March 1933, the new president Franklin D. Roosevelt asked Congress for additional funds for relief; the 1932 appropriation of $300 million planned for the entire year would only last, he told them, two more months.[42] The New Deal, which took shape in Roosevelt's first term, tackled the economic emergency and mobilized thousands of Americans in a new partnership of state and federal governments and community advocates. Less obvious but as important, Roosevelt motivated a new coalition of supporters with diverse religious connections, linking urban working class Catholics, Jews, and African Americans with traditional Democrats.[43]

Mainstream churches held out hope that the Depression would lead Americans back to church, where membership and participation had declined through the twenties. To some extent, it did. Religious activism in the New Deal took many forms. New Deal programs did not prohibit involvement of religious denominations or organizations from participating in some fashion, despite Constitutional barriers between state and religion. For example, parochial schools became eligible for food subsidies, and for the Pittsburgh Diocese of the western Pennsylvania Catholic Church, a priest to accompany the local Civilian Conservation Corps recruits, 70 percent of whom were Catholics. In other ways, however, religion demarcated how activists worked to assist communities. For African American women, private aid remained the chief source of relief and support for the needy, and much of that support still centered in organizations with religious connections. In contrast, white female reformers utilized the expanding public services established through the New Deal. These differences meant that African American women remained outside of the informal governmental networks that provided for political or occupational mobility for white reformers. At the same time, African American women still confronted racial restrictions that limited their access beyond largely segregated institutions. The importance of religious connections in social service and activism also meant that future efforts could draw upon the solid resources of African American churches.

The Young Women's Christian Association, transported from London to New York in 1858, remained one organization that attempted to bridge the racial divide among religious women. Despite officially remaining segregated until 1946, the Y leadership urged local affiliations to work with each other, and championed anti-lynching laws throughout the 1930s. In cities with large populations of immigrants, Y chapters opened employment bureaus, such as the Akron, Ohio, International Institute, which assisted in placing over two thousand applicants; the Harrisburg, Pennsylvania, Y offered courses in recent legislative reforms and programs. Increasingly, the YWCA lost much of its religious character, instead assuming the function of a social service agency.

Women in fundamentalist denominations in the 1930s also experienced the restrictions of gender; congregations did not abandon the belief that women should remain subordinate to men as ministers or husbands. Such limitations did not discourage Kathryn Kuhlman, an itinerant preacher who established a gospel tabernacle and radio show in 1935. Henrietta Mears followed suit in 1938, creating a mission and the Gospel Light Press.

For Dorothy Day and Peter Marin, the challenges of the Depression led to organizing the Catholic Worker Movement in 1933. A former socialist, Day converted to Catholicism after the birth of her daughter, and her new faith served as the motivation for a different form of radicalism. She and Marin established houses of hospitality to offer food, shelter, and support for the working poor, and communal farms to further a Catholic mission. The *Catholic Worker*, a newspaper run by Day and Marin, began in 1933, and continues today at the original price of one cent. Slowly, the Catholic Worker movement established a tradition of support for the poor and for political pacifism. Day and Marin challenged the Catholic Church for its failures to support workers and its conservative course in the 1920s, but insisted that violence in the union movement betrayed the "doctrine of the brotherhood of man and the dogma of the Mystical Body."[44] Remaining critical of capitalism and what she perceived as the alienation of work, Day nonetheless continued to advocate a spiritual course of challenge in place of socialism. This type of religious activism for social justice formed a distinct type of politics in the United States that brought adherents into civil rights work and subsequent anti-war efforts.

The social service efforts of women's religious associations continued through World War II. The YWCA worked with the USO to offer respite centers for service men and women, for example, while other organizations created networks of aid and support. Within the Jewish communities, advocacy for European refugees and challenges to Germany's discriminatory policies (and later, those of extermination) motivated thousands to petition and plead for American intervention. Yet not all Americans stood behind the war effort, and for pacificists, this period presented significant challenges. Dorothy Day and the Catholic Worker Movement remained firmly opposed to military force, and the organization suffered as pacificism became increasingly unpopular nationally. Other religions, such as the Seventh Day Adventists and the Jehovah's Witnesses, also insisted on maintaining their beliefs against armed conflict. For women, exempt from the draft, upholding religious principles meant support for male family members and friends who sought religious deferments or alternative service.[45]

The war's end in 1945 ushered in a new age of American politics and new prosperity. America's religions also underwent a period of contradictory change. On one hand, fundamentalism began to grow again even as the nation as a whole appeared to be more secular than ever. The G.I. Bill and expanding college opportunities meant better-educated Americas, but mystical beliefs and opposition to evolution still character- ized some religious groups. The prosperity of the nation also allowed con- gregations to erect lavish churches to celebrate a divinity who espoused simplicity and charity. Those incongruities have been seen as reflecting the tensions within Christian denominations during the fifties. The extra- ordinary diversity within the Christian faith, with nuanced interpretations of such issues as communion, the nature of the priesthood, or salvation itself, did not obscure the growing trend toward a liberal theology for most of the mainstream Protestants, however. Slowly a consensus emerged about a "Judeo-Christian" tradition, linking dominant faiths in a new, tolerant pluralism. This placed other religious groups outside of accepted practice, however, suggesting that the arriving Muslims, Sikhs, Buddhists, and others were somehow less religious than their Judeo- Christian counterparts.[46] The National Council of Churches, established in 1949, reflected this trend of exclusion.

Through the 1950s, Americans went to their churches and synagogues with the same regularity they had shown in the past. While attendance grew, however, commentators worried about a more secular society. Per- haps in response, Congress added the phrase "under God" to the Pledge of Allegiance, which assumed a new prominence in schools and public events. Religion seemed a particularly useful bulwark against the spread of communism in the Cold War; the atheists of the Soviet Union would not be able to breach the devotion of an assertively Christian (or Judeo- Christian) nation.

Largely outside of such mainstream religion, fundamentalists again returned to the astute use of media to spread an evangelical message. Billy Graham rapidly became one of the nation's most famous ministers, preaching a message of optimism and redemption from tent meetings to radio. Graham did not dwell openly on the foundations of his faith, such as a concept of dispensationalism that described the world's end, the rise of "the Beast," and a battle between Christ and Satan. Instead, Graham emphasized the importance of family and the home as a place of respect, retreat, and nurture. Other fundamentalists contributed to a new focus on family as the center of fulfillment. Outside secular pressures endan- gered family life, evangelicals insisted, and only the turn to be "born again" would ensure its protection and each individual's satisfaction in family life.[47] For women, the evangelical definition of family offered little support for work outside of the home or expanding gender-specific rights. Women ideally remained wives and mothers devoted to the home, con- tent in knowing their fulfillment came from service to family and church.

Increasingly, Americans responded to the evangelical argument; by the 1960s, Graham's radio program attracted millions of listeners worldwide, and he became part of what would be termed a "mainstream" evangelical movement. This also provided a foundation for the rapid expansion of evangelicalism in the 1970s, as the movement took a more political form.

The 1960s intensified the issues of religion for Americans in dramatically new ways. The Civil Rights movement continued to use the African American churches as a stepping stone for political organization, for example. From the Montgomery bus boycott of 1955, which led to the creation of the Southern Christian Leadership Conference, to the development of the Student Nonviolent Coordinating Committee (SNCC), ministers and parishioners utilized church networks to mobilize supporters. Civil rights politicized both African American congregations and white liberal Protestants and Catholics, who joined the movement. Women played key roles in both churches and political organizations. Fannie Lou Hamer cited her religious convictions as a motivation for her work in the Mississippi rights struggle, saying "we can't separate Christ from freedom."[48] Ella Baker, one of the organizers of SNCC, cited her mother's influence in shaping her determination to work for civil rights; Georgiana Ross Baker remained active in the Black Baptist Church's missionary work throughout her adult life.

Victoria DeLee, active in the South Carolina NAACP and vice president of the prorights United Citizens' Party of South Carolina, insisted that "God in front leading us all" provided the will to confront segregation and reactionary violence.[49]

The Nation of Islam, founded in 1930, attracted other African Americans with a similar message of self-determination and pride. Women's roles in the Nation reflected traditional assumptions about domesticity and men's roles as heads of faith and family. Women adopted head coverings and conservative dress, reflecting their devotion. Throughout the twentieth century, women in the Nation of Islam did not hold significant leadership roles, but in 2005, Ava Muhammad became the minister of the faith's Atlanta mosque. Another woman, Dora Muhammad, also rose as an editor on *The Call*, the Chicago paper of the Nation of Islam.

Women in the Civil Rights movement and in the Nation of Islam dealt with repeated refusals by male leaders to allow them into leadership position. Key female activists in SCLC and SNCC argued that a woman should be able to speak from the podium of the 1963 civil rights March on Washington, for example, suggesting that SNCC's Diane Nash be given that role. Instead they were told that women were included, activist Pauli Murray recalled, because Marion Anderson and Mahalia Jackson were scheduled to sing. In part, the political traditions of the past decades limited women's positions, but to some extent, the connections with religious traditions also constrained women. Feminist author Alice Walker responded to this history in the 1980s with arguments for a *womanist* theology, celebrating black women's independence, creativity, and spirituality. Adherents have contended that the distinctive place of African American women constitutes a unique historical experience which centers on community and mutuality.[50]

As the Civil Rights movement allowed Americans to reconsider the construction of citizenship, other questions of rights emerged. Through the 1960s, challenges to the Vietnam war; reaction to cultural conventions surrounding sex, drugs, and family; and the rise of a "counter-culture" meant confusion and anxiety to many. Two foundations of society seemed especially threatened, gender roles and religion.

By the mid-1960s, liberal clergy were questioning a range of ideas and practices, from the construction of liturgies to the composition of congregations. Following in the wake of Vatican II and the Catholic Church's loosening of such traditions as Latin mass and no-meat Fridays, Catholic parishioners responded to the less restrictive guidelines with horror or greater involvement. The assumptions of Christianity seemed unmoored, never more so than when Episcopal bishop James A. Pike of California openly questioned assumptions about a holy Trinity and the power of God. In 1966, *Time* magazine posed the question, "Is God Dead?", citing the popularity of Buddhism, atheism, and other spiritual alternatives.[51]

Another bombshell hit the American religious community in 1968, when Pope Paul VI issued a new encyclical, *Humanae Vitae*, or "On Human Life." The Pope declared that observant Catholics should refuse contraception, abortion, and other forms of reproductive control; marital sexuality was ordained for procreation, the Pope said. The impact on American Catholics was "devastating." Many Catholics found the choice between obedience and contraceptive difficult, as it presented new limits on both couples' decisions to limit family size and women's opportunities to work. Those who determined that the use of contraception did not violate their faith knew that the Church did not sustain that view; those who accepted the Pope's guidance found themselves at odds with other Americans determined to allow women some means of reproductive control. This debate intensified in 1973, when the Supreme Court overturned laws barring women's access to abortion services in *Roe v. Wade*. Those who disagreed strongly organized politically, creating the National Right to Life Committee in 1973.[52]

The women's movement that emerged in the 1960s and early 1970s had other dramatic effects on American religion. In mainstream Protestant congregations, women questioned their secondary role in church organization and spiritual life. Although some denominations already allowed women to be ministers, those who were made up fewer than 3 percent of ordained clergy. Congregationalists, the Disciples of Christ, the Assemblies of God, and Unitarian Universalists could describe a heritage of female ministers going back to the nineteenth century, and some pentecostalist and evangelical churches also accepted women preachers. For Presbyterians, Episcopalians, and other mainstream Protestants, the path to women in the priesthood came in largely hesitant steps. The Episcopal Church allowed women to be deacons (lay ministers) in 1970, but the refusal of the Church to move farther led to a protest in 1973, when eleven women received "ordination" by retired bishops. Finally, in 1976, the Church authorized dioceses to ordain women at will, and the next year, 1977, mandated women's acceptance. Pauli Murray became the first ordained African American woman priest in the faith in 1977, and in 1989, Barbara Harris became the first female Episcopal bishop (and the first American female bishop of any faith). In 2006, Katharine Jefferts Schori was elected to head the national church, the first woman to serve in that capacity in any mainstream denomination.

Christian theology became a deepening concern for women as well. In 1968, Mary Daly published an analysis of sexism in religion titled *The Church and the Second Sex*, and followed it with *Beyond God the Father* in 1973 and *Gyn/Ecology* in 1978. She challenged the assumptions of most Christians that God was male, provoking other feminists to reconsider gender and the foundations of faith. The re-examination of women in religion prompted by Daly and other writers such as Rosemary Ruether, a theology professor at the Claremont School of Theology, contributed to a rethinking of gender in many congregations and denominations. Between the 1970s and 1990s, liturgies, prayer books, hymns, and bible translations appeared which used inclusive language, ending an insistence on the maleness of God. In the Catholic Church, for example, the International Commission on English (ICEL) in the Liturgy attempted in 1997 to revise prayers. One that read "Behold the Lamb of God, who takes away the sins of the world. Blessed are those who are called to his supper" was under ICEL guidelines changed to read, "Behold the Lamb of God, who takes away the sin of the world. Blessed are those who are called to the banquet of the Lamb." These efforts led to disagreements within American congregations with the Vatican and with each other. Some bishops noted that even more conservative denominations used more gender-neutral language than the Vatican was then willing to accept; others rejected attempts to remove traditional words and phrases. The issue underlying such debates, the nature of gender and divinity, continues to provoke sharp discussions among the faithful.[53]

In Judaism, women gained access to the rabbinate after 1970. Sally Priesand became a rabbi in Reform practice in 1972; Sandy Eisenberg Sasso was the first female rabbi in the Reconstructionist tradition.

Women were allowed to become rabbis for Conservative synagogues in 1985. Despite those milestones, the first women rabbis faced obstacles. Sally Priesand, for example, did not find a congregation for two years before she became the rabbi at Monmouth Reform Temple in Tinton Falls, New Jersey.

Divinity schools that had been reluctant to include women also shifted admissions policies and programs. In 1973, Harvard University opened the Women's Studies in Religion Program, for example, and other major universities such as Duke and Yale added similar programs. By 2000, almost one-quarter of students at the nation's divinity schools were women. At the same time, the Catholic Church refused to accept women to the priesthood. The Church of Jesus Christ of Latter-Day Saints and Missouri Synod Lutherans retain their prohibitions against women as ministers.

The women's movement promoted some women to explore other avenues of spirituality. Zen Buddhism, Hare Krishna, and Transcendental Meditation drew practitioners in the 1970s. Other women participated in pagan practices, and Wicca, a traditional form of witchcraft, also attracted adherents who sought a more naturalistic or woman-centered faith. Others considered a less formalized spiritual path, considering a rejection of male-defined traditions through "matriarchal" practices that celebrate nature, a goddess, or other mystical forms. One practitioner of feminist spirituality described her belief in the earth as a living manifestation of the goddess, a naturalistic force of healing and love.[54]

These beliefs became inflammatory to some religious Americans. The conservative fundamentalist movement found much in the 1960s and 1970s that was objectionable and disturbing, from open witchcraft and pagan spirituality to a more relaxed nonmarital sexuality. Abortion and women's rights seemed to suggest women assuming male roles and violating maternal imperatives. Through the 1970s, Americans ill at ease with apparent confusion in gender roles and liberal faith found more comfort in fundamentalist faith. The ideas of premillennialism of fundamentalist denominations also convinced followers that the disorder in America might signal the day of worldly life. This created a different anxiety. As one analyst noted, a focus on Jesus's arrival prior to the millennium, a premise of premillennialism, meant that one should not divert attention toward politics and worldly things; the critical task for Christians would instead be to prepare for Christ's arrival. Yet the conflicting values at play in a diverse society aroused concern and anger. Then evangelicals realized that they could be more effective in achieving their religious goals, and social change, through political organization.

The rise of the religious right in the United States developed from the liberal politics of the 1960s, the strength of the women's movement, and the traditions of fundamentalism of earlier decades. The Supreme Court's

Tammy Faye Bakker and her husband, Jim Bakker, were television evangelists from 1976 to 1987. AP photo/Lou Krasky.

willingness to uphold the separation of church and state in cases such as *Engel* v. *Vitale* in 1962, which prohibited directed prayers in public schools, also suggested a need for political solutions. In 1979, Virginia minister Jerry Falwell formed the Moral Majority, and conservative political organizers such as Richard Viguerie responded by linking evangelicals with politicians such as Ronald Reagan. The new conservative coalition contributed significantly to the election of Reagan in 1980. Other conservative Christian groups appeared, such as Christian Voice, formed in California to oppose pornography and gay rights. By 1987, minister Pat Robertson, who founded the 700 Club on television, attempted to run for president. Although Robertson was unsuccessful, his effort led to the formation of the Christian Coalition in 1989.

The Christian Right vocally opposed changes in gender roles, rights for gays and lesbians, and public access to reproductive services. Focus on the Family, created by psychologist James Dobson, actively linked Christian messages to political action and support for "traditional" marriage. Dobson clarified the nature of the ideal family, one in which men and women retain biblically established, gender specific roles. For women's rights activists and those supporting reproductive rights, Christian politics seemed a distinct threat to the legal and personal advances won since the 1960s. Erosion of *Roe*, for example, came in a series of challenges through state legislatures and Congress, with strong backing from Christian Right organizations.[55]

By 2000, the Christian Right continued to influence politics, yet within the next five years, its reach diminished. Fragmented by scandals of sexual or financial impropriety in evangelical churches, the evangelical community also showed signs of moderating on social issues. A widening divide between "purists and pragmatists" reflected differences over whether there should be exceptions in laws against abortion to protect women's lives and health, over the need for environmental regulations, and over assistance to the poor worldwide. Some evangelical congregations appeared weary of political engagement, viewing it as detrimental from the true mission of their churches.[56]

In the new century, women continued to press for opportunities to express their religious convictions fully. In the Roman Catholic Church, for example, some women remained determined to win access to the priesthood; by 2007, approximately forty women had been "ordained" in defiance of canon law. Practitioners of womanist theology included prominent female professors at mainstream divinity schools; Delores Williams, the Paul Tillich Professor of Feminist Theology at Union Theological Seminary, described herself as a womanist theologian concerned with race, class, and gender, for example.

Religious discrimination remains a challenging question for Muslim women in the United States. By 2007, approximately 2,000 mosques served a population of seven to nine million American Muslims, a community that included immigrants and native-born citizens. Following the 2001 bombings of the World Trade Center and the Pentagon, religious tolerance for Muslims grew more fragile. Practices by Muslim women, such as the wearing of the hijab, a head-covering used by the observant, or modesty in exposing female bodies to men, continue to cause controversies. Some employers, from airlines to fitness clubs, refuse to allow Muslim women to wear the hijab, although such practice is protected by law. At the same time, however, some facilities accommodate the needs of Muslim women, such as providing segregated exercise classes or female-only athletic events.[57] Dissident Muslim American women have attempted to lead prayers in progressive mosques, while others cite their comfort with traditional practices of female reticence, arranged marriage, and modesty. The practice of faith in a society hesitant to accept differences remains fraught with difficulty for all Muslim women in America, as they seek to define themselves and their religion.

The questions of spirituality and faith raised by American women in the twentieth century remain central to the nation's identity. The Constitutional protections for religious freedom revered by generations and heralded by immigrants provide no special insight on gender. How Americans interpret the intersections between faith and women's roles remain matters of choice and contest.

NOTES

1. Betty A. DeBerg, *Ungodly Women: Gender and the First Wave of American Fundamentalism* (Macon, GA: Mercer University Press, 2000); Daniel Mark Epstein, *Sister Aimee: The Life of Aimee Semple McPherson* (New York: Harcourt Trade, 1994); Matthew Avery Sutton, *Aimee Semple McPherson and the Resurrection of Christian America* (Cambridge, MA: Harvard University Press, 2007).

2. Anne Braude, *Women and American Religion* (New York: Oxford University Press, 2000).

3. Braude, *Women and American Religion*, 3; Barbara Welter, "She Hath Done What She Could: Protestant Women's Missionary Careers in Nineteenth-Century America," in *Women in American Religion*, ed. Janet Wilson James (Philadelphia: University of Pennsylvania Press, 1980), 111–126.

4. Lois A. Boyd and R. Douglas Brackenridge, *Presbyterian Women in America* (Westport, CT: Greenwood Press, 1983), 31–41.

5. Karla Goldman, *Beyond the Synagogue Gallery: Finding a Place for Women in American Judaism* (Cambridge, MA: Harvard University Press, 2001).

6. Elizabeth Hayes Turner, *Women, Culture, and Community: Religion and Reform in Galveston, 1880–1920* (New York: Oxford University Press, 1997): 68.

7. Nancy Woloch, *Women and the American Experience* (New York: McGraw Hill, 2006): 287.

8. Dean George Hodges, "Religion in the Settlement," *Proceedings of the National Conference of Charities and Correction* (Boston: Geo. H. Ellis and P. S. King & Son, 1896), 150–153, http://tigger.uic.edu/htbin/cgiwrap/bin/urbanexp/main.cgi?file=new/show_doc.ptt&doc=894&chap=24.

9. Elizabeth Lasch-Quinn, *Black Neighbors: Race and the Limits of Reform in the American Settlement House Movement, 1890–1945* (Chapel Hill: University of North Carolina Press, 1993), 10.

10. Paul Harvey, *Redeeming the South: Religious Cultures and Racial Identities Among Southern Baptists, 1865–1925* (Chapel Hill: University of North Carolina Press, 1997).

11. Evelyn Brooks Higginbotham, *Righteous Discontent: The Women's Movement in the Black Baptist Church, 1880–1920* (Cambridge, MA: Harvard University Press, 1993), 14.

12. Braude, *Women and American Religion*, 100.

13. Melissa Walker et al., *Southern Women at the Millennium: A Historical Perspective* (Columbia: University of Missouri Press, 2003), 59.

14. Braude, *Women and American Religion*, 102.

15. Anne Braude, "Jewish Women in the Twentieth Century: Building a Life in America," in *Women and Religion in America, Volume Three: 1900–1968*, ed. Rosemary Radford Ruether and Rosemary Skinner Keller (New York: Harper and Row, 1986), 132.

16. Norma Fain Pratt, "Transitions in Judaism: The Jewish American Woman through the 1930s," in *Women in American Religion*, ed. Janet Wilson James (Philadelphia: University of Pennsylvania Press, 1980), 207–228.

17. Susan A. Glenn, *Daughters of the Shtetl: Life and Labor in the Immigrant Generation* (Ithaca, NY: Cornell University Press, 1991).

18. Ronald Takaki, *A Different Mirror: A History of Multicultural America* (Boston: Little, Brown, 1993): 247–255; Braude, *Women and American Religion*, 77.

19. Kay Parker, "American Indian Women and Religion on the Southern Plains," in *Women and Religion in America*, ed. Rosemary Radford Ruether and Rosemary Skinner Keller (New York: Harper and Row, 1986), 48–79.

20. Gordon B. Hinkley, "The Family: A Proclamation to the World," The Church of the Latter-day Saints, http://www.lds.org/library/display/0,4945,161-1-11-1,00.html.

21. Claudia L. Bushman, *Contemporary Mormonism: Latter-Day Saints in Modern America* (Westport, CT: Praeger, 2006).

22. Ibid., 23.

23. Ibid., 13, 23.

24. George M. Marsden, *Fundamentalism and American Culture: The Shaping of Twentieth-Century Evangelicalism, 1870–1925* (New York: Oxford University Press, 1982).

25. Marsden, *Fundamentalism and American Culture.*

26. Michael Lienesch, *In the Beginning: Fundamentalism, the Scopes Trial, and the Making of the Antievolution Movement* (Chapel Hill: University of North Carolina, 2007), 57–58.

27. Margaret Lamberts Bendroth, *Fundamentalism and Gender, 1875 to the Present* (New Haven, CT: Yale University Press, 1993), 65.

28. I Corinthians 14:34.

29. DeBerg, *Ungodly Women*, 46.

30. Bendroth, *Fundamentalism and Gender*, 64.

31. DeBerg, *Ungodly Women.*

32. Randall Balmer, "Religion in Twentieth Century America," in *Religion in American Life: A Short History*, ed. Jon Butler, Grant Wacker, and Randall Balmer (New York: Oxford University Press, 2000), 352.

33. Ibid.

34. Jualyne E. Dodson and Cheryl Townsend Gilkes, "Something Within: Social Change and Collective Education in the Sacred World of Black Christian Women," in *Women and Religion in America, Volume Three: 1900–1968*, ed. Rosemary Radford Ruether and Rosemary Skinner Keller (New York: Harper and Row, 1986), 80–130.

35. Sarah Deutsch, *Women and the City: Gender, Space, and Power in Boston, 1870–1940* (New York: Oxford University Press, 2000), 39, 41.

36. Timothy Walch, *Immigrant America: European Ethnicity in the United States* (London: Taylor & Francis, 1994), 142.

37. Mary Jo Weaver, "American Catholics in the Twentieth Century," in *Perspectives on American Religion and Culture: A Reader*, ed. Peter W. Williams (New York: Blackwell, 1999), 154–168.

38. Cited in Ruether and Keller, *Women and Religion in America*, 185, 188.

39. James J. Kenneally, "Eve, Mary, and the Historians: American Catholicism and Women," in *Women in American Religion*, ed. Janet Wilson James (Philadelphia: University of Pennsylvania Press, 1980), 191–206.

40. Maureen Fitzgerald, *Habits of Compassion: Irish Catholic Nuns and the Origins of New York's Welfare System, 1830–1920* (Urbana: University of Illinois Press, 2006); Suellen M. Hoy, *Good Hearts: Catholic Sisters in Chicago's Past* (Urbana: University of Illinois Press, 2006); Carol Coburn and Martha Smith, *Spirited Lives: How Nuns Shaped Catholic Culture and American Life, 1836–1920* (Chapel Hill: University of North Carolina Press, 1999).

41. Rosemary Radford Ruether, *Christianity and the Making of the Modern Family: Ruling Ideologies, Diverse Realities* (Boston: Beacon Press, 2001), 123.

42. T. H. Watkins, *The Hungry Years: A Narrative History of the Great Depression in America* (New York: Henry Holt, 1999), 158.

43. Peter W. Williams, *America's Religions: From Their Origins to the Twenty-First Century* (Urbana: University of Illinois Press, 2008), 252.

44. Dorothy Day, "Wealth, the Humanity of Christ, Class War," *Catholic Worker*, June 1935, http://www.catholicworker.org/dorothyday/daytext.cfm?TextID=290.

45. Martin E. Marty, *Modern American Religion: Under God, Indivisible, 1941–1960* (Chicago: University of Chicago Press, 1999).

46. Balmer, "Religion in Twentieth Century America," 367; Robert Wuthnow, *After Heaven: Spirituality in America Since the 1950s* (Berkeley: University of California Press, 2000).

47. David Harrington Watt, "The Private Hopes of American Fundamentalists and Evangelicals, 1925–1975," *Religion and American Culture* Vol. 1, No. 2 (Summer 1991): 155–175.

48. Cited in Vicki L. Crawford et al., *Women in the Civil Rights Movement: Trailblazers and Torchbearers, 1941–1965* (Bloomington: Indiana University Press, 1993): 45.

49. Rosetta E. Ross, *Witnessing and Testifying: Black Women, Religion, and Civil Rights* (Minneapolis, MN: Fortress Press, 2003): 132.

50. Michael Battle, *The Black Church in America: African American Christian Spirituality* (New York: Blackwell, 2006); Charles Eric Lincoln and Lawrence H. Mamiya, *The Black Church in the African-American Experience* (Durham, NC: Duke University Press, 1990).

51. "Toward a Hidden God," *Time Magazine*, April 8, 1966.

52. Balmer, "Religion in Twentieth Century America," 418.

53. Pamela Schaeffer, "Debate over Language Lingers," *National Catholic Reporter*, July 4, 1997.

54. Cynthia Eller, *Living in the Lap of the Goddess: The Feminist Spirituality Movement in America* (Boston: Beacon Press, 1995), 17.

55. Clyde Wilcox, *Onward Christian Soldiers? The Religious Right in American Politics* (Boulder, CO: Westview Press, 2000), 55.

56. Kevin Sack, "Religious Right's Tactician on Wider Crusade," *New York Times*, June 12, 1998; David D. Kirkpatrick, "The Evangelical Crackup," *New York Times*, October 28, 2007.

57. Oren Dorell, "Efforts to Accommodate Muslim Women's Modesty Spurs Debate," *USA Today*, June 13, 2007; Dana Lee Robert, *American Women in Mission: A Social History of Their Thought and Practice* (Macon, GA: Mercer University Press, 1997).

Selected Bibliography

Abel, Emily K. "Benevolence and Social Control: Advice from the Children's Bureau in the Early Twentieth Century." *Social Service Review* Vol. 68, No. 1 (1994): 1–19.

———. *Hearts of Wisdom: American Women Caring for Kin, 1850–1940.* Cambridge, MA: Harvard University Press, 2002.

———. "'Women Who Have No Men to Work for Them': Gender and Homelessness in the Great Depression." *Feminist Studies* Vol. 29, No. 1 (2003): 104–127.

Adler, Jeffrey S. "I Loved Joe, But I Had to Shoot Him": Homicide by Women in Turn-of-the-Century Chicago." *Journal of Criminal Law and Criminology* Vol. 92, No. 3/4 (2002): 867–898.

Allen, Ann Taylor. "'Let Us Live with Our Children': Kindergarten Movements in Germany and the United States, 1840–1914." *History of Education Quarterly* Vol. 28, No. 1 (1988): 23–48.

Anderson, Karen. *Wartime Women: Sex Roles, Family Relations, and the Status of Women during World War II.* Westport, CT: Greenwood Press, 1981.

Andersen, Kristi. *After Suffrage: Women in Partisan and Electoral Politics before the New Deal.* Chicago: University of Chicago Press, 1996.

Atkins-Sayre, Wendy. "'Naming Women': The Emergence of 'Ms.' as a Liberating Title." *Women and Language* Vol. 28, No. 1 (2005): 8–16.

Bailey, Beth. *From Front Porch to Back Seat: Courtship in Twentieth-Century America.* Baltimore: Johns Hopkins University Press, 1988.

———. *Sex in the Heartland.* Cambridge, MA: Harvard University Press, 2002.

Baker, Paula. "The Domestication of Politics: Women and American Political Society, 1780–1920." *American Historical Review* Vol. 89, No. 3 (1984): 620–647.

———. *Moral Frameworks of Public Life: Gender, Politics, and the State in Rural New York, 1870–1930.* New York: Oxford University Press, 1993.

Baron, Ava, ed. *Work Engendered: Toward a New History of American Labor.* Ithaca, NY: Cornell University Press, 1991.

Barrett, James R. "Americanization from the Bottom Up: Immigration and the Remaking of the Working Class in the United States, 1880–1930." *Journal of American History* Vol. 79, No. 3 (1992): 996–1020.

Bates, Gerri. "These Hallowed Halls: African American Women College and University Presidents." *Journal of Negro Education* Vol. 76 Issue 3 (2007): 373–390.

Behling, Laura. "'The Woman at the Wheel': Marketing Ideal Womanhood, 1915–1934." *Journal of American Culture* Vol. 20, No. 3 (1997): 13–30.

Bendroth, Margaret. *Fundamentalism and Gender, 1875 to the Present.* New Haven, CT: Yale University Press, 1993.

Benson, Susan Porter. *Counter Cultures: Saleswomen, Managers, and Customers in American Department Stores, 1890–1940.* Urbana: University of Illinois Press, 1986.

Berry, Mary Frances. *The Politics of Parenthood: Child Care, Women's Rights, and the Myth of the Good Mother.* New York: Viking Press, 1983.

Berube, Allan. *Coming Out under Fire: Coming Out Under Fire: The History of Gay Men and Women in World War II.* New York: Simon and Schuster, 2000.

Biondi, Martha. *To Stand and Fight: The Struggle for Civil Right in Postwar New York City.* Cambridge, MA: Harvard University Press, 2003.

Blackwelder, Julia Kirk. *Now Hiring: The Feminization of Work in the United States, 1900–1995.* College Station: Texas A&M University Press, 1997.

———. *Women of the Depression: Caste and Culture in San Antonio, 1929–1939.* College Station: Texas A&M University Press, 1999.

Blackenship, Kim M. "Bringing Gender and Race In U.S. Employment Discrimination Policy." *Gender and Society* Vol. 7, No. 2 (1993): 204–226.

Blee, Kathleen M. *Women and the Klan: Racism and Gender in the 1920s.* Berkeley: University of California Press, 1991.

Bolin, Winifred D. Wandersee. "The Economics of Middle-Income Family Life: Working Women during the Great Depression." *Journal of American History* Vol. 65, No. 1 (1978): 60–74.

Bolt, Christine. *Sisterhood Questioned?: Race, Class, and Internationalism in the American and British Women's Movements, 1880s–1970s.* New York: Routledge, 2004.

Boris, Eileen. *Home to Work: Motherhood and the Politics of Industrial Homework in the United States.* New York: Cambridge University Press, 1994.

Boyd, Robert L. "Race, Labor Market Disadvantage, and Survivalist Enterpreneurship: Black Women in the Urban North during the Great Depression." *Sociological Forum* Vol. 15, No. 4 (2000): 647–670.

Bradley, Patricia. *Women and the Press: The Struggle for Equality.* Evanston, IL: Northwestern University Press, 2005.

Brekus, Catherine A., ed. *The Religious History of American Women: Reimagining the Past.* Chapel Hill: University of North Carolina Press, 2007.

Brodkin, Kimberly. "'We Are Neither Male Nor Female Democrats': Gender Difference and Women's Integration within the Democratic Party." *Journal of Women's History* Vol. 19, Issue 2 (2007): 111–137.

Brown, Dorothy Marie, et al. *The Poor Belong to Us: Catholic Charities and American Welfare.* Cambridge, MA: Harvard University Press, 1997.

Brown, Elsa Barkley. "'What Has Happened Here?': The Politics of Difference in Women's History and Feminist Politics." *Feminist Studies* Vol. 18, No. 2 (1992): 295–312.

Brown, Nikki. *Private Politics and Public Voices: Black Women's Activism from* World *War I to the New Deal*. Bloomington: Indiana University Press, 2006.

Brown, Victoria Bissell. "The Fear of Feminization: Los Angeles High Schools in the Progressive Era." *Feminist Studies* Vol. 16 Issue 3 (1990): 493–519.

Brumberg, Joan. *Fasting Girls: The History of Anorexia Nervosa*. Cambridge, MA: Harvard University Press, 1998.

Brumberg, Joan. "'Ruined' Girls: Changing Community Responses to Illegitimacy in Upstate New York, 1890–1920." *Journal of Social History* Vol. 18, No. 2 (1984): 247–272.

Brush, Lisa D. "Worthy Widows, Welfare Cheats: Proper Womanhood in Expert Needs Talk about Single Mothers in the United States, 1900 to 1988." *Gender and Society* Vol. 11, No. 6 (1997): 720–746.

Buhle, Mari Jo. *Women and American Socialism, 1870–1920*. Urbana: University of Illinois Press, 1983.

Caldwell, Katherine L. "Not Ozzie and Harriet: Postwar Divorce and the American Liberal Welfare State." *Law and Social Inquiry* Vol. 23, No. 1 (1998): 1–53.

Cameron, Ardis. "Cultures of Belonging: Women, Popular Culture, and Activism." *Journal of Women's History* 18(2006): 128–136.

Cameron, Ardis. *Radicals of the Worst Sort: Laboring Women in Lawrence, Massachusetts, 1860–1912*. Urbana: University of Illinois Press, 1993.

Campbell, D'Ann. "Women in Uniform: The World War II Experiment." *Military Affairs* Vol. 51, No. 3 (1987): 137–139.

Cancian, Francesca M., and Steven L. Gordon. "Changing Emotion Norms in Marriage: Love and Anger in U.S. Women's Magazines since 1900." *Gender and Society* Vol. 2, No. 3 (1988): 308–342.

Carlson, Robert A. "Americanization as an Early Twentieth-Century Adult Education Movement." *History of Education Quarterly* Vol. 10, No. 4 (1970): 440–464.

Carroll, Susan J., ed. *The Impact of Women in Public Office*. Bloomington: Indiana University Press, 2001.

Carson, Mina. *Settlement Folk: Social Thought and the American Settlement Movement, 1885–1930*. Chicago: University of Chicago Press, 1990.

Cauthern, Nancy K., and Edwin Amenta. "Not for Widows Only: Institutional Politics and the Formative Years of Aid to Dependent Children." *American Sociological Review* Vol. 61, No. 3 (1996): 427–448.

Chafe, William. *The American Woman: Her Changing Social, Economic, and Political Roles, 1920–1970*. New York: Oxford University Press, 1972.

Chafe, William. *The Paradox of Change: American Women in the 20th Century*. New York: Oxford University Press, 1992.

Chan, Susan K. "From the 'Muscle Moll' to the 'Butch' Ballplayer: Mannishness, Lesbianism, and Homophobia in U.S. Women's Sport." *Feminist Studies* Vol. 19, No. 2 (1993): 343–368.

Chapkis, Wendy. "Trafficking, Migration, and the Law: Protecting Innocents, Punishing Immigrants." *Gender and Society* Vol. 17, No. 6 (2003): 923–937.

Chin, Margaret May. *Sewing Women: Immigrants and the New York City Garment Industry*. New York: Columbia University Press, 2005.

Chused, Richard H. "Late Nineteenth Century Married Women's Property Law: Reception of the Early Married Women's Property Acts by Courts and Legislatures." *American Journal of Legal History* Vol. 29, No. 1 (1985): 3–35.

Clark, Claudia. *Radium Girls, Women and Industrial Health Reform, 1910–1935.* Chapel Hill: University of North Carolina Press, 1997.

Clark, David S. "American Legal Education: Yesterday and Today." *International Journal of the Legal Profession* Vol. 10 Issue 1 (2003): 93–108.

Clark, Mary L. "Women as Supreme Court Advocates, 1879–1979." *Journal of Supreme Court History* Vol. 30 (2005): 47–67.

Clarke, Deborah. *Driving Women: Fiction and Automobile Culture in Twentieth-Century America.* Baltimore: Johns Hopkins University Press, 2007.

Clemens, Elisabeth S. "Securing Political Returns to Social Capital: Women's Associations in the United States, 1880s–1920s." *Journal of Interdisciplinary History* Vol. 29, No. 4 (1999): 613–638.

Cobble, Dorothy Sue. *Dishing It Out: Waitresses and their Unions in the Twentieth Century.* Urbana: University of Illinois Press, 1991.

Cohen, Lizabeth. *A Consumers' Republic: The Politics of Mass Consumption in Postwar America.* New York: Alfred A. Knopf, 2003.

Collins, Patricia Hill. *Black Feminist Thought: Knowledge, Consciousness, and the Politics of Empowerment.* New York: Routledge, 1991.

Coontz, Stephanie. *The Way We Never Were: American Families and the Nostalgia Trap.* New York: Basic Books, 1993.

Cook, Blance Wiessen. "Women Alone Stir My Imagination": Lesbianism and the Cultural Tradition. " *Signs* Vol. 4, No. 4 (1979): 718–739.

Costa, Dora L. "From Mill Town to Board Room: The Rise of Women's Paid Labor." *Journal of Economic Perspectives* Vol. 14, No. 4 (2000): 101–122.

Cott, Nancy F. *The Grounding of Modern Feminism.* New Haven, CT: Yale University Press, 1987.

———. "Marriage and Women's Citizenship in the United States, 1830–1934." *American Historical Review* Vol. 3 (1998): 1440–1473.

———. "What's in a Name? The Limits of 'Social Feminism;' or, Expanding the Vocabulary of Women's History." *Journal of American History* Vol. 76, No. 3 (1989): 809–829.

Cott, Nancy F., ed. *No Small Courage: A History of Women in the United States.* New York: Oxford University Press, 2000.

———. *Public Vows: A History of Marriage and the Nation.* Cambridge, MA: Harvard University Press, 2000.

Cowan, Ruth Schwartz. *More Work for Mother: The Ironies of Household Technology from the Open Hearth to the Microwave.* New York: Basic Books, 1983.

Creager, Angela H., et al. *Feminism in Twentieth-Century Science, Technology, and Medicine.* Chicago: University of Chicago Press, 2001.

Critchlow, Donald T. *Phyllis Schlafly and Grassroots Conservatism: A Woman's Crusade.* Princeton, NJ: Princeton University Press, 2005.

Crocker, Ruth Hutchinson. *Social Work and Social Order: The Settlement Movement in Two Industrial Cities, 1889–1930.* Urbana: University of Illinois Press, 1992.

Cuordileone, K. A. "'Politics in an Age of Anxiety': Cold War Political Culture and the Crisis in American Masculinity, 1949–1960." *Journal of American History* Vol. 87, No. 2 (2000): 515–545.

Curran, Laura. "Social Work's Revised Maternalism: Mothers, Workers, and Welfare in Early Cold War America, 1946–1963." Journal of Women's History Vol. 17 Issue 1 (2005): 112–136.

Dagbovie, Pero Gaglo. "Black Women Historians from the Late 19th Century to the Dawning of the Civil Rights Movement." *Journal of African American History.* Vol. 89, No. 3 (2004): 241–261.

Danzi, Angela D., and Susan Cotts Watkins. "Women's Gossip and Social Change: Childbirth and Fertility Control among Italian and Jewish Women in the United States, 1920–1940." *Gender and Society* Vol. 9, No. 4 (1995): 469–490.

Davis, Allen. *Spearheads for Reform: The Social Settlements and the Progressive Movement, 1890–1914.* New York: Oxford, 1967.

Deckman, Melissa Marie. *School Board Battles: The Christian Right in Local Politics.* Washington, DC: Georgetown University Press, 2004.

D'Emilio, John D., and Estelle B. Freedman. *Intimate Matters: A History of Sexuality in America.* Chicago: University of Chicago Press, 1988.

Dellinger, Kirsten. "Makeup at Work: Negotiating Appearance Rules in the Workplace." *Gender and Society* Vol. 11, No. 2 (1997): 151–177.

Devlin, Rachel. *Relative Intimacy: Fathers, Adolescent Daughters, and Postwar American Culture.* Chapel Hill: University of North Carolina Press, 2005.

Deitch, Cynthia. "Gender, Race, and Class Politics and the Inclusion of Women in Title VII of the 1964 Civil Rights Act." *Gender and Society* Vol. 7, No. 2 (1993): 183–203.

Deutsch, Sarah. "Learning to Talk More Like a Man: Class-Bridging Organizations, 1870–1940." *American Historical Review* Vol. 97, No. 2 (1992): 379–404.

———. *Women and the City: Gender, Space, and Power in Boston, 1870–1940.* New York: Oxford University Press, 2000.

Dodson, Debra L. *The Impact of Women in Congress.* New York: Oxford University Press, 2006.

Dolgin, Janet L. "The Constitution as Family Arbiter: A Moral in the Mess?" *Columbia Law Review* Vol. 102, No. 2 (2002): 337–407.

Dorr, Lisa Lindquist. "Black-on-White Rape and Retribution in Twentieth-Century Virginia: 'Men, Even Negroes, Must Have Some Protection.'" *Journal of Southern History* 66 (2000): 711–748.

———. *White Women, Rape, and the Power of Race in Virginia, 1900–1960.* Chapel Hill: University of North Carolina Press, 2004.

Douglas, Davidson M. *Jim Crow Moves North: The Battle over Northern School Segregation, 1865–1954.* New York: Cambridge University Press, 2005.

Douglas, Deborah G. *American Women and Flight since 1940.* Lexington: University Press of Kentucky, 2004.

Douglas, Susan Jeanne. *Where the Girls Are: Growing Up Female with the Mass Media.* New York: Times Books, 1994.

Drachman, Virginia G. *Enterprising Women: 250 Years of American Business.* Chapel Hill: University of North Carolina Press, 2002.

———. *Sisters in Law: Women Lawyers in Modern American History.* Cambridge, MA: Harvard University Press, 1998.

Dubler R. Ariela. "In the Shadow of Marriage: Single Women and the Legal Construction of the Family and the State." *Yale Law Journal* Vol. 112, No. 7 (2003): 1641–1715.

DuBois, Ellen Carol. *Feminism and Suffrage: The Emergence of an Independent Women's Movement in America.* Ithaca, NY: Cornell University Press, 1979.

DuBois, Ellen Carol, and Vicki L. Ruiz, eds. *Unequal Sisters: A Multicultural Reader in U.S. Women's History.* New York: Routledge, 1990.

———. "Working Women, Class Relations, and Suffrage Militance: Harriot Stanton Blatch and the New York Woman Suffrage Movement, 1894–1909." *Journal of American History* Vol. 74, No. 1 (1987): 34–58.

Durst, Anne. "'Of Women, by Women, and for Women': The Day Nursery Movement in the Progressive Era United States." *Journal of Social History* Vol. 39, No. 1 (2005): 141–159.

Dye, Nancy S., and Noralee Frankel, eds., *Gender, Class, Race, and Reform in the Progressive Era.* Lexington: University Press of Kentucky, 1995.

Echols, Alice. *Shaky Ground: The '60s and Its Aftershocks.* New York: Columbia University Press, 2002.

Eisenmann, Linda. *Higher Education for Women in Postwar America, 1945–1965.* Baltimore: Johns Hopkins University Press, 2006.

Enstad, Nan. *Ladies of Labor, Girls of Adventure: Working Women, Popular Culture, and Labor Politics at the Turn of the Century.* New York: Columbia University Press, 1999.

Evans, Sara M. *Born for Liberty: A History of Women in America.* New York: Simon and Schuster, 1997.

Evans, Sara. *Personal Politics: The Roots of Women's Liberation in the Civil Rights Movement and the New Left.* New York: Vintage Books, 1979.

———. *Tidal Wave: How Women Changed America at Century's End.* New York: Free Press, 2003.

Evans, Stephanie Y. *Black Women in the Ivory Tower, 1850–1954: An Intellectual History.* Gainesville: University Press of Florida, 2007.

Faderman, Lillian. *Odd Girls and Twilight Lovers: A History of Lesbian Life in Twentieth-Century America.* New York: Columbia University Press, 1991.

Fairclough, Adam. *A Class of Their Own: Black Teachers in the Segregated South.* Cambridge, MA: Harvard University Press, 2007.

Fass, Paula. *The Beautiful and the Damned: American Youth in the 1920's.* New York: Oxford University Press, 1975.

Feldstein, Ruth. *Motherhood in Black and White: Race and Sex in American Liberalism, 1930–1965.* Ithaca, NY: Cornell University Press, 2000.

Fessler, Ann. *The Girls Who Went Away: The Hidden History of Women Who Surrendered Children for Adoption in the Decades Before Roe V. Wade.* New York: Penguin, 2007.

Fields, Jill. "Fighting the Corsetless Evil: Shaping Corsets and Culture, 1900–1930." *Journal of Social History* Vol. 33, No. 2 (1999): 355–384.

Findlay, Eileen J. Suarez. *Imposing Decency, The Politics of Sexuality and Race in Puerto Rico, 1870–1920.* Durham, NC: Duke University Press, 1999.

Fine, Michelle, and Lois Weis. "Disappearing Acts: The State and Violence against Women in the Twentieth Century." *Signs* Vol. 25, No. 4 (2000): 1139–1146.

Finkelstein, Barbara. "A Crucible of Contradictions: Historical Roots of Violence against Children in the United States." *History of Education Quarterly* Vol. 40, No. 1 (2000): 1–21.

Ford, Lynne E. *Women and Politics: The Pursuit of Equality.* Boston: Houghton Mifflin, 2006.

Formanek-Brunell, Miriam. *Made to Play House: Dolls and the Commercialization of American Girlhood, 1830–1930.* New Haven, CT: Yale University Press, 1993.

Fox, Bonnie J. "Selling the Mechanized Household: 70 Years of Ads in Ladies Home Journal." *Gender and Society* Vol. 4, No. 1 (1990): 25–40.

Frank, Dana. "Housewives, Socialists, and the Politics of Food: The 1917 New York Cost-of-Living Protests." *Feminist Studies* Vol. 11, No. 2 (Summer 1985): 255–285.

Franklin, V. P. "Hidden in Plain View: African American Women, Radical Feminism, and the Origins of Women's Studies Programs, 1967–1974." *Journal of African American History* Vol. 87 (2002): 433–445.

Freedman, Estelle. "The New Woman: Changing Views of Women in the 1920s." *Journal of American History* Vol. 61, No. 2 (1974): 372–393.

———. *Their Sisters' Keepers: Women's Prison Reform in America, 1830–1930.* Ann Arbor: University of Michigan Press, 1984.

Freeman, Susan K. *Sex Goes to School: Girls and Sex Education Before the 1960s.* Urbana: University of Illinois Press, 2008.

Friedan, Betty. *The Feminine Mystique.* New York: Norton, 1963.

Friedman, Barbara. "'The Soldier Speaks': *Yank* Coverage of Women and Wartime Work." *American Journalism* Vol. 22, No. 2 (2005): 63–82.

Friedman, Lawrence M. *Private Lives: Families, Individuals, and the Law.* Cambridge, MA: Harvard University Press, 2004.

Furstenberg, Frank F. "History and Current Status of Divorce in the United States." *Future of Children* Vol. 4, No. 1 (1994): 29–43.

Gabaccia, Donna R. *From the Other Side: Women, Gender, and Immigrant Life in the U.S., 1820–1990.* Bloomington: Indiana University Press, 1994.

Gabin, Nancy F. *Feminism in the Labor Movement: Women and the United Auto Workers, 1935–1975.* Ithaca, NY: Cornell University Press, 1990.

———. "'They Have Placed a Penalty on Womanhood': The Protest Actions of Women Auto Workers in Detroit-Area UAW Locals, 1945–1947." *Feminist Studies* Vol. 8, No. 2 (1982): 373–398.

Gallagher, Julie. "Waging the 'Good Fight': The Political Career of Shirley Chisholm, 1953–1982." *Journal of African American History* Vol. 92, Issue 3 (2007): 392–416.

Gerhard, Jane F. *Desiring Revolution: Second-Wave Feminism and the Rewriting of American Sexual Thought, 1920 to 1982.* New York: Columbia University Press, 2001.

Giddings, Paula. *When and Where I Enter: The Impact of Black Women on Race and Sex in America.* New York: Morrow, 1984.

Gilboy, Janet A. "Deciding Who Gets In: Decisionmaking by Immigration Inspectors." *Law and Society Review* Vol. 25, No. 3 (1991): 571–600.

Gilmore, Glenda. *Gender and Jim Crow: Women and Politics of White Supremacy in North Carolina, 1896–1920.* Chapel Hill: University of North Carolina Press, 1996.

Ginzberg, Lori. *Women and the Work of Benevolence: Morality, Politics, and Class in the Nineteenth Century U.S.* Cambridge, MA: Harvard University Press, 1975.

Glenn, Evelyn NakaNo. "Cleaning Up/Kept Down: A Historical Perspective on Racial Inequality." *Stanford Law Review* Vol. 43, No. 6 (1991): 1333–1356.

———. "The Dialectics of Wage Work: Japanese-American Women and Domestic Service, 1905–1940." *Feminist Studies* Vol. 6, No. 3 (1980): 432–471.

———. *Unequal Freedom: How Race and Gender Shaped American Citizenship and Labor.* Cambridge, MA: Harvard University Press, 2002.

Goldin, Claudia. "The Changing Economic Role of Women: A Quantitative Approach." *Journal of Interdisciplinary History* Vol. 13, No. 4, (1983): 707–733.

———. "The Role of World War II in the Rise of Women's Employment." *American Economic Review* Vol. 81, No. 4 (1991): 741–756.

——. *Understanding the Gender Gap: An Economic History of American Women.* New York: Oxford University Press, 1990.

Goldin, Claudia, and Lawrence F. Katz. "The Shaping of Higher Education: The Formative Years in the United States, 1890 to 1940." *Journal of Economic Perspectives* Vol. 13, No. 1 (1999): 37–62.

Goodwin, Joanne L. *Gender and the Politics of Welfare Reform: Mothers' Pensions in Chicago, 1911–1929.* Chicago: University of Chicago Press, 1997.

Gordon, Ann D., and Bettye Collier-Thomas, eds. *African-American Women and the Vote, 1837–1965.* Amherst: University of Massachusetts Press, 1997.

Gordon, Linda. "Black and White Visions of Welfare: Women's Welfare Activism, 1890–1945." *Journal of American History* Vol. 78, No. 2 (1991): 559–590.

——. "Family Violence, Feminism, and Social Control." *Feminist Studies* Vol. 12, No. 3 (1986): 452–478.

——. *The Great Arizona Orphan Abduction.* Cambridge, MA: Harvard University Press, 1999.

——. *Heroes of Their Own Lives: The Politics and History of Family Violence: Boston, 1880–1960.* Urbana: University of Illinois Press, 2002.

——. *The Moral Property of Women: A History of Birth Control Politics in America.* Urbana: University of Illinois Press, 2007.

Gordon, Linda, and Ellen DuBois. "Seeking Ecstasy on the Battlefield: Danger and Pleasure in Nineteenth-Century Feminist Sexual Thought." *Feminist Studies* Vol. 9, No. 1 (1983): 7–25.

——. "Social Insurance and Public Assistance: The Influence of Gender in Welfare Thought in the United States, 1890–1935." *American Historical Review* Vol. 97, No. 1 (1992): 19–54.

Gordon, Linda, ed., *Women, the State, and Welfare.* Madison: University of Wisconsin Press, 1990.

Gordon, Lynn D. "The Gibson Girl Goes to College: Popular Culture and Women's Higher Education in the Progressive Era, 1890–1920." *American Quarterly* Vol. 39, No. 2 (1987): 211–230.

Graham, Laurel D. "Domesticating Efficiency: Lillian Gilbreth's Scientific Management of Homemakers, 1924–1930." *Signs* Vol. 24, No. 3 (1999): 633–675.

Graham, Sara Hunter. *Woman Suffrage and the New Democracy.* New Haven, CT: Yale University Press, 1996.

Grant, Julia. *Raising Baby by the Book: The Education of American Mothers.* New Haven, CT: Yale University Press, 1998.

Griswold, Robert L. *Fatherhood in America: A History.* New York: Basic Books, 1993.

Grossman, Joanna L. "Women's Jury Service: Right of Citizenship or Privilege of Difference?" *Stanford Law Review* Vol. 46, No. 5 (1994): 1115–1160.

Hall, Jacquelyn Hall. "Disorderly Women: Gender and Labor Militancy in the Appalachian South." *Journal of American History* Vol. 73, No. 2 (1986): 354–382.

——. *Revolt Against Chivalry: Jesse Daniel Ames and the Women's Campaign Against Lynching.* New York: Columbia University Press, 1993.

Harrison, Cynthia E. "A 'New Frontier' for Women: The Public Policy of the Kennedy Administration." *Journal of American History* Vol. 67, No. 3 (1980): 630–646.

——. *On Account of Sex: The Politics of Women's Issues, 1945–1968.* Berkeley: University of California Press, 1988.

Hartmann, Susan M. *From Margin to Mainstream: American Women and Politics Since 1960.* New York: Knopf, 1989.

——. *The Home Front and Beyond: American Women in the 1940s.* Boston: Twayne, 1982.

Harvey, Anna. *Votes without Leverage: Women in American Electoral Politics, 1920–1970.* New York: Cambridge University Press, 1998.

Harvey, Brett. *The Fifties: A Women's Oral History.* New York: HarperCollins, 1993.

Haskell, Molly. *From Reverence to Rape: The Treatment of Women in the Movies.* Chicago: University of Chicago Press, 1987.

Heinicke, Craig W. "One Step Forward: African-American Married Women in the South, 1950–1960." *Journal of Interdisciplinary History* Vol. 31, No. 1 (2000): 43–62.

Hembold, Lois Rita. "Beyond the Family Economy: Black and White Working-Class Women During the Great Depression." *Feminist Studies* Vol. 13, No. 3 (1987): 629–655.

Helmbold, Lois Rita, and Ann Schofield. "Women's Labor History, 1790–1945." *Reviews in American History.* Vol. 17, No. 4 (1989): 501–518.

Hewitt, Nancy. *Southern Discomfort: Women's Activism in Tampa, Florida, 1880s to 1920s.* Urbana: University of Illinois Press, 2001.

Hewitt, Nancy A., and Suzanne Lebsock, eds. *Visible Women: New Essays on American Activism.* Urbana: University of Illinois Press, 1993.

Hicks, Cheryl D. "'In Danger of Becoming Morally Depraved': Single Black Women, Working-Class Black Families, and New York State's Wayward Minor Laws, 1917–1928." *University of Pennsylvania Law Review* Vol. 151, No. 6 (2003): 2077–2121.

Higginbotham, Evelyn Brooks. *Righteous Discontent: The Women's Movement in the Black Baptist Church, 1880–1920.* Cambridge, MA: Harvard University Press, 1993.

——. "African-American Women's History and the Metalanguage of Race." *Signs* Vol. 17, No. 2 (1992): 251–274.

Hine, Darlene Clark. *Black Women in White: Racial Conflict and Cooperation in the Nursing Profession, 1890–1950.* Bloomington: Indiana University Press, 1989.

Hine, Darlene Clark, ed. *Black Women in America.* Oxford ; New York: Oxford University Press, 2005.

Hondagneu-Sotelo, Pierrette. *Gendered Transitions: Mexican Experiences of Immigration.* Berkeley: University of California Press, 1994.

Honey, Maureen. *Creating Rosie the Riveter: Class, Gender, and Propaganda during World War II.* Amherst: University of Massachusetts Press, 1984.

Howard, Walter T., and Virginia M. Howard. "Family, Religion, and Education: A Profile of African-American Life in Tampa, Florida, 1900–1930." *Journal of Negro History* Vol. 79, No. 1 (Winter 1994): 1–17.

Hunter, Tera. *To 'Joy My Freedom: Southern Black Women's Lives and Labors After the Civil War.* Cambridge, MA: Harvard University Press, 1997.

Irving, Katrina. *Immigrant Mothers: Narratives of Race and Maternity, 1890–1925.* Urbana: University of Illinois Press, 2000.

Jacobs, Meg. "'How About Some Meat?': The Office of Price Administration, Consumption Politics, and State Building from the Bottom Up." *Journal of American History* Vol. 84, No. 3 (1997): 910–941.

Jacobson, Lisa. *Raising Consumers: Children and the American Mass Market in the Early Twentieth Century.* New York: Columbia University Press, 2004.

Jeansonne, Glen. *Women of the Far Right: The Mothers' Movement and World War II.* Chicago: University of Chicago Press, 1996.

Johnson, Joan Marie. "'Drill into Us . . . the Rebel Tradition': The Contest over Southern Identity in Black and White Women's Clubs, South Carolina, 1898–1930." *Journal of Southern History* Vol. 66, No. 3 (2000): 525–562.

Johnson, Kathleen. "Women Defend the Nation." The Cold War Museum, http://www.coldwar.org/articles/50s/women_civildefense.html.

Jones, Beverly W. "Mary Church Terrell and the National Association of Colored Women, 1896 to 1901." *Journal of Negro History* Vol. 67, No. 1 (1982): 20–33.

Jones, Jacquelyn. *Labor of Love, Labor of Sorrow: Black Women, Work, and the Family from Slavery to the Present.* New York: Vintage, 1985.

Kaledin, Eugenia. *Mothers and More: American Women in the 1950s.* Boston: Twayne, 1984.

Kaplan, E. Ann. *Motherhood and Representation: The Mother in Popular Culture and Melodrama.* New York: Routledge, 1992.

———. *Rocking Around the Clock: Music Television, Postmodernism, and Consumer Culture.* New York: Methuen, 1987.

Katz, Michael B., ed. *Education in American History: Readings on the Social Issues.* New York: Praeger, 1973.

Katz, Michael B., Mark J. Stern, and Jamie J. Fader. "Women and the Paradox of Economic Inequality in the Twentieth Century." *Journal of Social History* Vol. 39, No. 1 (2005): 65–88.

Kay, Herma Hill. "From the Second Sex to the Joint Venture: An Overview of Women's Rights and Family Law in the United States during the Twentieth Century." *California Law Review* Vol. 88, No. 6 (2000): 2017–2093.

Kennedy, Elizabeth, and Madeline Davis. *Boots of Leather, Slippers of Gold: The History of a Lesbian Community.* New York: Routledge, 1993.

Kerber, Linda. *No Constitutional Right to Be Ladies: Women and the Obligations of Citizenship.* New York: Hill and Wang, 1998.

———. "Separate Spheres, Female Worlds, Woman's Place: The Rhetoric of Women's History." *Journal of American History* Vol. 75, No. 1 (1988): 9–39.

Kerber, Linda, et al. *U.S. History as Women's History.* Chapel Hill: University of North Carolina Press, 1991.

Kesselman, Amy. "Women's Liberation and the Left in New Haven, Connecticut, 1968–1972." *Radical History Review* Issue 81 (2001): 15–33.

Kessler-Harris, Alice. *In Pursuit of Equity: Women, Men, and the Quest for Economic Citizenship in Twentieth-Century America.* New York: Oxford University Press, 2001.

———. *Out to Work: A History of Wage-Earning Women in the United States.* New York: Oxford University Press, 2003.

———. "Reframing the History of Women's Wage Labor: Challenges of a Global Perspective." *Journal of Women's History* 15(2004): 186–206.

Kitch, Carolyn. *The Girl on the Magazine Cover: The Origins of Visual Stereotypes in American Mass Media.* Chapel Hill: University of North Carolina Press, 2001.

Klatch, Rebecca E. *Women of the New Right.* Philadelphia: Temple University Press, 1987.

Kleinberg, S. J. "Children's and Mothers' Wage Labor in Three Eastern U.S. Cities, 1880–1920." *Social Science History* Vol. 29 Issue: Number 1(2005): 45–76.

Kleinberg, S. J., et al. *The Practice of U.S. Women's History: Narratives, Intersections, and Dialogues.* Brunswick, NJ: Rutgers University Press, 2007.

Koven, Seth, and Sonya Michel. "Womanly Duties: Maternalist Politics and the Origins of Welfare States in France, Germany, Great Britain, and the United States, 1880–1920." *American Historical Review.* Vol. 95, No. 4 (1990): 1076–1108.

———, eds., *Mothers of a New World: Maternalist Politics and the Origins of the Welfare State.* New York: Routledge, 1993.

Kraditor, Aileen. *The Ideas of the Woman Suffrage Movement, 1890–1920.* New York: Columbia University Press, 1965.

Kunzel, Regina. *Fallen Women, Problem Girls: Unmarried Mothers and the Professionalization of Social Work, 1890–1945.* New Haven, CT: Yale University Press, 1993.

———. "Pulp Fictions and Problem Girls: Reading and Rewriting Single Pregnancy in the Postwar United States." *American Historical Review* Vol. 100, No. 5 (1995): 1465–1487.

Ladd-Taylor, Molly. *Mother-Work: Women, Child Welfare, and the State, 1890–1930.* Urbana: University of Illinois Press, 1995.

———. *Raising a Baby the Government Way: Mothers' Letters to the Children's Bureau, 1915–1932.* New Brunswick, NJ: Rutgers University Press, 1986.

Lagemann, Ellen Condliffe. *A Generation of Women: Education in the Lives of Progressive Reformers.* Cambridge, MA: Harvard University Press, 1979.

Landay, Lori. *Madcaps, Screwballs, and Con Women: The Female Trickster in American Culture.* Philadelphia: University of Pennsylvania Press, 1998.

Landes, Elisabeth M. "The Effect of State Maximum-Hours Laws on the Employment of Women in 1920." *Journal of Political Economy* Vol. 88, No. 3 (1980): 476–494.

Larson, Edward J. "In The Finest, Most Womanly Way: " Women in The Southern Eugenics Movement. " *American Journal of Legal History* Vol. 39, No. 2 (1995): 119–147.

Lasch-Quinn, Elizabeth. *Black Neighbors: Race and the Limits of Reform in the American Settlement House Movement, 1890–1945.* Chapel Hill: University of North Carolina Press, 1993.

Laslett, Barbara, and Johanna Brenner. "Gender and Social Reproduction: Historical Perspectives." *Annual Review of Sociology* Vol. 15 (1989): 381–404.

Lassonde, Stephen A. "Should I Go, or Should I Stay?: Adolescence, School Attainment, and Parent-Child Relations in Italian Immigrant Families of New Haven, 1900–1940." *History of Education Quarterly* Vol. 38, No. 1 (1998): 37–60.

Law, Sylvia A. "Women, Work, Welfare, and the Preservation of Patriarchy." *University of Pennsylvania Law Review* Vol. 131, No. 6 (1983): 1249–1339.

Leach, William R. "Transformations in a Culture of Consumption: Women and Department Stores, 1890–1925." *Journal of American History* Vol. 71, No. 2 (1984): 319–342.

Leavitt, Judith. *Brought to Bed: Child Bearing in America, 1750–1950.* New York: Oxford University Press, 1985.

Lehrer, Susan. *Origins of Protective Labor Legislation for Women, 1905–1925.* Albany: SUNY Press, 1987.

Lemons, Stanley. *The Woman Citizen: Social Feminism in the 1920s.* Urbana: University of Illinois Press, 1973.

Leroux, Karen. "'Lady Teachers' and the Genteel Roots of Teacher Organization in Gilded Age Cities." *History of Education Quarterly* Vol. 46, No. 2 (2006): 164–191.

Lieberman, Robert C. *Shifting the Color Line: Race and the American Welfare State.* Cambridge, MA: Harvard University Press, 1998.

Linden, Blanche M. G. *American Women in the 1960s: Changing the Future.* New York: Twayne, 1993.

Lindsay, Matthew J. "Reproducing a Fit Citizenry: Dependency, Eugenics, and the Law of Marriage in the United States, 1860–1920." *Law and Social Inquiry* Vol. 23, No. 3 (1998): 541–585.

Lipartito, Kenneth "When Women Were Switches: Technology, Work, and Gender in the Telephone Industry, 1890–1920." *American Historical Review* Vol. 99, No. 4 (1994): 1076–1111.

Lissak, Rivka Shpak. *Pluralism and Progressives: Hull House and the New Immigrants, 1890–1919.* Chicago: University of Chicago Press, 1989.

Lopez, Nancy. *Hopeful Girls, Troubled Boys: Race and Gender Disparity in Urban Education.* New York: Routledge, 2003.

Lotz, Amanda D. *Redesigning Women: Television after the Network Era.* Urbana: University of Illinois Press, 2006.

Lucas, Kristin. *Dubious Conceptions: The Politics of Teenage Pregnancy.* Cambridge, MA: Harvard University Press, 1997.

Lunardini, Christine A. *From Equal Suffrage to Equal Rights: Alice Paul and the National Woman's Party, 1910–1928.* New York: New York University Press, 1986.

Lynn, Susan. *Progressive Women in Conservative Times: Racial Justice, Peace, and Feminism, 1945 to the 1960s.* New Brunswick, NJ: Rutgers University Press, 1992.

MacLean, Nancy. *Freedom Is Not Enough: The Opening of the American Workplace.* Cambridge, MA: Harvard University Press, 2007.

MacDonald, Victoria Marie. "The Paradox of Bureaucratization: New Views on Progressive Era Teachers and the Development of a Woman's Profession." *History of Education Quarterly* Vol. 19, No. 4 (1999): 427–453.

Mahar, Karen Ward. *Women Filmmakers in Early Hollywood.* Baltimore: Johns Hopkins University Press, 2006.

Marling, Karal Ann. *As Seen on TV: The Visual Culture of Everyday Life in the 1950s.* Cambridge, MA: Harvard University Press, 1998.

Marsh, Margaret. "From Separation to Togetherness: The Social Construction of Domestic Space in the American Suburbs, 1840–1915." *Journal of American History* Vol. 76, No. 2 (1989): 506–527.

Mannis, Valerie S. "Single Mothers by Choice." *Family Relations* Vol. 48, No. 2 (1999): 121–128.

Matthaei. Julie A. *An Economic History of Women in America: Women's Work, the Sexual Division of Labor, and the Development of Capitalism.* New York: Schocken Books, 1982.

Matthews, Glenna. *Just a Housewife: The Rise and Fall of Domesticity in America.* New York: Oxford University Press, 1987.

May, Ann Mari. "'Sweeping the Heavens for a Comet': Women, the Language of Political Economy, and Higher Education in the U.S." *Feminist Economics* Vol. 12, Issue 4 (2006): 625–640.

May, Elaine Tyler. *Barren in the Promised Land: Childless Americans and the Pursuit of Happiness.* Cambridge, MA: Harvard University Press, 1997.

———. *Homeward Bound: American Families in the Cold War Era.* New York: Basic Books, 1999.

McCammon, Holly J. "Stirring up Suffrage Sentiment: The Formation of the State Woman Suffrage Organizations, 1866–1914." *Social Forces* Vol. 80, No. 2 (2001): 449–480.

McCune, Mary. "Creating a Place for Women in the Socialist Brotherhood: Class and Gender Politics in the Workmen's Circle." *Feminist Studies* Vol. 28, No. 3 (2002): 585–610.

McElya, Micki. *Clinging to Mammy: The Faithful Slave in Twentieth-Century America.* Cambridge, MA: Harvard University Press, 2007.

McFeely, Mary Drake. *Can She Bake a Cherry Pie?: American Women and the Kitchen in the Twentieth Century.* Amherst: University of Massachusetts Press, 2001.

McGerr, Michael. "Political Style and Women's Power, 1830–1930." The Journal of *American History* Vol. 77, No. 3 (1990): 864–885.

Mettler, Suzanne. *Soldiers to Citizens: The G.I. Bill and the Making of the Greatest Generation.* New York: Oxford University Press, 2005.

Meyerowitz, Joanne. "Beyond the Feminine Mystique: A Reassessment of Postwar Mass Culture, 1946–1958." *Journal of American History* Vol. 79, No. 4 (1993): 1455–1484.

———. *Not June Cleaver: Women and Gender in Postwar America, 1945–1960.* Philadelphia: Temple University Press, 1994.

———. *Women Adrift: Independent Wage-Earners in Chicago, 1880–1930.* Chicago: University of Chicago Press, 1998.

———. "Women, Cheesecake, and Borderline Material: Responses to Girlie Pictures in the Mid-Twentieth Century U.S." *Journal of Women's History* Vol. 8, No. 3 (1996): 9–35.

Milkman, Ruth. *Gender at Work: The Dynamics of Job Segregation by Sex during World War II.* Urbana: University of Illinois Press, 1987.

Milkman, Ruth, ed. *Women, Work, and Protest: A Century of Women's Labor History.* New York: Routledge, 1985.

Miller, Marc. "Working Women and World War II." *New England Quarterly* Vol. 53, No. 1 (1980): 42–61.

Mink, Gwendolyn. *The Wages of Motherhood: Unequal in the Welfare State, 1917–1942.* Ithaca, NY: Cornell University Press, 1995.

Minow, Martha. "We, the Family: Constitutional Rights and American Families." *Journal of American History* Vol. 74, No. 3 (1987): 959–983.

Mintz, Steven. *Huck's Raft: A History of American Childhood.* Cambridge, MA: Harvard University Press, 2004.

Misra, Joya, et al. "Envisioning Dependency: Changing Media Depictions of Welfare in the 20th Century." *Social Problems* Vol. 50 Issue 4 (2003): 482–504.

Moller, Stephani. "Supporting Poor Single Mothers." *Gender and Society* Vol. 16 Issue 4 (2002): 465–484.

Morantz-Sanchez, Regina. *Sympathy and Science: Women Physicians in American Medicine.* New York: Oxford University Press, 1985.

Morello, Karen Berger. *The Invisible Bar: The Woman Lawyer in America: 1638 to the Present.* Boston: Beacon Press, 1986.

Muncy, Robyn. *Creating A Female Dominion in American Reform, 1890–1935.* New York: Oxford University Press, 1991.

Murphy, Marjorie. *Blackboard Unions: The AFT and the NEA, 1900–1980.* Ithaca, NY: Cornell University Press, 1990.

Novkov, Julie. *Constituting Workers, Protecting Women: Gender, Law, and Labor in the Progressive Era and New Deal Years.* Ann Arbor: University of Michigan Press, 2001.

Oberman, Michelle. "Turning Girls into Women: Re-Evaluating Modern Statutory Rape Law." *Journal of Criminal Law and Criminology* Vol. 85, No. 1 (1994): 15–79.

Odem, Mary. *Delinquent Daughters: Protecting and Policing Adolescent Female Sexuality in the United States, 1885–1920.* Chapel Hill: University of North Carolina Press, 1995.

Oliveri, Rigel. "Statutory Rape Law and Enforcement in the Wake of Welfare Reform." *Stanford Law Review* Vol. 52, No. 2 (2000): 463–508.

O'Neill, William L. *Everyone Was Brave.* Chicago: Quadrangle Books, 1971.

Orleck, Annelise. *Common Sense and a Little Fire: Women and Working-Class Politics in the United States, 1900–1965.* Chapel Hill: University of North Carolina Press, 1995.

———. "Feminism Rewritten: Reclaiming the Activism of Working-Class Women." *Reviews in American History* Vol. 32, No. 4 (2004): 591–601.

———. "'We Are That Mythical Thing Called the Public': Militant Housewives during the Great Depression." *Feminist Studies* Vol. 19, No. 1 (1993): 147–172.

Orloff, Ann Shola. "Gender and the Social Rights of Citizenship: The Comparative Analysis of Gender Relations and Welfare States." *American Sociological Review* Vol. 58, No. 3 (1993): 303–328.

Orloff, Ann. "Gender in the Welfare State" *Annual Review of Sociology* Vol. 22 (1996): 51–78.

Pagnini, Deanna L., and S. Philip Morgan. "Racial Differences in Marriage and Childbearing: Oral History Evidence from the South in the Early Twentieth Century." *American Journal of Sociology* Vol. 101, No. 6 (1996): 1694–1718.

Parker, Alison M. *Purifying America: Women, Cultural Reform, and Pro-Censorship Activism, 1873–1933.* Urbana: University of Illinois Press, 1997.

Pascoe, Peggy. "Miscegenation Law, Court Cases, and Ideologies of 'Race' in Twentieth-Century America." *Journal of American History* Vol. 82, No. 1 (1996): 44–69.

———. *Relations of Rescue: The Search for Female Moral Authority in the American West.* New York: Oxford University Press, 1990.

Patterson, Martha. *Beyond the Gibson Girl: Reimaging the American New Woman.* Bloomington: Indiana University Press, 2005.

———. "Survival of the Best Fitted: Selling the American New Woman as Gibson Girl, 1895–1910." *ATQ* Vol. 9, No. 2 (1995): 73–88.

Peiss, Kathy. *Cheap Amusements: Working Women and Leisure in Turn-of-the-Century New York.* Philadelphia: Temple University Press, 1986.

———. *Hope in a Jar: The Making of America's Beauty Culture*. New York: Metropolitan Books, 1998.

Reagan, Leslie J. "About to Meet Her Maker": Women, Doctors, Dying Declarations, and the State's Investigation of Abortion, Chicago, 1867–1940. " *Journal of American History* Vol. 77, No. 4 (1991): 1240–1264.

———. *When Abortion Was a Crime: Women, Medicine, and the Law in the United States, 1867–1973*. Berkeley: University of California Press, 1994.

Rehak, Melanie. *Girl Sleuth: Nancy Drew and the Women Who Created Her*. New York: Harcourt, 2005.

Resnik, Judith. "Asking About Gender in the Courts." *Signs* 21(1996): 952–990.

Rhodes, Deborah. *Gender and Justice*. Cambridge, MA: Harvard University Press, 1989.

Rich, Adrienne. "Compulsory Heterosexuality and Lesbian Existence." *Signs* Vol. 5, No. 4 (1980): 631–660.

Riley, Glenda. *Divorce: An American Tradition*. New York: Oxford University Press, 1991.

Ritter, Gretchen. "Jury Service and Women's Citizenship before and after the Nineteenth Amendment." *Law and History Review* Vol. 20, No. 3 (2002): 479–515.

Roberts, Mary Louise. "Gender Consumption and Commodity Culture." *American Historical Review* Vol. 103, No. 3 (1998): 817–844.

Rose, Elizabeth. *A Mother's Job: The History of Day Care, 1890–1960*. New York: Oxford University Press, 1999.

Rosen, Marjorie. *Popcorn Venus: Women, Movies, and the American Dream*. New York: Avon, 1973.

Rosenberg, Rosalind. *Divided Lives: American Women in the Twentieth Century*. New York: Hill and Wang, 1992.

Rossiter, Margaret W. *Women Scientists in America: Before Affirmative Action, 1940–1972*. Baltimore: Johns Hopkins University Press, 1995.

Roth, Louise Marie. *Selling Women Short: Gender Inequality on Wall Street*. Princeton, NJ: Princeton University Press, 2006.

Rothman, Ellen K. *Hands and Hearts: A History of Courtship in America*. New York: Basic Books, 1984.

Roy-Fequiere, Magali. "Contested Territory: Puerto Rican Women, Creole Identity, and Intellectual Life in the Early Twentieth Century." *Callaloo* Vol. 17, No. 3 (1994): 916–934.

Ruether, Rosemary, and Rosemary S. Keller. *Women and Religion in America, Vol. 3: 1900–1968*. New York: Harper and Row, 1986.

Ruggles, Steve. "The Origins of African-American Family Structure." *American Sociological Review* Vol. 59, No. 1 (1994): 136–151.

Ruiz, Vicki L. *From Out of the Shadows: Mexican Women in Twentieth Century America*. New York: Oxford University Press, 1998.

Rumbaut, Ruben G. "Origins and Destinies: Immigration to the United States Since World War II." *Sociological Forum*, Vol. 9, No. 4 (1994): 583–621.

Rupp, Leila J. "Feminism and the Sexual Revolution in the Early Twentieth Century: The Case of Doris Stevens." *Feminist Studies* Vol. 15, No. 2 (1989): 289–309.

———. *Survival in the Doldrums: The American Women's Rights Movement, 1945 to the 1960s*. New York: Oxford University Press, 1987.

Rury, John. "Education in the New Women's History." *Educational Studies* Vol. 17 Issue 1 (1986): 1–15.

———. *Education and Social Change: Themes in the History of American Schooling.* New York: Routledge, 2005.

———. "Vocationalism for Home and Work: Women's Education in the United States, 1880–1930." *History of Education Quarterly* Vol. 24, No. 1 (1984): 21–44.

Rymph, Catherine E. *Republican Women: Feminism and Conservatism from Suffrage Through the Rise of the New Right.* Chapel Hill: University of North Carolina Press, 2006.

Rynbrandt, Linda J. "The 'Ladies of the Club' and Caroline Bartlett Crane: Affiliation and Alienation in Progressive Social Reform." *Gender and Society* Vol. 11, No. 2 (1997): 200–214.

Scanlon, Jennifer. *Inarticulate Longings: The Ladies' Home Journal, Gender, and the Promises of Consumer Culture.* New York: Routledge, 1995.

Scanlon, Jennifer. "Material Girls: Women and Popular Culture in the Twentieth Century." *Radical History Review* Vol. 66 (1996): 172–183.

Scott, Anne Firor. "Most Invisible of All: Black Women's Voluntary Associations." *Journal of Southern History* Vol. 56, No. 1 (1990): 3–22.

Scharf, Lois. *To Work and to Wed: Female Employment, Feminism, and the Great Depression.* Westport, CT: Greenwood Press, 1980.

Schlossman, Steven, and Brian Gill. "'A Sin against Childhood': Progressive Education and the Crusade to Abolish Homework, 1897–1941." *American Journal of Education* Vol. 105, No. 1 (1996): 27–66.

Schuyler, Lorraine Gates. *The Weight of Their Votes: Southern Women and Political Leverage in the 1920s.* Chapel Hill: University of North Carolina Press, 2006.

Schwager, Sally. "Educating Women in America." *Signs* Vol. 12, No. 2 (1987): 333–372.

Scott, Anne Firor. *Natural Allies: Women's Associations in American History.* Urbana: University of Illinois Press, 1991.

Shaw, Stephanie. *What a Woman Ought to Be and Do: Black Professional Women Workers during the Jim Crow Era.* Chicago: University of Chicago Press, 1996.

Shklar, Judith. *American Citizenship: The Quest for Inclusion.* Cambridge, MA: Harvard University Press, 1991.

Siegel, Reva B. "She the People: The Nineteenth Amendment, Sex Equality, Federalism, and the Family." *Harvard Law Review* Vol. 115, No. 4 (2002): 947–1046.

———. "The Modernization of Marital States." *Georgetown Law Journal* (1994): 2127–2211.

Sirgo, Henry B. "Women, Blacks, and the New Deal." *Women and Politics* Vol. 14, No. 3 (1994): 57–77.

Sklar, Kathryn Kish. *Florence Kelley and the Nation's Work: The Rise of Women's Political Culture, 1830–1900.* New Haven, CT: Yale University Press, 1995.

Skocpol, Theda. "The Enactment of Mothers' Pensions: Civic Mobilization and Agenda Setting or Benefits of the Ballot?: Response." *American Political Science Review* Vol. 89, No. 3 (1995): 720–730.

Skocpol, Theda, et al. "Women's Associations and the Enactment of Mother's Pensions in the United States." *American Political Science Review* Vol. 87, No. 3 (1993): 686–701.

Sloan, Kay. "Sexual Warfare in the Silent Cinema: Comedies and Melodramas of Woman Suffrage." *American Quarterly* Vol. 33, No. 4 (1981): 412–436.

Smith, Daniel Scott. "'The Number and Quality of Children': Education and Marital Fertility in Early Twentieth-Century." *Journal of Social History* Vol. 30 Issue 2 (1996): 367–393.

Smith-Rosenberg, Carroll. *Disorderly Conduct: Visions of Gender in Victorian America.* New York: A. A. Knopf, 1985.

Sochen, June. *From Mae to Madonna: Women Entertainers in Twentieth-century America.* Lexington: University Press of Kentucky, 1999.

Solinger, Rickie. *Pregnancy and Power: A Short History of Reproductive Politics in America,* New York: New York University Press, 2005.

Spain, Daphne. "Gendered Spaces and Women's Status." *Sociological Theory* Vol. 11, No. 2 (1993): 137–151.

Spellman, Susan V. "All the Comforts of Home: The Domestication of the Service Station Industry, 1920–1940." *Journal of Popular Culture* 37(2004): 463–477.

Strasser, Susan. *Never Done: A History of American Housework.* New York: Henry Holt, 2000.

Stearns, Peter. "Girls, Boys, and Emotions: Redefinition and Historical Change." *Journal of American History* Vol. 80, No. 1 (1993): 36–74.

Stein, Marc. *City of Sisterly and Brotherly Loves: Lesbian and Gay Philadelphia, 1945–1972.* Chicago: University of Chicago Press, 2000.

Sterett, Susan. "Constitutionalism and the Common Law—Nineteenth-Century Social Welfare in the United States." *Oxford Journal of Legal Studies* Vol. 17, No. 4 (1997): 587–610.

Strasser, Susan. *Satisfaction Guaranteed: The Making of Mass Marketing in America.* New York: Pantheon Books, 1989.

Strom, Sharon Hartman. *Beyond the Typewriter: Gender, Class, and the Origins of Modern American Office Work, 1900–1930.* Urbana: University of Illinois Press, 1994.

———. "Challenging 'Woman's Place': Feminism, the Left, and Industrial Unionism in the 1930s." *Feminist Studies* Vol. 9, No. 2 (1983): 359–386.

———. "Leadership and Tactics in the American Woman Suffrage Movement: New Perspectives from Massachusetts." *Journal of American History* Vol. 62, No. 2 (1975): 296–315.

Storrs, Landon R. Y. "Left-Feminism, the Consumer Movement, and Red Scare Politics in the United States, 1935–1960." *Journal of Women's History* Vol. 18, No. 3 (2006): 40–67.

Swerdlow, Amy. *Women's Strike for Peace: Traditional Motherhood and Radical Politics in the 1960s.* Chicago: University of Chicago Press, 1993.

Takacs, Stacy. "Alien-Nation: Immigration, National Identity, and Transnationalism." *Cultural Studies* Vol. 13, Issue 4 (1999): 591–620.

Tax, Meredith. *The Rising of the Women: Feminist Solidarity and Class Conflict, 1880–1917.* Urbana: University of Illinois Press, 2001.

Thelin, John R. *A History of American Higher Education.* Baltimore: Johns Hopkins University Press, 2004.

Thomas, Sue. *How Women Legislate.* New York: Oxford University Press, 1994.

Thomas, Sue, and Clyde Wilcox, eds. *Women and Elective Office: Past, Present, and Future.* New York: Oxford University Press, 2005.

Thompson, Becky. "Multiracial Feminism: Recasting the Chronology of Second Wave Feminism." *Feminist Studies* Vol. 28, No. 2 (2002): 336–360.

Ulrich, Laurel. *Well-behaved Women Seldom Make History.* New York: Alfred A. Knopf, 2007.

Urban, Wayne J. Gender, *Race and the National Education Association: Professionalism and Its Limitations.* New York: Taylor and Francis, 2000.

VanBurkleo, Sandra F. *"Belonging to the World": Women's Rights and American Constitutional Culture.* New York: Oxford University Press, 2001.

Vandenberg-Daves, Jodi. "The Manly Pursuit of a Partnership between the Sexes: The Debate over YMCA Programs for Women and Girls, 1914–1933." *Journal of American History* Vol. 78, No. 4 (1992): 1324–1346.

Vogel, Lise. *Mothers on the Job: Maternity Policy in the U.S. Workplace.* New Brunswick, NJ: Rutgers University Press, 1993.

Walsh, Andrea S. *Women's Film and Female Experience, 1940–1950.* Westport, CT: Praeger, 1984.

Waters, Pamela Barnhouse, and David R. James. "Schooling for Some: Child Labor and School Enrollment of Black and White Children in the Early Twentieth-Century South." *American Sociological Review* Vol. 57, No. 5 (1992): 635–650.

Ware, Susan. *Beyond Suffrage: Women in the New Deal.* Cambridge, MA: Harvard University Press, 1981.

Ware, Susan. *Holding Their Own: American Women in the 1930s.* Boston: Twayne, 1982.

Weiler, Kathleen. "Women and Rural School Reform: California, 1900–1940." *History of Education Quarterly* Vol. 34, No. 1 (1994): 25–47.

Welke, Barbara Y. "Unreasonable Women: Gender and the Law of Accidental Injury, 1870–1920." *Law and Social Inquiry* Vol. 19, No. 2 (1994): 369–403.

Wells, Sandra. *Police Women: Life with the Badge.* Westport, CT: Praeger, 2005.

Wexler, Laura. *Tender Violence: Domestic Images in the Age of U.S. Imperialism.* Chapel Hill: University of North Carolina Press, 2001.

White, Deborah Gray. *Too Heavy a Load: Black Women in Defense of Themselves, 1894–1994.* New York: W. W. Norton, 1999.

Wiese, Andrew. *Places of Their Own: African American Suburbanization in the Twentieth Century.* Chicago: University of Chicago Press, 2004.

Whitt, Jan. *Women in American Journalism: A New History.* Urbana: University of Illinois Press, 2008.

Witt, Linda, et al., *Running as a Woman: Gender and Power in American Politics.* New York: Free Press, 1995.

Woloch, Nancy. *Women and the American Experience.* New York: McGraw Hill, 2006.

Wood, Molly M. "Diplomatic Wives: The Politics of Domesticity and the 'Social Game' in the U.S. Foreign Service, 1905–1941." *Journal of Women's History* Vol. 17, No. 2 (2005): 142–165.

Yellin, Emily. *Our Mothers' War: American Women at Home and at the Front During World War II.* New York: Simon and Schuster, 2004.

Zelizer, Viviana A. *Pricing the Priceless Child: The Changing Social Value of Children.* Princeton, NJ: Princeton University Press, 1994.

Zimmerman, Joan G. "The Jurisprudence of Equality: The Women's Minimum Wage, the First Equal Rights Amendment, and Adkins v. Children's Hospital, 1905–1923." *Journal of American History* Vol. 78, No. 2 (1991): 188–225.

Zylan, Yvonne. "Maternalism Redefined: Gender, the State, and the Politics of Day Care, 1945–1962." *Gender and Society* Vol. 14, No. 5 (2000): 608–629.

Index

228   Index

Peter, Paul, and Mary, 79
Peterson, Elly, 146
Peterson, Esther, 141
Philips v. Martin Marietta Corporation,
    25, 171
Pickford, Mary, 41, 69
Pierce, Sarah, 88
Planned Parenthood v. Casey, 169
Portia Law School, 159
Pregnancy Disability Act, 25, 50, 103,
    156
Presidential Commission on the Status
    of Women, 22, 141
President's Commission on Higher
    Education, 100
Priesand, Sally, 200–201
Progressive era, 114
prostitution, 67
protective legislation, 8
Puerto Rico, 138

Radcliffe College, 98
Rainey, Gertrude, 67
Ramo, Roberta Cooper, 166
Rankin, Jeanette, 126, 128
Ray, Charlotte E., 158
Reagan, Ronald, 146, 148
Red Scare, 64, 135–137
Reed v. Reed, 25, 156, 165, 172
Rehl, Jodi, 170
Reno, Janet, 149, 166
Rice, Condoleeza, 150
Rice, Harriet Alleyne, 93
Richards, Ellen Swallow, 35
Robbins, Margaret Dreier, 115, 118
Roberts, John, 176
Robertson, Alice Mary, 128
Robertson, Pat, 202
Robinson, Lelia Josephine, 158
Roe v. Wade, 52, 145, 155, 168–169, 199
Rogers, Ginger, 70
Roosevelt, Eleanor, 12, 21–22, 73,
    131–135, 141
Roosevelt, Franklin Delano, 11, 135
Rosenberg, Ethel, 136
Rosenwald, Julius, 93
Rosie the Riveter, 14, 18
Ross, Nellie Tayloe, 129

Rostker v. Goldberg, 174
Rubinstein, Helena, 5
Rudkin, Margaret, 22
Ruether, Rosemary, 200
Russell, Lillian, 57
Russell, Rosalind, 73

Salt-n-Peppa, 83
same-sex marriage, 176–177
Sanctified church, 191
Sandler, Bernice, 104
Sanger, Margaret, 39, 66, 127
Sarandon, Susan, 80
Sasso, Sally Eisenberg, 200
Sawyer, Diane, 84
Schlafly, Phyllis, 52, 145–146
Schneiderman, Rose, 118, 131
school suffrage, 122
Schulman, Cathy, 80
scientific housekeeping, 35
Sears Roebuck, 59
Second Vatican Council, 193
settlement houses, 115–116
Sexual Abuse Act of 1986, 170
sexuality, 38, 46, 48, 51, 66, 74
Shanti, Roxanne, 83
Shaw, Anna Howard, 124
Sheppard Towner Act, 129, 130
Simkovitch, Mary, 38, 95, 116
Sisters of Mercy, 193
Skinner v. Oklahoma, 167
Slick, Grace, 80
Smith, Bessie, 68
Smith, Hilda, 132
Smith, Howard, 141
Smith, Margaret Chase, 22, 129,
    134–137
Smith, Mary Louise, 146
Smith Lever Act, 35
Snowe, Olympia, 170
Social Security Act, 12, 42
Soldier Brides Act of 1947, 163
Southern Christian Leadership
    Conference, 140, 198
Spahr, Margaret, 166
Spelling, Margaret, 151
Spelman College, 94, 120
Spencer, Anne, 68

About the Author

MARTHA MAY is an associate professor of history at Western Connecticut State University.